Marketing Through Search Optimization

Marketing Through Search Optimization
How to be found on the Web

Alex Michael and Ben Salter

ELSEVIER
BUTTERWORTH
HEINEMANN

AMSTERDAM   BOSTON   HEIDELBERG   LONDON   NEW YORK   OXFORD
PARIS   SAN DIEGO   SAN FRANCISCO   SINGAPORE   SYDNEY   TOKYO

Butterworth-Heinemann
An imprint of Elsevier
Linacre House, Jordan Hill, Oxford OX2 8DP
200 Wheeler Road, Burlington, MA 01803

First published 2003

British Library Cataloguing in Publication Data
Michael, Alex
   Marketing through search optimization: how to be found on the Web
   1. Internet marketing   2. Web search engines
   I. Title   II. Salter, Ben
   658.8'02854678

Library of Congress Cataloguing in Publication Data
A catalogue record for this book is available from the Library of Congress

ISBN 0 7506 5979 3

For information on all Butterworth-Heinemann publications
visit our website at www.bh.com

Composition by Genesis Typesetting Limited, Rochester, Kent
Printed and bound in Italy

Contents

Acknowledgements

Alex Michael:

I would like to thank the team at Toni&Guy Marketing and Design, and in particular Linda Evans and Mark Nicholls for all their support and help over the years. I would also like to thank Karl Murphy, Andrew Teale and Raj Ahuja for having vision and confidence in employing Sprite to handle EMB's digital marketing.

I would like to thank Vinton Cerf and Robert Kahn for inventing the Internet.

Ben Salter:

I would like to thank everyone at Sprite, particularly Alex and Rob for the support over the years. I'd also like to thank Barry Salter (my dad) for his useful insights, and the rest of my family and friends.

Introduction

Search engines provide one of the primary ways by which Internet users find websites. That's why a website with good search engine listings may see a dramatic increase in traffic. Everyone wants those good listings. Unfortunately, many websites appear poorly in search engine rankings, or may not be listed at all because they fail to consider how search engines work. In particular, submitting to search engines is only part of the challenge of getting good search engine positioning. It's also important to prepare a website through 'search engine optimization'. Search engine optimization means ensuring that your web pages are accessible to search engines and are focused in ways that help to improve the chances that they will be found.

How search engines work

The term 'search engine' is often used generically to describe both crawler-based search engines and human-powered directories. These two types of search engines gather their listings in very different ways.

This book provides information, techniques and tools for search engine optimization. This book does not teach you ways to trick or 'spam' search engines. In fact, there is no such search engine magic that will guarantee a top listing. However, there are a number of small changes you can make that can sometimes produce big results.

The book looks at the two major ways search engines get their listings:

1 Crawler-based search engines
2 Human-powered directories

Crawler-based search engines

Crawler-based search engines, such as HotBot, create their listings automatically. They 'crawl' or 'spider' the Web and create an index of the results; people then search through that index. If you change your web pages, crawler-based search engines eventually find these changes, and that can affect how you are listed. This book will look at the spidering process and how page titles, body copy and other elements can all affect the search results.

Human-powered directories

A human-powered directory, such as Yahoo!, depends on humans for its listings. The editors at Yahoo! will write a short description for sites they review. A search looks for matches only in the descriptions submitted.

Changing your web pages has no effect on your listing. Things that are useful for improving a listing with a search engine have nothing to do with improving a listing in a directory. The only exception is that a good site, with good content, might be more likely to get reviewed for free than a poor site.

'Hybrid' search engines or mixed results

In the Web's early days, it used to be that a search engine either presented crawler-based results or human-powered listings. Today it is extremely common for both types of results to be presented, although usually, a hybrid search engine will favour one type of listings over another. For example, Yahoo! is more likely to present human-powered listings. However, it does also present crawler-based results as provided by Google.

The parts of a crawler-based search engine

Crawler-based search engines have three major elements. The first is the spider, also called the crawler, which visits a web page, reads it, and then follows links to other pages within the site. This is what it means when someone refers to a site being 'spidered' or 'crawled'. The spider returns to the site on a regular basis, perhaps every month or two, to look for changes. Everything the spider finds goes into the second part of the search engine, the index. The index, sometimes called the catalog, is like a giant book containing a copy of every web page that the spider finds. If a web page changes, then this book is updated with new information. Sometimes it can take a while for new pages or changes that the spider finds to be added to the index, and thus a web page may have been 'spidered' but not yet 'indexed'. Until it is indexed – added to the index – it is not available to those searching with the search engine. Search engine software is the third part of a search engine. This is the program that sifts through the millions of pages recorded in the index to find matches to a search and rank them in order of what it believes is most relevant.

Major search engines: the same, but different

All crawler-based search engines have the basic parts described above, but there are differences in how these parts are tuned. That is why the same search on different search engines often produces different results. Some of the significant differences between the major crawler-based search engines are summarized on the search engine features page. Information on this page has been drawn from the help pages of each search engine, along with knowledge gained from articles, reviews, books, independent research, tips from others, and additional information received directly from the various search engines.

How search engines rank web pages

Search for anything using your favourite crawler-based search engine. Almost instantly, the search engine will sort through the millions of pages it knows about and present you with ones that match your topic. The matches will even be ranked, so that the most relevant ones come first. Of course, the search engines don't always get it right. Non-relevant pages make it through, and sometimes it may take a little more digging to find what you are looking for. But by and large, search engines do an amazing job. So, how do crawler-based search engines go about determining relevancy, when confronted with hundreds of millions of web pages to sort through? They follow a set of rules, known as an algorithm. Exactly how a particular search engine's algorithm works is a closely kept trade secret. However, all major search engines follow the general rules below.

Location, location, location . . . and frequency

One of the main rules in a ranking algorithm involves the location and frequency of keywords on a web page – let's call it the location/frequency method, for short. Pages with the search terms appearing in the HTML title tag are often assumed to be more relevant than others to the topic. Search engines will also check to see if the search keywords appear near the top of a web page, such as in the headline or in the first few paragraphs of text. They assume that any page relevant to the topic will mention those words right from the beginning. Frequency is the other major factor in how search engines determine relevancy. A search engine will analyse how often keywords appear in relation to other words in a web page. Those with a higher frequency are often deemed more relevant than other web pages.

Spice in the recipe

Now it's time to qualify the location/frequency method described above. All the major search engines follow it to some degree, in the same way that cooks may follow a standard chilli recipe. However, cooks like to add their own secret ingredients. In the same way, search engines add spice to the location/frequency method. Nobody does it exactly the same, which is one reason why the same search on different search engines produces different results.

To begin with, some search engines index more web pages than others. Some search engines also index web pages more often than others. The result is that no search engine has the exact same collection of web pages to search through, and this naturally produces differences when comparing their results.

Many web designers mistakenly assume that META tags are the 'secret' in propelling their web pages to the top of the rankings. However, not all search engines read META tags. In addition, those that do read META tags may chose to weight them differently. Overall, META tags can be part of the ranking recipe, but they are not necessarily the secret ingredient.

Search engines may also penalize pages, or exclude them from the index, if they detect search engine 'spamming'. An example is when a word is repeated hundreds of times on a page, to increase the frequency and propel the page higher in the listings. Search engines watch for common spamming methods in a variety of ways, including following up on complaints from their users.

Off-the-page factors

Crawler-based search engines have plenty of experience now with webmasters who constantly rewrite their web pages in an attempt to gain better rankings. Some sophisticated webmasters may even go to great lengths to 'reverse engineer' the location/frequency systems used by a particular search engine. Because of this, all major search engines now also make use of 'off-the-page' ranking criteria.

Off-the-page factors are those that a webmaster cannot easily influence. Chief among these is link analysis. By analysing how pages link to each other, a search engine can determine both what a page is about and whether that page is deemed to be 'important', and thus deserving of a ranking boost. In addition, sophisticated techniques are used to screen out attempts by webmasters to build 'artificial' links designed to boost their rankings.

Another off-the-page factor is clickthrough measurement. In short, this means that a search engine may watch which results someone selects for a particular search, then eventually drop high-ranking pages that aren't attracting clicks while promoting lower-ranking pages that do pull in visitors. As with link analysis, systems are used to compensate for artificial links generated by eager webmasters.

Chapter 1
Introduction to search engine optimization

To implement search engine optimization (SEO) effectively on your website you will need to have a knowledge of what people looking for your site are searching for, your own needs, and then how to best implement these. Each SEO campaign is different, depending on a number of factors – including the goals of the website, and the budget available to spend on the SEO. The main techniques and areas that work today include:

- Having easily searchable content on your site
- Having links to and from your site from other high profile websites
- The use of paid placement programs
- Optimized site content to make site users stay after they have visited.

This book will teach you about all this, but initially Chapter 1 will take you through the background to search optimization. First of all we will look at the history of search engines, to give you a context to work in, and then we'll take a look at why people use search engines, what they actually search for when they do, and how being ranked highly will benefit your organization. Next we will provide a critical analysis of choosing the right SEO consultancy (if you have to commission an external agency).

The history of search engines on the Web

Back in 1990 there was no World Wide Web, but there was still an Internet, and there were many files around the network that people needed to find. The main way of receiving files was by using File Transfer Protocol (FTP), which gives computers a common way to exchange files over the Internet. This works by using FTP servers, which a computer user sets up on his or her computer. Another computer user can connect to this FTP server using a piece of software called an FTP client. The person retrieving the file has to specify an address and usually a username and password to log onto the FTP server. This was the way most file sharing was done; anyone who wanted to share a file had first to set up an FTP server to make the file available. The only way people could find out where a file was stored was by word-of-mouth; someone would have to post on a message board where a file was stored. The first ever search engine was called Archie, and was created in 1990 by a man called Alan Emtage. Archie was the solution to the problem of finding information easily; the engine combined a data gatherer, which compiled site listings of FTP sites, with an expression matcher that allowed it to retrieve files from a user typing in a search term or query. Archie was the first search engine; it 'spidered' the Internet, matched the files it had found with search queries, and returned results from its database.

In 1993, with the success of Archie growing considerably, the University of Nevada developed an engine called Veronica. These two became affectionately known as the grandfather and grandmother of search engines. Veronica was similar to Archie, but was for Gopher files rather than FTP files. Gopher servers contained plain text files that could be retrieved in the same way as FTP files. Another Gopher search engine also emerged at the time, called Jughead, but this was not as advanced as Veronica. Archie no longer exists, but Figure 1.1 provides an example of an Archie Gateway page that is no longer functional.

The next major advance in search engine technology was the World Wide Web Wanderer, developed by Matthew Gray. This was the first ever robot on the Web, and its aim was to track the Web's growth by counting web servers. As it grew it began to count URLs as well, and this

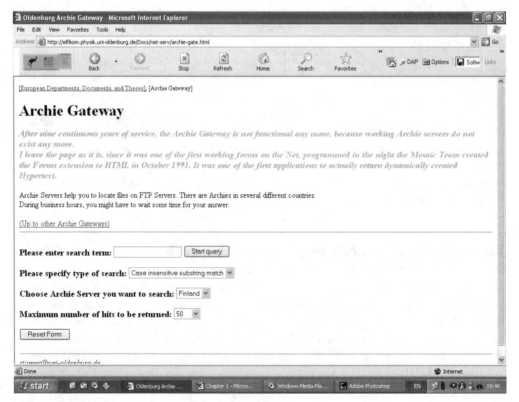

Figure 1.1 *An Archie gateway page (reproduced with permission)*

eventually became the Web's first database of websites. Early versions of the Wanderer software did not go down well initially, as they caused loss of performance as they scoured the Web and accessed single pages many times in a day; however, this was soon fixed. The World Wide Web Wanderer was called a robot, not because it was a robot in the traditional sci-fi sense of the word, but because on the Internet the term robot has grown to mean a program or piece of software that performs a repetitive task, such as exploring the net for information. Web robots usually index web pages to create a database that then becomes searchable; they are also known as 'spiders', and you can read more about how they work in relation to specific search engines in Chapter 2.

After the development of the Wanderer, a man called Martijn Koster created a new type of web indexing software that worked like Archie and was called ALIWEB. ALIWEB was developed in the summer of 1993. It was evident that the Web was growing at an enormous rate, and it became clear to Martijn Koster that there needed to be some way of finding things beyond the existing databases and catalogues that individuals were keeping. ALIWEB actually stood for 'Archie-Like Indexing of the Web'. ALIWEB did not have a web-searching robot; instead of this, webmasters posted their own websites and web pages that they wanted to be listed. ALIWEB was in essence the first online directory of websites; webmasters were given the opportunity to provide a description of their own website and no robots were sent out, resulting in reduced performance loss on the Web. The problem with ALIWEB was that webmasters had to submit their own special index file in a specific format for ALIWEB, and most of them did not understand or did not bother to learn how to create this file. ALIWEB therefore suffered from the problem that people did not use the service, as it was only a relatively small directory. However, it was still a landmark, having been the first database of websites that existed.

The World Wide Web Wanderer inspired a number of web programmers to work on the idea of developing special web robots. The Web continued growing throughout the 1990s, and more and more powerful robots were needed to index the growing number of web pages. The main concept behind spiders was that they followed links from web page to web page – it was logical to assume that every page on the Web was linked to another page, and by searching through each page and following its links a robot could work its way through the pages on the Web. By continually repeating this, it was believed that the Web could eventually be indexed. At the end of December 1993 three search engines were launched that were powered by these advanced robots; these were the JumpStation, the World Wide Web Worm, and the Repository Based Software Engineering Spider (RBSE). JumpStation is no longer in service, but when it was it worked by collecting the title and header from web pages and then using a retrieval system to match these to search queries. The matching system searched through its database of results in a linear fashion and became so slow that, as the Web grew, it eventually ground to a halt. The World Wide Web Worm indexed titles and URLs of web pages, but like the JumpStation it returned results in the order that it found them – meaning that results were in no order of importance. The RBSE spider got around this problem by actually ranking pages in its index by relevance.

All the spiders that were launched around this time, including Architext (the search software that became the Excite engine), were unable to work out actually what it was they were indexing; they lacked any real intelligence. To get around this problem, a product called Elnet Galaxy was launched. This was a searchable and browsable directory, in the same way Yahoo is today (you can read more about directories in Chapter 3). Its website links were organized in a hierarchical structure, which was divided into subcategories and further subcategories until users got to the website they were after. Take a look at the Yahoo directory for an example of this in action today. The service, which went live in January 1994, also contained Gopher and Telnet search features, with an added web page search feature. The next significant stage came with the creation of the Yahoo directory in April 1994, which began as a couple of students' list of favorite web pages, and grew into the worldwide phenomenon that it is today. You can read more about the growth of Yahoo in Chapter 3 of this book, but basically it was developed as a searchable web directory. Yahoo guaranteed the quality of the websites it listed because they were (and still are) accepted or rejected by human editors. The advantage of directories, as well as their guaranteed quality, was that users could also read a title and description of the site they were about to visit, making it easier to make a choice to visit a relevant site.

The first advanced robot, which was developed at the University of Washington, was called WebCrawler (Figure 1.2). This actually indexed the full text of documents, allowing users to search through this text, and therefore delivering more relevant search results.

Figure 1.2 *The WebCrawler website*

WebCrawler was eventually adopted by America Online (AOL), who purchased the system. AOL ran the system on its own network of computers, because the strain on the University of Washington's computer systems had become too much to bear, and the service would have been shut down otherwise. WebCrawler was the first search engine that could index the full text of a page of HTML; before this all a user could search through was the URL and the description of a web page, but the WebCrawler system represented a huge change in how web robots worked.

The next two big guns to emerge were Lycos and Infoseek. Lycos had the advantage in the sheer size of documents that it indexed; it launched on 20 July 1995 with 54 000 documents indexed, and by January 1995 had indexed 1.5 million. When Infoseek launched it was not original in its technology, but it sported a user-friendly interface and extra features such as news and a directory, which won it many fans. In 1999, Disney purchased a 45 per cent stake of Infoseek and integrated it into its Go.com service (Figure 1.3).

In December 1995 AltaVista came onto the scene, and was quickly recognized as the top search engine due to the speed with which it returned results (Figure 1.4). It was also the first search engine to use natural language queries, which meant users could type questions in much the same

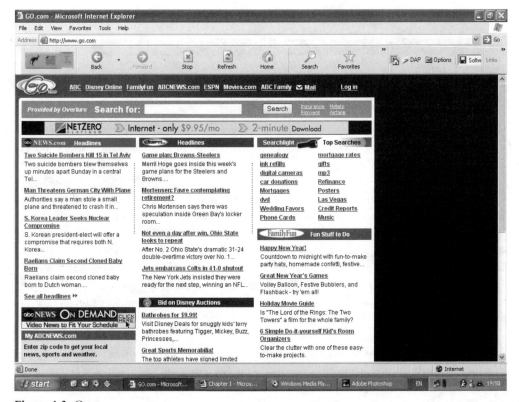

Figure 1.3 *Go.com*

Figure 1.4 *The AltaVista website (reproduced with permission)*

way as they do with Ask Jeeves today, and the engine would recognize this and not return irrelevant results. It also allowed users to search newsgroup articles, and gave them search 'tips' to help refine their search.

On 20 May 1996 Inktomi Corporation was formed, and HotBot was created (Figure 1.5). Inktomi's results are now used by a number of major search services, which are covered in the Inktomi section of Chapter 2 of this book. Hotbot has recently been redesigned for streamlined service and results, and searchers can now choose to search from a variety of sources. When it was launched it was hailed as the most powerful search engine, and it gained popularity quickly. Hotbot claimed to be able to index 10 million web pages a day; it would eventually catch up with itself and re-index the pages it had already indexed, meaning its results would constantly stay up to date.

Around the same time a new service called MetaCrawler was developed, which searched a number of different search engines at once (Figure 1.6). This got around the problem, noticed by many people, of the search engines pulling up completely different results for the same search. MetaCrawler promised to solve this by forwarding search engine queries to search engines such

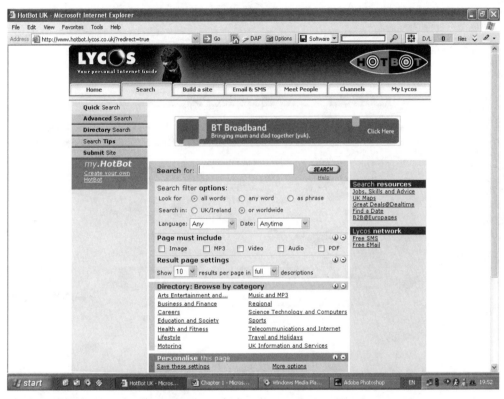

Figure 1.5 *Hotbot (reproduced with permission of Inktomi)*

as AltaVista, Excite and Infoseek simultaneously, and then returning the most relevant results possible. Today MetaCrawler still exists, and covers About, Ask Jeeves, FAST, FindWhat, LookSmart and Overture to get its results.

By mid-1999, search sites had begun using the intelligence of web surfers to improve the quality of search results. This was done through monitoring clicks. The DirectHit search engine introduced a special new technology that watched which sites surfers chose, and the sites that were chosen regularly and consistently for a particular keyword rose to the top of the listings for that keyword. This technology is now in general use throughout the major search engines. DirectHit is now integrated in to the Teoma search service (Figure 1.7).

Next, Google was launched at the end of 1998 (Figure 1.8). Google has grown to become the most popular search engine in existence, mainly owing to its ease of use, the number of pages it indexes, and the relevancy of it results. Google introduced a new way of ranking sites, through link analysis – which means that sites with more links to and from them rank higher. You can read more about Google in Chapter 3 of this book.

Figure 1.6 *The MetaCrawler website (©2003 InfoSpace, Inc. All rights reserved. Reprinted with permission of InfoSpace, Inc.)*

A newcomer to the scene, and certainly a site to look out for in the future, is WiseNut (Figure 1.9). This site was launched in September 2001, and has been hailed as the successor to Google. WiseNut places a lot of emphasis on link analysis to ensure accurate and relevant results. It is covered in more depth in Chapter 2, and can be found at www.wisenut.com.

Other notable landmarks that will be discussed later in the book include the launch of LookSmart in October 1996, the Open Directory in June 1998 and, in April 1997, Ask Jeeves, which was intended to create a unique user experience emphasizing an intuitive easy-to-use system. Also launched around this time was GoTo, later to be called Overture, which was the first pay-per-click search engine (see Chapter 4).

There we have it, a brief history of search engines. Some have been missed out, of course, but the ones covered here show the major developments in the technology, and serve as an introduction to the main topics that are covered in a lot more detail later in this book.

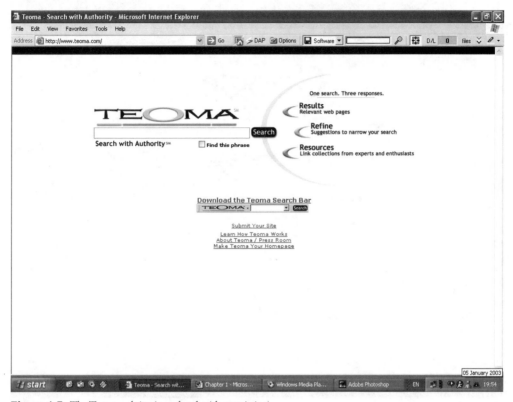

Figure 1.7 *The Teoma website (reproduced with permission)*

Why do people search?

Having a page indexed is the first stage of being recognized by search engines, and is essential – we can go as far as to say that until it is indexed, your site does not exist. Unless the surfer has seen your web address on a piece of promotional material or as a link from another site, he or she will try to find your website by using a search engine – most likely Google or Yahoo. If your site is not listed in the index of a search engine, then the surfer cannot access it. Many URLs are not obvious or even logical, and for most searches we have no idea of the URL we are trying to find. This is why we use search engines – they create an index of the World Wide Web and build a giant database by collecting keywords and other information from web pages. This database links page content with keywords and URLs, and is then able to return results depending on what keywords or search terms a web surfer enters as search criteria. Our research shows that around 80 per cent of websites are found through search engines. This makes it clear why companies want to come up first in a listing when a web surfer performs a related search. People use search engines to find specific content, whether a company's website or their favorite particular recipe. What you need to do through your website SEO is ensure that you make it easy for surfers to find your site, by ranking highly in search engines, being listed in directories, and having relevant links to and from your site across the World Wide Web. Essentially, you are trying to make your website search-engine friendly.

Figure 1.8 *Familiar to most of us, the Google homepage (reproduced with permission)*

Search engines have become extremely important to the average web user, and research shows that around eight in ten web users regularly use search engines on the Web. The Pew Internet Project Data Memo (which can be found at www.pewinternet.org), released in July 2002, reveals some extremely compelling statistics. It states that more than one in four (or about 33 million) adults use a search engine on a daily basis in the USA, and that 85 per cent of American Internet users have used an online search engine to find information on the Web. The report states that 'search engines are the most popular way to locate a variety of types of information online'. The only online activity to be more popular than using a search engine is sending and receiving emails. Some other statistics that the report revealed were:

- College graduates are more likely to use a search engine on a typical day (39 per cent, compared to 20 per cent of high school graduates).
- Internet users who have been online for three or more years are also heavy search engine users (39 per cent on a typical day, compared to 14 per cent of those who gained access in the last six months).
- Men are more likely than women to use a search engine on a typical day (33 per cent, compared to 25 per cent of women).

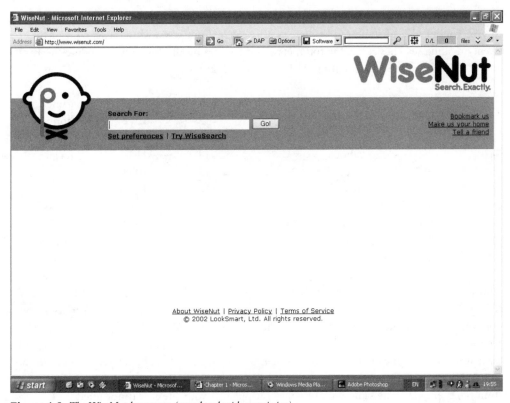

Figure 1.9 *The WiseNut homepage (reproduced with permission)*

If you not convinced already of the importance of SEO as part of the eMarketing mix, here are some more interesting statistics:

- The NPD Group, a research group specializing in consumer purchasing and behavior study, has shown that search engine positions are around two to three times more effective for generating sales than banner ads (http://www.overture.com/d/about/advertisers/slab.jhtml).
- 81 per cent of UK users find the websites they are looking for through search engines (Source: UK Internet User Monitor. Forrester Research Inc., June 2000).
- According to a report published by the NPD Group, 92 per cent of online consumers use search engines to shop and/or purchase online.
- A study conducted by IMT Strategies found that search engines are the number one way (46 per cent) by which people find websites; random surfing and word-of-mouth were ranked equal second (20 per cent each).

Finding out what people search for

Sites that allow you to see what people are searching for are listed at the end of Chapter 7. As well as being a bit of fun, these sites can be quite revealing; they let you see the top search terms for particular searches across various search engines, and the terms that are doing the best overall. Just to give you an idea of some results, here is a list taken from www.wordtracker.com of the top twenty ranking searches across the top metasearch engines on the Internet (including the Excite and MetaCrawler search engines) on 24 December 2002:

1	3958	autos	11	1369	games
2	2909	travel	12	1272	hotmail
3	2223	Google	13	1199	hotmail.com
4	1995	Yahoo	14	1122	recipes
5	1957	jokes	15	1098	cars
6	1869	ebay	16	1029	christmas
7	1858	hotels	17	1011	books
8	1586	health	18	1008	white pages
9	1411	yahoo.com	19	1005	powerball
10	1405	lyrics	20	972	mortgages

This is interesting reading – particularly that people are actually searching on search engines for 'Google', 'Yahoo' and even 'Yahoo.com'. This goes to show that even if web surfers know a company's name (in the case of the 1411 searches for 'Yahoo.com' they knew practically the whole web address) they will still search for it on a search engine. These searchers were using one particular search engine in order to find another. If Google and Yahoo, therefore, do not have good search engine positioning, then they will lose a lot of users who cannot find their site in searches from other engines. The same will, of course, happen to your site if it is not listed.

So what's so great about being ranked highly?

Getting listed in a search engine doesn't do you much good if you're number 298 of 900 524 results, and it also doesn't help much if you rank at number eleven. Most search engines display ten results per page, and this is where you have to be aiming for. So once your site is indexed, you will need to turn your attention to ranking. Realistically you want to be aiming for the top ten to twenty positions on any given search engine, and these are the most treasured positions by webmasters. You will read more about positioning on specific engines and directories as you read through this book, but take the top ten as a general rule of thumb. Some webmasters go as far as to employ 'dirty tricks' to get their site into the top positions, but why do they do this?

To find the answer, you need to put yourself into the position of a searcher. When searchers are confronted with a page of results, their immediate reaction is to look down that list and then stop looking when they see a relevant site. No major studies exist regarding the importance of top ranking, but common sense dictates that searchers will visit the first two or three relevant sites found rather than trawling through pages of search results to find your site listed at position 298. Our own research shows that around 50 per cent of search engine users expect to find the answer to their query on the first page, or within the top ten search engine results. Another 20 per cent revealed that they would not go past the second page of search results to find the site they were looking for. Therefore, if your website is not ranked towards the top you will essentially be invisible to most search engine users. Most search engine software uses both the position and the frequency of keywords to work out the website ranking order – so a web page with a high frequency of keywords towards the beginning will appear higher on the listing than one with a low frequency of keywords further down in the text. Another major factor that is taken into account is link popularity. All these topics are covered in more detail in Chapter 6.

Today's search engine promotion requires a multifaceted approach. To achieve a site's full potential, site promotion must incorporate target audience research and analysis, competitor analysis, pay-per-click optimization, and professional copywriting. SEO also requires a sharp eye and an ear to the ground; search engine technology is constantly changing, so you will need to keep up with the changes and reassess your search engine strategy accordingly.

Should you use an SEO consultancy or do it yourself?

By buying this book you have already taken the first steps towards DIY SEO, but for some of you the use of an SEO consultancy will be unavoidable and perhaps you have chosen this book to arm you with the knowledge you need to approach an SEO company confidently. In any case, if you do decide to use an SEO consultant there are a number of issues that you will need to be aware of.

Specialist marketing firms, like Sprite Interactive, live and breathe search engine marketing, and understand fully what it takes to generate traffic for your site and to achieve a top ranking. By investing in the services of one of the many highly skilled SEO consultants available you can reap considerable rewards, but you need to have the knowledge to choose the company that is right for you. There are a number of companies who will use underhand tactics to attempt to promote your site, or who will not promote your site well at all. You should start with the basics when you approach an SEO company. Ask the consultant to explain the difference between a directory and a search engine (which you, of course, will know after reading this book). Then ask what type of approach will be taken when the company optimizes your site – which should be done within the site's existing structure. SEO consultants should be able to explain to you how the different search engines find their content, and have a good working knowledge of web design and development – including HTML and Flash. You should be able to ask them questions about the site architecture (see Chapter 6) and expect answers, as this information is essential to any SEO campaign.

Credible SEO consultants should outline a plan where they will spend time working with you to develop the relevant site keywords and phrases that you expect people to use when searching for you. Consultants should also be skilled in writing quality, concise copy. Building link popularity for your site is another important service provided by SEO consultants, as it will boost your ranking on certain search engines – in a nutshell, you should make sure any links you exchange with other sites are relevant, and that the consultant does not use automated linking software (see Chapter 5). Be very wary of consultants who advocate 'spamming' techniques, such as using hidden text on your web pages or submitting your site multiple times over a short period of time. They will only be found out by the search engine in question, and thus run the risk of getting your site banned altogether. Legitimate SEO consultants will work well within the rules set by the search engines, and will keep up to date with these rules through industry sources.

An investment in professional SEO consultancy is likely to be cheaper than one month of a print advertising campaign. For that your site will be optimized across three to five key phrases. Your contract will probably last from six months to a year, as it will take this long for the optimization to take full effect. Expect your chosen SEO consultants to be able reliably to inform you about the latest rates on all the pay-for-placement engines (see Chapter 4). If you choose correctly, your SEO consultant can save you a considerable amount of time and effort, and will generate quality targeted traffic for your site.

Watch out for companies that offer guarantees against rankings achieved. Many of these are pretty worthless, and generally have a number of 'let-out' clauses. There is no guarantee of success, but there are ways greatly to increase the odds of being ranked highly. The main factor in measuring the success of an SEO campaign is the increase in traffic to your website.

You need to ask yourself a few questions when choosing an SEO professional. Is it the consultant's job to increase your sales? Is the consultant there to increase your traffic? Or just to get you a high ranking? Most SEO professionals would agree that they are there to get their client's site ranked highly, and many will state up front that this is their main aim; however, generally speaking the first two options will result as a knock-on effect of having a highly ranked site. What happens if this is not the case? The client will often assume that high rankings will immediately result in extra traffic and additional sales, but in some cases this does not happen, and the finger of blame is pointed. So who is to blame? The answer will lie in what the original agreement and expectations were between the SEO consultant and the client. There are a number of reasons why sales or traffic might not increase, and these may be the fault of either the SEO company or the client.

For example, it would be the SEO company's fault if the wrong keywords were targeted. A client's website may be listed highly but for the wrong keywords and search terms, and therefore would not generate any relevant traffic, or any traffic at all. So make sure you agree on what keywords you are going to use first, to avoid any conflicts later on. There is no real excuse for an SEO professional to target the wrong keywords, especially after having consulted you and doing the necessary research.

There are two immediate ways in which the client could be in the wrong. First, the client may decide that he or she knows best, fail to pay attention to the SEO advice offered, and choose unrelated keywords for the website. It is up to the client to follow the advice of the SEO consultant. Secondly, a client may have a badly designed site, which does not convert visitors into sales; an SEO consultant can advise on this, but in the end it is down to the client to act and to commission a site redesign.

It's important to know exactly what you'll be getting from your SEO company right from the start, and here is a checklist of questions to ask a potential SEO consultant:

1 How long have you been providing search engine optimization services?
2 Are you an individual consultant, or are you part of a team?
3 How long have you and your team been online?
4 What types of websites do you *not* promote?
6 Can you describe and/or produce recent successful campaign results?
7 Do you have website design experience?
8 What are your opinions with regard to best practices for the SEO industry, and how do you try to keep to these?
9 How many search engine optimization campaigns have you been involved with? What was your role for those projects? How many are still active? How many are inactive? If inactive, why?
10 Are there any guarantees for top search engine positions? (The answer to this question will depend on whether or not you choose a pay-per-click program; see Chapter 4 for more information.)
11 Do you have experience managing bid management campaigns?
12 What strategies would you use to increase our website's link popularity?
13 Explain to me how Google's PageRank software works, and how you could increase our website's rating. (The answer to this will involve building quality inbound links to your website.)
14 How would you orchestrate a links popularity campaign?
15 What changes can we expect you to make to our website to improve our positioning in the search engines?
16 Will there be changes in the coding of our website to make it rank better?
17 What type of reporting will you provide us with, and how often?

This checklist provides a useful starting point for you when approaching an SEO professional. At Sprite we make sure that all the consultants can answer these questions and more whenever they are approached for new SEO business. Most importantly, however, if you choose to use SEO professionals, be patient with them. You need to remember that SEO is a long-term process, and it will take around six months before you have any real measure of success. If you are not happy with the results after this time, then it is probably time to move on. Appendix A provides an example SEO presentation; although this is more of an internal presentation, it will give you an idea of some of the issues you should be looking out for.

Natural traffic

If you are going to use an agency for SEO, then you will also need to tap into your site's natural traffic. You can see how you need to employ a variety of tools and methods in order to develop a successful campaign by looking at the pie chart at the start of Chapter 7 (Figure 7.1). Your natural traffic is web traffic that will develop outside of the optimization services provided by an SEO company. It is not traffic that is 'directed' to your site by good search engine ranking and positioning; it is traffic that will find your site in other ways, such as through printed advertising or through having a shared interest in your website. You need to bear this in mind throughout your SEO process, as it is part of the full marketing mix that will result in quality traffic for your website. Make sure your print advertising (and any other promotional material for that matter) features your web address in a prominent position. Target relevant publications with your advertisements, and make sure that any groups that share an interest in your website are well informed. If you want to track the success of a print campaign, one technique you can use is to feature an alternative URL; you can then track the amount of hits to this URL, which will tell you how successful the print ad or campaign has been. Tapping into your site's natural traffic may take more thought and planning than just optimizing your site and hoping that people will find it by searching for it, but the hits that you will receive from 'natural' traffic will be of a higher quality, and will be more likely to spend longer on your site than those coming from search engine results alone. Another way to increase your 'natural' traffic is by building your site's link popularity (see Chapter 5).

In conclusion

This chapter has been designed as a basic introduction to some of the concepts surrounding SEO. It is clear from reading the statistics quoted that getting listed on search engines is essential to promote your website effectively, and that ranking highly is essential if you want your site to be noticed by surfers performing searches. If you do choose to use an SEO consultancy, then be sure to follow the guidelines outlined above, and read this book first to give you the knowledge to approach an agency confidently and make sure you are able to get the most out of them. Remember that SEO is a long-term process; it cannot happen overnight, and it is something that you need to commit to fully to get the most out of it.

Chapter 2

Web crawlers

A web crawler is a program that automatically surfs the Internet looking for links. It then follows each link and retrieves documents that in turn have links, recursively retrieving all further documents that are referenced. Web crawlers are sometimes referred to as web wanderers, web robots, or spiders. These names give the impression that the software itself moves between sites, although this is not the case. A crawler simply visits sites by requesting documents from them, and then automatically visits the links on those documents.

Unlike directories, where you subscribe a URL, with a crawler you are likely to have several (if not many) pages listed. Crawler-based search engines automatically visit web pages to compile their listings. This means that by taking care in how you build your pages, you can rank well in crawler-produced results.

Web crawlers start from a list of URLs, such as server lists. Most indexing services also allow you to submit URLs manually, which will then be visited by the crawler. Crawlers can select URLs to visit and index, and to use as a source for new URLs. Robots may index the HTML titles, or the first few paragraphs, or parse the entire HTML and index all words, prioritizing the HTML constructs (see Chapter 6 for more on HTML construction and page architecture). Some parse the META tag, or other special hidden tags. To register your site with a robot, you need to find the link to a URL submission form on the crawler's search page. Fortunately you don't have to submit your URL manually to every service: Submit-it <URL: http://www.bcentral.com/products/si/default.asp> will do it for you.

You can always check to see if a crawler has visited your site by looking at your server logs. If your server supports user-agent logging, you can check for retrievals by looking at the user-agent header values. If you notice a site repeatedly checking for the file '/robots.txt', chances are it is a robot.

You will notice lots of entries to 'robots.txt' in your log files. This is because the log files are automatically generated by your server robots, which are trying to see if you have specified any rules for them using the Standard for Robot Exclusion. If you don't care about robots and want to prevent the messages in your error logs, simply create an empty file called robots.txt in the root level of your server (see Chapter 6 for more information regarding robots.txt files).

The alternative to using robots.txt is a new standard for using HTML META tags to keep robots out of your documents. To learn more about META tags, refer to Chapter 6.

It is true that listing pages or directories in the robots.txt file may invite curiosity as to why you are keeping people out. So, you can put all the files you don't want robots to visit in a separate subdirectory and make it unlistable, then list only the directory name in the robots.txt. A robot can't traverse that directory unless a link is placed from a file on the Web.

Submitting to Google

Arguably the most important crawler-based search engine is Google. Yahoo and AOL Search have their main results 'powered' by Google. The best way to get listed with Google is to build links to your website – in fact, this is the way to get listed for free with all the major crawlers on the Web. Crawlers' only purpose in life is to follow links, so the more links you have pointing to your site,

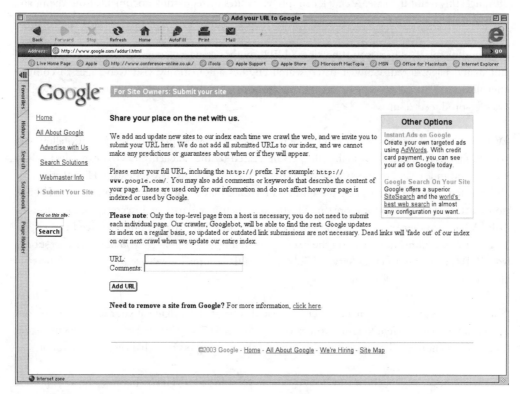

Figure 2.1 *The Google Add URL page (reproduced with permission)*

the more likely it is that the crawlers will find and include your pages. This of course means that if you have submitted your site to the major directories, then Google and other crawlers will almost certainly have found the URL that was listed – thus you can benefit in two ways from subscribing to the directories. Basic tips on building good links are covered in Chapter 6, and Chapter 3 discusses submitting to directories. You can Add URL in Google, which lets you submit a URL directly to its crawler: http://www.google.com/addurl.html. Figure 2.1 shows you the page and its contents.

Whilst you cannot guarantee that Google will include a URL submitted to it in this way, it is the only means by which you can submit your site details. If you do submit, then you should submit your home page and perhaps one or two other URLs from 'inside' your website via the Add URL page. The main reason for submitting some of your inside pages is that this increases the target for the crawler, which may miss your home page, and gives Google a number of alternate routes into your site. It could take up to a month before Google lists the web pages of a new site, and because of this you might consider making use of its paid placement program (see Chapter 4).

How does Google manage to find the right results for every query so quickly? The engine behind Google's search technology is PigeonRank™, which is a system for ranking web pages developed by Google founders Larry Page and Sergey Brin at Stanford University. Brin argued that low-cost pigeon clusters (PCs) could be used to compute the relative value of web pages faster than human editors or machine-based algorithms. PigeonRank gets its name from the domestic pigeon (*Columba livia*) and its unique capacity to recognize objects regardless of spatial orientation – the common grey pigeon can easily distinguish among items displaying the smallest differences. In the same way, Google has the ability to select relevant websites from among thousands of similar pages. By collecting clusters of computers, Google is able to process search queries at speeds superior to those of traditional search engines. When a search query is submitted to Google, it is routed to a data store where monitors flash result pages at tremendous speeds. When one computer in the cluster identifies a relevant result it assigns the page a rank value of one, and for each result the rank increases. Those pages receiving the most hits are returned at the top of the user's results page, with the other results displayed below. A Google search is a way of finding high-quality websites with information relevant to your search.

Submitting to Inktomi

Inktomi (Figure 2.2) is a crawler-based search engine, and adds to its content in two ways; by link crawling and paid inclusion. It discontinued its free Add URL page in September 2002. Inktomi does not make its search engine available to the public through its own site, but is instead licensed to other companies. These companies are then able to offer web-wide searching without having to build the crawler-based listings themselves.

Inktomi provides back-up results to MSN Search. Most search engines provide human-powered 'directory' results in some way. A search at Google going through the 'category' links leads to a

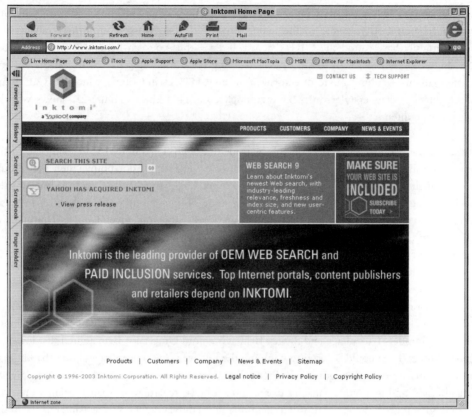

Figure 2.2 *The Inktomi website (reproduced with permission)*

human-compiled result always appearing at the very top of the search results page. The human-compiled search engines always have a back-up partnership with a crawler-based search engine.

Link crawling

The Inktomi crawler finds the pages naturally as it moves around the Web following links, and by far the best way of being listed is for the crawler to find your site in its own time in this way. The more links you have, the more likely it is that a crawler will find your site. Once you start featuring links from other sites this will in turn generate more links, because webmasters will see that your site is rating highly for a particular topic relevant to their content and so will link to you. The quality of the content is important as a basis for propagating links; if your content is good, relevant and regularly updated, then websites will link to it. Inktomi will not index pages that are delivered dynamically; Chapter 6 covers this issue and how to get around it.

Inktomi's crawler may eventually find and index your pages with just one link from somebody else's site. The amount of pages Inktomi will include may vary, and it is more likely to index single pages within your site that have a single link pointing at them. To help it with this,

Inktomi maintains a 'WebMap' from across the Web. The WebMap is made up of links from the Web, and can determine which pages are linked to most often. It is also more likely to index documents that are 'elevated' in your site, rather than buried deeply in a complicated directory structure.

Index Refresh

Inktomi revisits every non-paid inclusion page in its index at least once during a two- to three-week period – on average, around every ten days, although it has been known for pages to be revisited far more frequently than this. Pages may be tagged for fast refresh if they are seen as popular or if they've been observed to change often over time. You can sometimes have pages dropped after they have been revisited. If the Inktomi crawler tries to reach a page repeatedly but has trouble accessing it, then the page will be dropped from the listings; this could be due to server problems and network delays.

Paid inclusion

If your pages are not 'picked up' by the crawler, then you have to use 'paid inclusion' programs. Paid inclusion allows you to pay to ensure that your pages are listed, but does *not* guarantee that your pages will rank well for particular terms. The upside is that you know that your pages will be included in the index and will appear somewhere in response to searches. All new commercial sites should use the program, as they will be ranked quickly in Inktomi for a modest sum of money (see Chapter 4 for more on paid inclusion).

Inktomi's Search/Submit

http://www.inktomi.com/products/web_search/submit.html

You should at least use 'Search/Submit' to get your home page listed. This program is designed for smaller websites, and uses a self-serve model, charging a fee per page. You pick the pages that you want indexed, then use a form to submit them along with your credit card details, paying a set amount per page. Once the pages are accepted, they'll appear within the Inktomi Paid Inclusion index within two days and will be revisited for up to a year (see Chapter 4). If you build up some links, then it's more likely that your site will not be dropped by the crawler. Home pages are very important to all crawlers; paying the fee is really only speeding up the process of getting the home page listed for a new site. 'Search Submit' is not sold by Inktomi, but rather through its partners. The fees work on a sliding scale, with it being cheaper to submit subsequent pages than the first one.

Index Connect

Inktomi's Index Connect program is designed for those who wish to list 1000 or more pages with the service. It can present your entire catalogue of products, services, and premium content through leading search portals. It offers your most relevant pages to a large, qualified audience, and helps your customers find you – not your competitors. Instead of a fee per page, as with the Search/Submit program described above, Index Connect uses cost-per-click (CPC) pricing (see Chapter 4).

Changing URLs

All Inktomi's partners should allow you to change your URLs without additional cost. For example, if you paid to include 50 URLs and then monitored your website logs to discover that only ten of these were receiving measurable traffic attributable to Inktomi partners, it would mean you were paying for 40 URLs but not recovering their cost in visitors to your site. In this situation, the first thing you should do is see if you can optimize those URLs and get better results. This will take time. Alternatively, you can drop those 40 URLs from the program and instead change to 40 new URLs. It may be that some of these will just naturally rank well, saving you from having to perform optimization work. Clickthrough reporting is now offered to all paid inclusion partners by Inktomi. Be aware that there is no advantage to submitting the same URLs to more than one partner; all of them feed into the Inktomi index, so using more than one for the same URL is a waste of money.

Relevancy and content

Inktomi indexes the full-text of documents, but ignores certain common words during phrase searches; there is no way to override their exclusion.

As with most major crawler-based search engines, Inktomi will rank pages better in reply to particular queries if they contain the search terms in their HTML body copy with some degree of occurrence. The particular terms you want a page to be found for should appear in the title tag of that page. A ranking boost is also given to pages that contain the search terms in their META tags – in the META keywords tag, the META description tag, or both. However, probably the biggest role in ranking is that of link analysis. The engine analyses links from across the Web to determine both the importance of a page and the terms it might be relevant for. Clickthrough measurements are also used to determine if a page should be given a boost in rankings for particular terms. In addition, Inktomi has internal editorial staff who constantly run large numbers of searches and then select relevant documents. Inktomi then uses these human data to tweak its various relevancy controls to try automatically to match the human selections. In this way, the company hopes to model the human qualities of what's relevant into its ranking software.

Inktomi news index – Moreover

http://www.moreover.com/

Inktomi has a news index that is refreshed every fifteen minutes, and is provided to partners that wish to carry it. This news content is gathered by Moreover. Moreover provides news coverage in about 300 different categories or 'webfeeds', ranging from biotech to Coca Cola news. When you visit the site, you'll find a list of webfeeds via dropdown boxes on the left side of the home page. Choosing a webfeed displays current headlines online, and you can also enter your email address to receive headlines on a daily or weekly basis.

To create its webfeeds, Moreover crawls about 1500–2000 different sources. Some of these are news sites, such as CNN or the *New York Times*; others are sites about a particular subject rather than exclusively about news. It's this inclusion of subject-oriented sites that gives Moreover its edge. Moreover has a staff of about eight editors who establish the different webfeeds. They create keywords and definitions designed to locate relevant stories for each webfeed, and also establish which websites (or sections of particular websites) have content related to a particular webfeed.

Submitting to FAST Search (AllTheWeb.com)

FAST Web Search is a crawler-based search engine that uses its own technology to create a web page index. Not only is FAST Web Search a web crawler-based search engine that powers the primary results for Lycos; it also maintains its own search engine called AllTheWeb.com, which the general public can use. This serves as a 'showcase' site for FAST. Again, as with the other crawlers, building links is the best way to get listed for free. If you submit your site via an Add URL

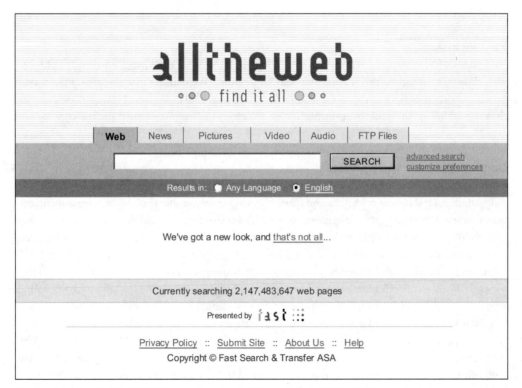

Figure 2.3 *The FAST Add URL page (reproduced with permission of AlltheWeb)*

page (http://www.alltheweb.com/add_url.php) it can take up to six weeks to see the results, assuming your pages accepted – which is not guaranteed. Figure 2.3 demonstrates how easy it is to add your URL to this free listing.

FAST will guarantee to include your pages within two days if you use its paid inclusion program. As with Inktomi, new sites need to use the program to get their home pages listed quickly. The cost is modest, and means that the page will be revisited every two days for up to a year. It's possible that your page might be dropped if you don't renew, but this is highly unlikely to happen to a home page.

FAST inclusion is sold by FAST's portal partners. Currently, the best way to sign up is via the Lycos program (http://search.lycos.com/searchservices/) or through PositionTech.com.

Most people will encounter FAST results through its key partner, Terra Lycos. FAST adds content to its web page index in three major ways: by link crawling, paid inclusion and free Add URL submissions. FAST's crawler will index dynamic pages, to some degree. If it reads a static page that links to a dynamic page (as defined by those with &, %, =, $ or ? symbols in their URLs), the crawler will then read that dynamic page but not follow any links from it. Dynamic pages can also be submitted through the paid inclusion program.

Paid inclusion

Paid inclusion is the guaranteed way to have your site indexed. If your pages constantly fail to get picked up naturally, then this is your only way to be listed. Remember that the program does not guarantee that the pages you pay for will rank well for particular phrases. However, by ensuring they are included, this will bring in traffic (see Chapter 4 for more on paid inclusion).

Content Indexed and Refresh

FAST will read and store both URL text and body text in its index. Invisible and 'small' text is indexed, though it is subject to the same spam filters as is more visible text. META tag information is not indexed, including the description or META keywords tags; META description content is used for display purposes only. FAST refreshes about 20 to 30 per cent of its web page index every seven to ten days, using an 'adaptive' crawl. These pages get selected in three key ways. First, FAST monitors its clickthrough logs to see which pages are coming up most often in search results. These pages are likely to get refreshed more often, so as to avoid users encountering '404 page not found' errors. Second, FAST looks to link popularity data to identify which pages seem most important. Finally, it visits newly found sites on a more regular basis initially, to watch how often they change. If they change frequently, then they may be added to the adaptive crawl. Most of the remaining pages are refreshed every month, although about 15 per cent of the index may take longer than a month to refresh. The exception is paid inclusion URLs, which will be revisited and refreshed in the web page index every two days.

Relevancy ranking

Page descriptions

META keyword tags are not indexed. FAST generates page descriptions in one of three ways:

1 It will use your META description tag
2 It will use your page's description from the Open Directory, if it is listed there
3 If you are not in the Open Directory, it will default to using the first 200 characters or so that appear in your visible HTML body copy.

FAST will also examine the location and frequency of your terms on a page, in determining whether it should rank well.

Link analysis

The FAST relevancy ranking system is based on link analysis as part of its 'FirstPage'. In the early days of the Web, search engines made use of 'link popularity' as part of their ranking mechanisms. In a pure link popularity system, sheer numbers count – the more links point at your page, the more important your page is considered to be. Today, the major search engines have moved on from sheer numbers. Because some site owners create 'artificial' links for boosting their rankings, major search engines make use of 'link analysis' rather than link popularity.

With link analysis, a search engine tries to determine the relative importance of each link and its context. By leveraging both of these aspects, a search engine can make better use of link structures than pure link popularity permits.

Directory structures

According to FAST, Pages in 'higher' levels are more likely to be ranked better. For example, here are pages at various levels in the Sprite website:

http://www.sprite.net/process.htm
http://www.sprite.net/process/design/index.htm
http://www.sprite.net/process/design/methodology/index.htm

The first page is at the top level of the website, as the page name 'process.htm' comes after the first slash following the domain name 'www.sprite.net'. The second page is on the second level, and the third page is on the third level. The third page is 'buried' within the site, and therefore might not rank as well.

Spam detection

FAST tries to eliminate spam by watching for unusual linkages – sites that appear to be linking together for purposes of making themselves more popular. It also examines the frequency of terms on pages, and removes those that seem excessively unusual for that language. FAST checks to see if terms appear excessively in different locations of a document and at a high frequency, which can be suggestive of 'doorway' style pages that target a particular term.

The main advice from FAST is not to try and overly engineer your pages. Make use of the terms you want to be found for in your body copy and in your title tags. Keep your terms relevant to your content.

AllTheWeb site

FAST runs its own search site called AllTheWeb. Relatively few people actually use this site, in comparison to those run by FAST partners, such as Lycos.com. However, it can be helpful to understand some of the specifics at AllTheWeb. It uses clustering, or what it calls 'site collapsing'. This means that you shouldn't see more than two pages in the top results from any particular site when doing a web search. AllTheWeb also watches for 'nonsense' pages, where the text may make no sense to a human reader, despite having a sentence structure intended to make it appear normal and relevant to crawlers.

Other search indexes

FAST has separate indexes for multimedia content, such as pictures, video and MP3 files, FTP listings, and news content. News content comes from 3000 news websites that have been identified as such by Jupiter Media Metrix. This information is gathered from across the Web, so if you publish it you could show up in these indexes.

Partners

FAST distributes its listings to a wide variety of partners. Among these, Terra Lycos is key. It runs the Lycos.com website, which makes heavy use of FAST's crawler-based results. Lycos Europe is another major FAST partner, which uses the results for its sites in Europe. Also in Europe, World Online, Wind and the Scandinavia Online network of sites use FAST listings.

When you are listed in the FAST web page index your pages are made available to all the various partners, so you don't need to submit to each partner. However, be aware that different partners may implement the use of FAST's results in various ways. This is why you may see ranking differences, if you compare results between partners. For example, there may be slight differences between the results at Lycos.com and AllTheWeb, both in ranking and in counts reported.

Submitting to Teoma

Ask Jeeves owns Teoma, and Teoma is an important crawler-based search engine because it powers the Ask Jeeves website. Teoma has no free Add URL page; it creates its index from crawling the Web, so if you have links pointing at your website you will get included naturally some time down the line. However, Teoma will guarantee to include your pages if you use its paid inclusion program, and it has been known to list sites within three days. This appears to be the only feasible route for a commercial website. For a small fee, the page will be revisited each week for up to a year. It's possible that your page could be dropped if you don't renew, but this is highly unlikely to happen to a home page. To sign up for the program, visit http://ask.ineedhits.com/

Teoma and Ask Jeeves results

A major group of listings on the Ask Jeeves results page is headed 'You may find my search results helpful'. The listings in this section come from Teoma (see Figure 2.4).

Teoma is a very good search engine, but cannot compete with the breadth of Google and its dominance of the Web. Teoma offers three kinds of results for each query. On the left of the results page are 'relevant web pages', which are typical of other engines. On the right are two other kinds of results: 'Refine', a list of 'Suggestions to narrow your search', and 'Resources', which are 'link collections from experts and enthusiasts'. All three types of results are generated using proprietary technology that makes them unique compared to those of other engines.

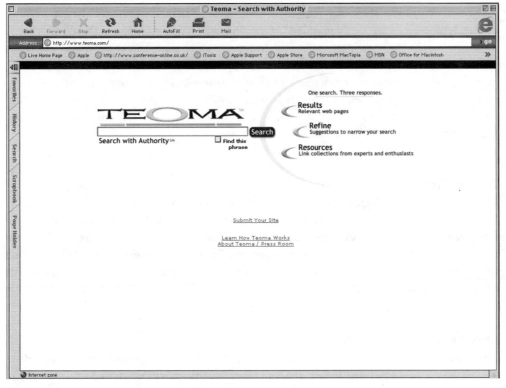

Figure 2.4 *www.teoma.com (reproduced with permission)*

Teoma's underlying technology is an extension of the HITS algorithm developed by researchers at IBM. Teoma seeks out 'hubs' and 'establishments' related to your query terms using a 'social network' of related content that forms a 'community' about the topic. This approach differs from Google's, which uses a similar but more static ranking system. It's also unlike the approach taken by Northern Light and other engines that classify web pages based on predefined categories.

The 'Refine' result is Teoma's exceptional feature. These links are automatically generated labels that 'define' a community for the query words entered by the user. So even if an initial query doesn't provide good results, the 'Refine' links allow the user to 'drill down' into a community, revealing information that would never be found using other search engines. This dynamic approach to content means that Teoma can find the beginnings of a new community for new or obscure pages. This is an alternative approach to that used by other search engines (including Google), which tend to rely on lots of links pointing to pages.

Teoma is a new type of hybrid between a search engine and a directory, incorporating the best features of both. Like most search engines, Teoma's scope is large enough to satisfy even the most obscure information need, but without overwhelming the user.

Ask Jeeves and Direct Hit

Ask Jeeves owns Direct Hit, which recently became integrated into the Teoma offering. Direct Hit provided Ask Jeeves with a version of the Open Directory, which is offered to those who choose the 'Browse by Subject' tab at the top of the Ask Jeeves home page. Direct Hit results were both provided to the Direct Hit site itself and distributed to partner sites. Direct Hit measures what pages users selected from the search results of all of its partners, plus those using its own site. It also measures how long they spend visiting these pages, and the more 'popular' pages rise to the top of its results. Direct Hit also crawls the Web, so that it can refine its own listings, rather than rely just on the clickthrough measured at its partners' sites.

Answer link

This is a paid inclusion program that allows sites to be listed in the Ask Jeeves knowledge base. Editors will review your site, determine the types of questions you would provide an answer for, and give you an estimate of the traffic they'd expect to send to you over six months. You will then pay for the forecast based on the perceived value of the search queries you may be relevant for and the overall amount of traffic expected to be generated. Your site must have 'quality content' and meet editorial guidelines to be involved in this program. Frames on your website are an absolute no-no.

DirectLinx

These are paid text ads that appear under the heading 'Featured Sponsor' on the Ask Jeeves site, usually to the right of the main listings. They must be purchased through the Ask Jeeves advertising department.

Submitting to AltaVista

AltaVista is primarily a crawler-based search engine, which uses its own technology to create a web page index that forms the bulk of the listings that appear in response to a search from the AltaVista home page. It is not as popular as it used to be, but a significant number of people still use it to search the Web. AltaVista's crawler will probably locate your site, follow links within it and add pages to its web page index. It will visit your site every four weeks to check for changes and new pages, so building links is the best way to get listed for free. You can then take advantage of other sites' investment in search optimization.

AltaVista does take submission via an Add URL page (http://addurl.altavista.com/addurl/new). You need only submit your home page and one or two inside pages, and should expect a delay of one month if your site gets accepted. There are no guarantees to those using the Add URL page.

The Add URL page will display a submission code that must be entered. The code is a series of letters and numbers displayed in a graphic format (see Figure 2.5); automatic submission tools cannot read the information. This has been done because AltaVista found that the vast majority of automated submissions were for low quality pages.

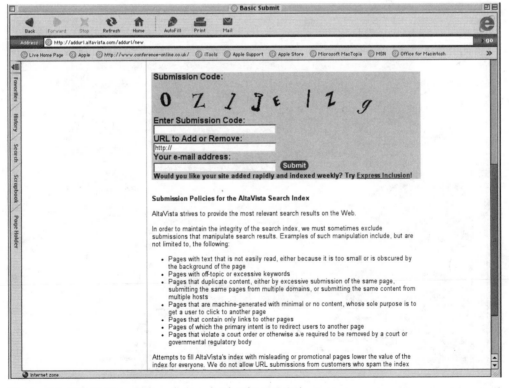

Figure 2.5 *The AltaVista graphic code (reproduced with permission)*

There is no limit to how many pages you may submit per day, per website; the only limitation is that after submitting five pages, the system will force you to generate a new submission code. You can use the new code to do another batch of five URLs, and so on. The graphic format of the submission code is designed to combat text recognition programs, but you may find it hard to read. To avoid this you can refresh the Add URL page to have a new one generated, which hopefully may be clearer.

AltaVista makes available other types of listings, such as human-powered directory information from LookSmart, paid listings from Overture (GoTo), and news headlines from Moreover. The results page is dominated by listings from AltaVista's own web page index, although paid listings from either Overture or AltaVista are also included.

Root page advantage

Breaking up a website into multiple sites gives you more 'root', sometimes described as multiple home pages that collectively tend to be more highly ranked than any other single home page. That's both due to search engine algorithms, and because root pages tend to attract the majority of links from other websites.

Figure 2.6 *The Sprite interactive home page*

The root page is whatever page appears when you enter the domain name of a site. Usually, this is the same as your home page. For instance, if you enter www.sprite.net into your browser, the page that loads is Figure 2.6 – both the Sprite home page and the 'root' page for the Sprite web server. However, if you have a site within someone else's web server, such http://www.ellenzak-.com/mysite/, then your home page is not the root page. That's because the server has only one root page, the page that loads when you enter 'ellenzak.com' into your browser.

In our example there used to be only one root page – the one that appeared when someone went to 'sprite.net' – and this page had to focus on all different product terms. Now, each of the new sites also has a root page – and each page can be specifically about a particular product type. Breaking up a large site might also help you with directories. Editors tend to prefer listing root URLs rather than long addresses that lead to pages buried within a website. So to some degree, breaking up your site into separate sites should give each site the same possibility of a ranking while collectively having a greater hit area.

Paid inclusion

AltaVista operates both a self-service paid inclusion program ('Express Inclusion') for those who wish to submit less than 500 web pages and a bulk program ('Trusted Feed') for those with many pages they'd like to submit on a cost-per-click basis. Both of these are explained in more detail in Chapter 4. Programs are described further below. With Express Inclusion, the pages will be visited on a weekly basis for up to six months. This means that a brand new page submitted to AltaVista through the program, or changes to existing pages, should show up in about a week. AltaVista will guarantee to include your pages in about a week to two weeks if you use its paid inclusion program. It's recommended that new sites use the program to get their home pages quickly listed, and for a relatively small fee the page will be revisited regularly for up to six months. It's possible that your page could be dropped, if you don't renew. To sign up for the program, visit the page https://www.infospider.com/av/app/

Overture sponsored listings

AltaVista also carries paid listings from Overture. These listings appear if AltaVista has sold the listings for a particular word through its own in-house program; in this case, up to the top six listings from Overture for that word will appear in the paid listings areas. If however, AltaVista has sold a term via an exclusive deal, then NO Overture listings will appear. So if you bought 'books' with AltaVista through an exclusive deal, then only your paid listing for 'books' would appear. To appear in any location where Overture links are shown, you need to be listed with Overture and among its top bidders.

Blended Search links

A 'Blended Search' link will be the first listing in the web page index results section. These currently appear in response to some shopping or news-related searches. Selecting the link brings back information from AltaVista's shopping search or from the Moreover news index.

Trusted feed

The Trusted Feed program allows businesses with large websites to submit 500 or more URLs via an XML feed directly to AltaVista's index. Webmasters have the option of submitting custom titles, keywords and descriptions for each URL, and other META data. Information submitted in a Trusted Feed replaces information gathered by AltaVista's crawler. While the Trusted Feed program allows webmasters to influence key components of each URL, AltaVista insists that the underlying pages will still be subject to the same relevancy algorithms as all other pages in the index. The META data contained in a Trusted Feed is just one of many factors used to compute relevance.

Extensive reporting tools exist, and are designed to reveal both how much traffic particular pages receive and where the traffic is coming from. Reports can be generated for overall traffic patterns, top queries, top URLs, 'clicks related to this word', 'clicks related to this URL', and other types of information.

Reports can be downloaded into Excel spreadsheets for further analysis. The program is particularly aimed to benefit sites that are traditionally difficult to crawl, such as those using frames or dynamically generated content. The program can be used to submit URLs to AltaVista from sites that block search engine crawlers with the robots.txt protocol.

The Trusted Feed program allows cloaking, in that the pages are different from those that the human visitor sees. AltaVista will compare the Trusted Feed META data with the destination pages themselves, and will also conduct periodic spot-checks of pages, comparing them with Trusted Feed META data. If the pages appear to be significantly different in meaning, then a spam penalty may be applied. You can sign up for the program via http://www.altavista.com/sites/search/trustedfeed

On the page factors

These are key factors within a page's content that influence rank. The phrase appears in the title of the web page, in the META description and keyword tags, and in the beginning of the body copy.

The number of search terms present on a page and their proximity are also considered for ranking purposes. In general, the ranking algorithm ensures that pages containing the exact phrases searched for will rise to the top of the results. AltaVista tends to place a stronger emphasis on a website's root page, and makes use of link analysis to boost page rankings.

Spamming

AltaVista imposes relevancy penalties or removes pages from its web index if the pages are found to be spamming the service. Here is a list of things AltaVista considers to be spamming:

- Using invisible text or text too small to read
- Repeating keywords over and over
- Being misleading about a page's content in the META description tag

- Padding pages with keywords unrelated to the page's actual content
- Submitting identical or near-identical pages, either from the same site or from mirror sites.

Spam penalties depend on the method of spamming, and include the following:

- Identical, near-identical pages, pages using META-refresh, and those with excessive keyword repetition are automatically excluded from the index if detected.
- Suspicious pages are placed on a report, then reviewed by an editor. If your page was listed in AltaVista and then disappeared, it may be that it was considered spam upon review and removed. All pages from a site may be removed and further submissions blocked, so respect the rules – otherwise there can be near-irreversible consequences.

Web page index: content and retrieval

- Comments are not indexed. Only the first 100K of text on a page is indexed, and after that only links are indexed, up to a maximum of 4MB. Since most web pages are less than 100K, these limitations should not be a problem.
- Pages heavy with text in a small font size may not get listed. Avoid using font size 2 or lower as the dominant size for your body copy.
- AltaVista considers words in the META description and keywords tags to be additional words on the page, just as if they appeared on the page in ordinary text.
- Text from the description META tag is used for page descriptions. If no META description tag exists, then AltaVista will create an 'abstract' based on text from the body copy of a web page. It may also use only a portion of a META description tag, as well as body copy, to form a description.

AltaVista allows for 'listing enhancements', which are logos, icons, taglines or text links that you choose. This facility is available through the paid inclusion program, and incurs an extra cost.

Language detection

AltaVista looks at a page to see if the bulk of the words match those of a particular language, and automatically categorizes web pages by language. Its crawler tries to determine the language of a web page at the time it is spidered, using dictionary-based technology. You cannot specify which language a page should be assigned to, not even using the Content-Type META tag. AltaVista also translates the text it finds into Unicode, which can store characters for all languages, not just Western European ones. This means that a single index serves users all over the world. A user can perform a search in English, then one in Chinese, without having to leave the service and go to a Chinese-only edition.

International editions

AltaVista operates a variety of non-US editions targeting countries worldwide. These editions offer access to both 'worldwide' and country-specific search results. Worldwide results come from

AltaVista's global search index, which is the same index that AltaVista.com uses. If you are listed with AltaVista.com, you will be listed in any AltaVista edition. Follow these two key rules for international listing:

1 Write pages in the language of the country you are targeting
2 List pages hosted under a domain name that matches the country you are targeting.

Porn filter detection

AltaVista provides a filtering mode for its users, which filters pages in three ways. First, AltaVista's spider will tag pages as distasteful if it finds certain words and phrases used in particular ways. Secondly, the search retrieval software uses a filtering process developed in partnership with SurfWatch to catch anything that makes it past the spider-based filter. Finally, AltaVista allows users to report on any pages that may have slipped through the first two barriers, via this URL: http://doc.altavista.com/help/search/report_off.html

AltaVista directory

AltaVista provides access to its own version of the LookSmart directory to those who browse categories from the AltaVista home page. To appear in AltaVista's directory information, you need to be listed with LookSmart. AltaVista refreshes its listings from LookSmart every day, so once you have been added to LookSmart you should appear in AltaVista's version within a day or two.

AltaVista multimedia index

AltaVista makes multimedia content – images, audio files and video files – available to searches from its multimedia indexes. Users access the multimedia index either through the tabs on AltaVista's results page, or by visiting the various multimedia services directly.

AltaVista's MP3/Audio Search service provides sound listings that come from crawling both web- and FTP sites, plus those available from partner sites such as CDNow and MP3.com. Music sites can be added through this URL: http://help.altavista.com/search/add_ftp

MP3/Audio Search can be reached directly via this URL: http://mp3.altavista.com/

AltaVista's Video Search content comes from crawling the Web as well as from video files provided by news, entertainment and financial broadcast companies. Video Search can be reached directly via this URL: http://video.altavista.com/

Image search and image enhanced results

The AltaVista spider cannot actually 'see' what's inside these images; instead, it guesses – so if you look for 'eiffel tower' using AltaVista image search, you'll get pictures of the Eiffel Tower or graphics with the word 'eiffel tower' in them. However, AltaVista doesn't retrieve these pictures because it can recognize what the Eiffel Tower looks like or because it can read the text inside an image. AltaVista remains mostly blind to what the actual image shows, and instead relies on the words that appear around the image or in the file name of the image to understand its content. Pictures with the word 'eiffel tower' in the file name or pictures that appear on web pages that make use of the word 'eiffel tower' in the HTML text give AltaVista the clues it needs to display results.

Known internally as Image Enhanced Results, or IER, this is where some listings in search results have images associated with them. Try a search for 'New York' or 'eiffel tower' at AltaVista France to see examples of this. AltaVista automatically chooses which listings should get images and what images it will use. It displays textual results. So in a search for 'Empire State Building' it will display quality results for those words, using all its usual criteria. It then sees whether any of the top results have pictures that succeed as a match for the search terms – which means the page needs an image on it. If there is no image, there is no chance of having an image displayed. Next, the image needs to be in .jpg or .gif format. If you get this far, you then need an image on your page that's associated with the search terms. This could mean that the search terms are in the image's file name – 'Empire State Building' would be an example of this. It could also mean that the search terms appear in the HTML copy near the image – perhaps you have the words 'Empire State Building' as part of a paragraph describing a picture on your page. In addition to crawling the Web, AltaVista presents images that come from partner sites such as Getty and Corbis.

Image Search can be reached directly via http://images.altavista.com/

WiseNut

WiseNut was launched in September 2001, and was seen in the media as a potential 'Google killer'. When San Francisco-based LookSmart purchased the search engine in April 2001, industry watchers wondered how a search engine using crawler-based technology fitted in with LookSmart's business model of using human editors to compile directories of the Web.

Like Google and most of the other major search engines, WiseNut puts a lot of emphasis on link analysis, but adds a few other ingredients for calculating relevance. In addition to link analysis, WiseNut also emphasizes the proximity of search terms in underlying documents, computing results in real time, based on specific queries.

WiseNut automatically categorizes results into 'wiseguides', which are semantically related to the words in your query. You can open up a wiseguide category by clicking its link, or click on an icon next to the category to conduct a new search automatically using the category as your query. WiseNut offers links for related queries, and clusters results from individual sites. Its clustering is unique; instead of the usual 'more results' from this site link, WiseNut lists the exact number of pages on a site that it has determined are relevant to your query. It also offers a

Figure 2.7 *The Sneak-a-Peek function (reproduced with permission of WiseNut)*

'Sneak–a–Peek' function, which lets you preview of a page without leaving the WiseNut's result page (see Figure 2.7). This eliminates a lot of 'mouse traffic' between the results page and the back button.

WiseNut's indexing technology has been designed to scale up to 1 trillion (a million million million) URLs. While this may seem like overkill given the current estimates of two to four billion pages on the Web, it means that Wisenut is serious about staying in the game as the Web continues to grow.

WiseNut's public search engine is just one part of its overall business, and is expected to generate only about 20 per cent of revenues. WiseNut's main emphasis is on providing site search to large websites, and enterprise search for intranets. This is where the real money and profit potential for search technology lies.

Submitting to the major search engines

Table 2.1 attempts to summarize the details of how to submit to the major crawler-based search engines. The terms used within it are explained here.

Table 2.1 Submitting to the major search engines

	AltaVista	*FAST*	*Google*	*Inktomi*	*Teoma*
Listing tied to submit	Yes	No	No	Yes	No free Add URL page
Submit limit	None	None	5–10	20	n/a
Page appear	4–6 weeks	2–6 weeks	Up to 5 weeks	Within 8 weeks	n/a
Search listings updates	1 day to 6 weeks	1 day to 6 weeks	1 day to 4 weeks	1 day to 8 weeks	Monthly refresh
Paid inclusion	Yes	Yes	No	Yes	Yes
Self-serve limit	500 URLs	500 URLs	n/a	1000 URLs	1000 URLs
Bulk program	Yes, CPC pricing	Yes, Custom quote & CPC pricing	n/a	Yes, CPC pricing	No
Drives content	AltaVista	FAST (AllTheWeb), Lycos	Google, Yahoo!, Netscape	AOL, MSN, HotBot, iWon, LookSmart, Overture	Ask Jeeves, Teoma

Listing tied to submit

Depending on the search engine, there is not always an advantage in submitting multiple pages from your website. All crawler-based engines will send out a crawler to your site and gather what they find of interest independently of your submission. With some search engines, directly submitting a page greatly increases the odds that the page will be listed. Table 2.1 shows which search engines operate in this way.

Submission limit

This shows the maximum number of submissions each search engine will allow per day for a single website. It is important to remember that there is usually no reason to submit each page from your website to search engines where the listing is not tied to submission. Our experience at Sprite is that the closer you approach the limit for submission, which is usually 50 URLs (unless otherwise stated) per day, the more likely it is that you may attract a review of your site.

Pages appear

This shows how soon you should expect pages to appear within the listings of a search engine. This is after initial registration of a new site, not using the paid inclusion program for that engine.

Search listings updates

It is almost impossible to be certain how up-to-date a search engine's data is. In fact the best guideline is to take what the search engines say and double it for all mission critical content. The statistics in Table 2.1 reflect how out-of-date a search engine may be for pages that are already listed in the index. There have been situations where pages on certain crawler sites were out-of-date by at least twice the amount that the search engines would normally allow.

Paid inclusion

This shows whether a search engine offers a paid inclusion program. In most instances, this is a guarantee that your pages are included in its listings.

Self-serve limit

This shows how many URLs you can submit when using 'self-serve' style programs that charge flat fees per URL, usually with credit card billing.

Bulk program

This identifies whether a 'bulk' inclusion program is available, which allows submission of thousands of URLs. Usually these programs operate on a cost-per-click basis.

Drives content

This identifies the main content drivers for listings from the crawler-based search engines. As you can see, this includes not only the own-branded content but also partner websites.

Doorway pages

Remember, even though you may submit doorway pages or any pages directly to a search engine there is no guarantee that they will be listed, especially with search engines where listing is not tied to submitting. Doorway pages need to be submitted individually, otherwise the search engine won't know how to find them because they do not have links pointing to them.

In conclusion

After all the effort invested in your favourite search engine, will it ever pay off? Is the search engine likely to be around tomorrow? For searchers, such losses could mean less diversity in search results. For web marketers, it could mean less likelihood of being found. The demise of Go was dramatic and simple – Open Text faced the search engine question of whether it should develop its technology as a product for businesses, concentrate on its consumer website, or try to do both. The company ultimately decided to concentrate on software, and the web search site was allowed to die slowly. Magellan was a rival to Excite, and was finally consumed in the mid-1990s. Magellan has never closed; it is just withering away essentially unsupported. Excite also acquired WebCrawler in 1996. WebCrawler is far more popular than Magellan, but it is no longer one of the Web's major search services. There haven't been service enhancements for ages; nor does Excite position the service toward users. Lycos acquired Point in 1996, and this never survived.

To survive, the search engines need content and services to keep users visiting their sites, and thus boost ad revenue. A big turnabout came in July 1997, when Amazon announced a landmark deal to be a preferred book merchant carried by Excite and Yahoo. All the big search engines were making online retailing deals; this apparently saved the search industry. By 1998, instead of the expected shakeout, the future of search engines seemed bright owing to their transformation into portals. Investors loved them. Searching was only a small part of what search engines offered.

In February 1998, the year when we were supposed to have only two or three search engines remaining, a new search engine was launched – GoTo. It sold paid listings. GoTo's business model was absolutely opposite to everything the portals had evolved into. Instead of trying to keep people at GoTo, the service wanted them to leave, because outbound departures were how GoTo earned its money. It was easy for GoTo to gamble with paid listings – it had no reputation to lose. The major search engines were more conservative. GoTo became Overture, and is as strong today as it ever was.

In addition to the loss of big retailing deals, the search engine portals also suffered from the decline in more ordinary banner advertising as a result of the crash of dotcom stocks in 2000. Both Go and AltaVista pulled back from wanting to be all-purpose portals in September 2000. The consolidation that had long been predicted was finally here.

Visit the LookSmart site today, and you'll only find the non-profit submission form after a struggle. In contrast, Yahoo's system of limiting mandatory fees to commercial categories makes sense. Perhaps we'll see a hybrid approach – some categories may cost more than others, allowing non-profits to pay a smaller fee while letting search engines capitalize further on what they charge to appear in popular commercial categories. Similarly, Inktomi offers a mechanism to ensure that non-profit sites are better included in its index, as a response in kind to the deeper indexing it does of some sites that pay.

As for Overture, which is the big winner these days, search can be inconsistent. AOL Search might convert well for one site, but the same link running at Lycos just does not give up the same results.

Google has been the shining example of a service offering a good search facility and that has attracted users without needing to spend large advertising budgets. The long-term strategy for all the search engines is to provide great search products to an ever more sophisticated market.

There are three main tips to achieve better ranking on search engines:

1 Register your site on all the engines, using commercial and non-commercial registration
2 Build good architecture for your site
3 Have a clear strategy for link building, and make sure it works.

Chapter 3

Directories

In this chapter we'll be looking at the three major search engine directories on the Web – Yahoo, the Open Directory, and LookSmart. As well as gaining an understanding of how each of these engines works, you will learn the best way to get your site listed at all three, and tips on how to improve your site listing. There is a marked distinction between how a directory-based search engine works and how a crawler-based search engine works, and this is discussed first.

What is a directory?

A directory is an approach to organizing information – one of the most common types of directory is a telephone directory. On the Web, a directory is essentially a subject guide, typically organized by major topics and subtopics. Results in a directory are taken from websites that have already been submitted to that directory, and have been listed through some kind of screening process. Many directories have web crawlers as a part of their service (most notably Yahoo! and Google), but directories are generally maintained and updated by humans, and to get your site listed you will have to go through some kind of approval process – so your site has to be both relevant and good (especially in the case of Yahoo).

Yahoo – www.yahoo.com

Yahoo (Figure 3.1) is the oldest search service on the Web, and is the most important place to begin site submission. There are a number of distinct advantages that sites on Yahoo have, and this will be covered later.

Yahoo is the perfect example of an idea that blossomed into something bigger than its founders could have hoped, and is now the brand name most associated with the Internet. For some users it *is* the Internet, owing to the portal-like services Yahoo now offers. Yahoo was started in 1994 by two electrical engineering students, David Filo and Jerry Yang. They began by building a list of their favourite websites, but it soon became evident that they needed more than their own personal time to manage the information they had accumulated.

41

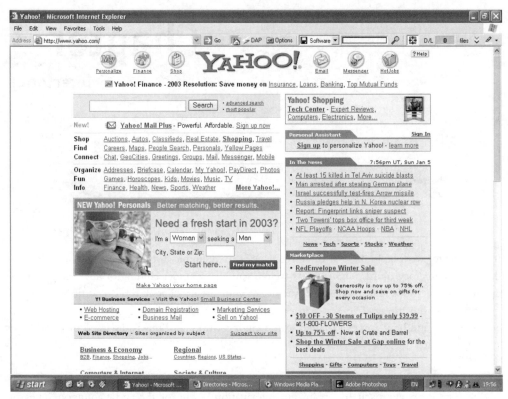

Figure 3.1 *Screen grab of yahoo.com (reproduced with permission)*

To accommodate all the information and resources they required, Filo and Yang moved Yahoo over to the Netscape facilities in early 1995. Netscape was a very large portal in its own right, and had vast technical resources. Yahoo continued to grow, and today is a public company with over 1 million sites in its directory. Yahoo has acquired a number of companies, including Geocities and Rocketmail, in order to provide free web pages and email to its subscribers. Yahoo continues to grow, and is now one of the biggest portal sites in existence.

As mentioned above, it is important to remember that Yahoo is not a search engine but a directory that is edited and maintained by humans; therefore, when you submit a site to Yahoo it will be reviewed by a human and not by a piece of software. Yahoo employs a number of full-time professional editors, whose job it is to visit the thousands of sites that submit to the directory and decide if they should be listed. Yahoo is also not the biggest directory service on the Internet; the Open Directory (see below) holds this crown, with around 2 million sites indexed.

Yahoo supplements its directory results with search engine spider results, which are supplied by Google (previously they were supplied by Inktomi). The reason that Yahoo (and every other directory service) supplements its own results is so that it does not return any results with 'no

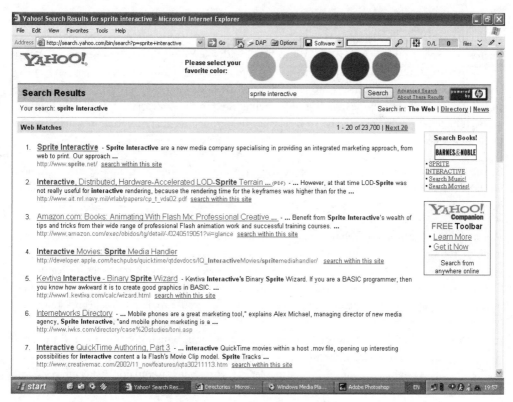

Figure 3.2 *The Yahoo results page (reproduced with permission)*

matches'. Because of the nature of a directory, with large sites having to be described in 25 words or less, there are bound to be words or phrases that return no results – and Google provides a back-up for when this happens.

How searches on Yahoo work

If you type a search into Yahoo, you will see that the results are split into three categories (Figure 3.2):

1 Directory category matches
2 Sponsor matches
3 Web matches.

You will notice that the main bulk of search results now come from the 'web matches'; this change happened in October 2002, whereas previously the bulk of the search results had come from the Yahoo directories themselves. This will be discussed more later.

The Yahoo directory

While the main results that Yahoo searchers see come from Google, Yahoo still holds its own database of over 1 million web pages. Being listed with the Yahoo directory poses advantages to site owners for a number of reasons. First, if you are listed in the directory then you stand more chance of being noticed by users browsing through or detouring through the directory listings after or before performing a search. Secondly, being listed in the directory can help your listing in the Web matches results. Thirdly, being listed may help your link analysis rating in search engines such as Google.

Before you learn about techniques for actually getting your site listed in the directory, it is important to delve a bit further into how the directory is put together and how the human editors decide where sites are placed in it.

Websites that are featured on Yahoo are either found by its human editors, or are reviewed and then submitted. Sites are placed into one or more of Yahoo's categories. If you browse around Yahoo, you will see that each of the categories is a stand-alone web page, with the websites featured in that category listed in alphabetical order. Pages are only in the Yahoo directory if they can be found in these alphabetical listings; many people think that just because their site has been listed in the 'web matches' section of the results page they are listed with Yahoo, but this is not always the case. In each category there is also usually a 'most popular' section, which contains the most popular websites in that category. This is useful if you are browsing around Yahoo and want to know what the best or most popular website is in a particular category, but it is a major disadvantage if your site is not listed in this section because these are the sites that are the most frequently visited. Yahoo uses an automatic system to select which sites are listed in this section and will not reveal its criteria, but it is most likely through the use of link analysis.

Yahoo also has a 'sponsor listings' section near the top of its commercial category pages (categories are split into commercial and non-commercial, and this will be covered in more depth later).

Icons

Some sites have small icons next to their name, or have their name in a different text format. These have the following meanings:

- The sunglasses icon means that Yahoo editors think a site is outstanding; you can only get this award by having an excellent site.
- 'Pick' icons mean that your site is one of Yahoo's daily or weekly picks.
- Bold listings indicate that there are sub-listings for that particular website. For example, there may be a shaving product manufacturer who has two separate websites, one for men and one for women. Its brand would be represented by the manufacturer's name in bold, and this would then link to a further page with the two individual websites on it.
- The @ symbol is used to indicate that a company has its own Yahoo page, and that this page is elsewhere in the directory structure. Clicking on a link with the @ symbol next to it will take you to that company's page.

Commercial versus non-commercial categories

Yahoo has both commercial and non-commercial categories, and when submitting your site you will need to decide which of these categories to submit to. Commercial websites are generally those that belong to profit-making organizations, and non-commercial sites are generally those that that are not run for profit and are there to serve a particular interest or hobby. To submit to the commercial categories costs money, but it is generally worth it to get your site listed.

Preparing your website for submission

Websites listed on Yahoo are chosen by humans, and therefore the listing criteria are a lot stricter than if your site were being selected by a spider. Yahoo will not index sites that are not of the highest quality for their particular category, and this means no broken links, spelling mistakes or 'under construction' signs. One good method for seeing how much of a chance your site has of being listed is to view the other sites in the category to which you're applying. If these sites are poorly designed and unattractive and yours is not, then you have a better than average chance of being listed. This technique is relative, and you will find that certain categories (such as heavyweight scientific sites) will feature poorer quality websites (which contain a lot of relevant content) than categories such as 'soft drink companies', where manufacturers will have invested a lot of money in developing their online presence.

It is important to make sure that your website is consistent with the description you submit to Yahoo. If the editors visiting your site expect one thing and then actually find another, this is a sure-fire way not to be listed. Also, be careful about using frames.

Click-through

An important feature of Yahoo's listing system is that it now tracks click-through behaviour as part of the ranking system. This means that when you click on a link in Yahoo it will count the click-throughs on that page. It will also log the fact that the user chose that page after searching with a particular keyword, and as more people select the site using the same keywords its ranking will rise. This can lead to some sites being listed above others that have more relevant keywords in their descriptions. Yahoo is also now tracking 'click away' behaviour; this means that it times how long a user stays at a site before returning to Yahoo – and the longer the user stays, the better it is for the site's ranking. This means that sites that have high quality, relevant content and design are more likely to fare well.

Submitting your website to the Yahoo directory

It is important to have a plan before actually submitting your site to Yahoo, so make sure you follow the subsequent instructions and create a strategy. This means when you do submit your site you will know exactly what to do and will thus ensure the best possible results. Throughout this section we're going to refer to a fictional Sports Shoes website as an example.

Keywords

First you need to decide what search terms are the most important to people searching for your website. You need to be careful when you are doing this, and perform a number of searches on Yahoo to test the words and phrases you have chosen – are they returning the same kind of website as yours? You need to use these keywords to write a site description that is no more than 25 words in length and will be submitted to Yahoo later. It is important to make sure this description is appealing; it's very tempting to submit a list of keywords to Yahoo, but if you submit something that reads well and describes your product effectively and succinctly it is more likely to be looked at by both editors and searchers, and also to generate a higher click-through rate – which in turn will lead to a higher ranking. Bearing all this in mind, choose four or five top keywords and phrases to describe your site. For our fictional sports shoes site these could be:

1 Sports shoes
2 Sports trainers
3 Running shoes
4 Shoes.

Decide which of these is the most important, as it will help you when choosing which category to submit to.

Choose the right category

Your website will be placed into one of Yahoo's categories, so it is helpful to have researched which category to submit your site to before starting the submission process. On Yahoo's search page a few categories will typically be listed at the top of the page, and users frequently detour into these categories when searching for sites. To research which is the best category for your site, you should go to Yahoo and search for the terms by which you hope to be found. Then look at the categories Yahoo returns on its results page, and choose the most appropriate one. It also helps to visit the categories you have short-listed to check the other sites there. Check whether your competitors are listed in that category, and whether the other sites listed are similar businesses to yours. You will probably find about six or seven relevant categories for your site; you need to choose the one that is the most 'obvious', bearing in mind that if the category you choose is not sufficiently relevant Yahoo can either reject your listing or put your site in a different category altogether. If your web page seems appropriate for two or more categories then you'll need to pick one, but you can suggest one of the others (this is covered in more detail later). If you have decided to use the Yahoo Express submission program, you don't need to choose a category; the editors will choose it for you.

Submission methods

To begin the submission process, you need to go to the category you have chosen and click on the 'suggest a site' link at the bottom of the page.

If you choose a non-commercial category, you'll next see a page asking you whether you'd like to use the 'Standard Submission' or 'Yahoo Express'. It is advisable to use the Yahoo Express program to get your site listed, as this method will almost certainly get you listed quickly. If you are submitting to a commercial category (within the Business and Economy section of the directory), then you have to use Yahoo Express.

The Yahoo Express service was introduced in February 1999 because Yahoo had received a number of complaints that certain sites were not being listed. For a fee, Yahoo will guarantee to review your submission and give you a yes or no answer within seven working days. It is very important to remember that this does not guarantee that your site will be listed; all you are getting is a yes or no answer. The service also does not guarantee where or how you will be listed. You are not given a refund if your site is not accepted.

Although this process may seem quite harsh, most of the sites that do submit via Yahoo Express are accepted, and by following the tips outlined in this chapter you can vastly increase your chances of being listed in your preferred category. A year after submitting your site you will be sent a renewal notice by Yahoo, prompting you to pay the annual fee.

One feature of Yahoo Express is that you can leave the choice of category up to the editors at Yahoo. However, it is recommended that you choose your own category. If you choose you are more likely to select somewhere that is relevant, and you will probably have done a lot of research than the Yahoo editor before choosing it. It is worth putting in the effort and research necessary to select the category that is relevant for you.

Overall, we recommend that you always use the Yahoo Express submission service, even when submitting to a non-commercial area. If you have determined that a Yahoo directory listing is essential to your website, then this gives you the best chance of getting there quickly.

Choosing a title

You are going to have to choose a title for your site when you get to 'Step 2: Site and contact information'. The title of your site is crucial to how it is ranked in the directory listings, and you want to choose a title that reflects the most important search terms and keywords associated with it. Your site title should not exceed 60 characters, and it is worth bearing in mind that Yahoo ranks sites alphabetically. Being towards the beginning of the alphabet is therefore advantageous; people are more likely to look at your site, as the typical user does not take the time to scroll down a page to check out all the results, but clicks on the first few sites that appear. If your company name is not high in the alphabet, try choosing one of your brands or products that is; however, do not be overt with your use of letters. If you choose something like 'A1 Sports Shoes' this will not go down well with the Yahoo editors, and they will probably likely use your real business name instead. If you are submitting your site for free you should be especially careful, as editors tend to ignore sites that use these tactics in favour of getting through the backlog of sites that have submitted properly.

There are exceptions to this rule, where sites are allowed to use alphabetical and numerical games to influence their listing. One high-profile case is the 'Viagra' category, where there are plenty of sites whose name begins with symbols and numbers. You will see in this section a lot of the sites begin with '!'; this is because of the way Yahoo ranks ASCII characters (see Table 3.3).

Your site description

The main mistake that people make when submitting to Yahoo is to create a 25-word description that is merely a list of relevant keywords, making no attempt to arrange these into a meaningful paragraph. If you do this the Yahoo editor can and will cut down your description, and in the process you will lose some of your valuable keyword phrases. A good start to defining your site is to look at the description of other relevant sites in the category to which you are submitting. If there is a prevailing trend in the site descriptions, then follow this – for example, all the descriptions might begin with the word 'Provides'. This means that the particular editor for the category likes that type of language, and as it is this editor you have to impress, it helps to use the kind of language he or she likes. Do all you can to make sure your description sounds like those in your chosen category, and if your main keyword is not listed in any of the site descriptions, then chances are that the editor does not like that keyword. If you use it it's likely it will be removed, so choose another word instead.

You need to make sure your site description reads well; if it is a 'clunky' paragraph that does not flow, then the editor is likely to alter it to make it read better. It is worth getting an experienced copywriter or editor to look at your description and make sure that it is written well. Your main aim is to create a site description that will not be edited by Yahoo, and to make something that is going to be enticing for someone surfing Yahoo's directory.

Additional category

The submission form also has an 'Additional information' box, and you can use this box to suggest one additional Yahoo category for your site. For example, if you sell running shoes but also provide information on health and running, then you could ask to be listed in a non-commercial category about health and fitness. You will need to provide a short explanation as to why Yahoo should include your site in the additional category, and there is no guarantee that you will be listed, but at the same time there is nothing to lose by trying.

If your site could be listed in both the business-to-business and the business-to-consumer sections of Yahoo, you should select the most appropriate of these when you submit and put the other in the additional category box, with an explanation as to why you should be in both. Yahoo should then comply and list you in both.

The listing

If you have used the Express submission, Yahoo will notify you via email within seven days regarding whether your site has been listed. You will not, however, know how it is going to be described until you see the listing in the directory. If Yahoo has not listed your site, has put you in a category that is not suitable for your site, or has given your site a poor or misleading description, you can appeal against the decision. Yahoo will then tell you why your site was not listed; if it was due to something repairable, like broken links, you should fix the problem and then resubmit. If the rejection was caused by something else, you should deal with this the best you can. If your site description was edited so much that you feel it no longer describes your site, Yahoo suggests that you change the URL form to update your listing. You need to have a good reason to change your listing, other than just making your site rank better. Reasons, if relevant, may include a change of company name, or that your business has shifted its focus. If your site has not appeared within seven days, Yahoo advises that you resubmit once. If after two weeks your site has still not appeared, then contact Yahoo support services at url-suport@yahoo-inc.com to find out what's wrong.

Sponsor matches

Yahoo also offers a sponsor matches section, which is a fee-based system that permits commercial sites listed in the directory to be placed at the top of results pages relevant to them. The sponsor matches provide a guarantee of being listed for certain keywords, and appear under the heading near the top of Yahoo's results page.

To get listed in the sponsor links at Yahoo.com, you must be listed highly at Overture.com (see Chapter 4) because the first three results for a particular search at Overture.com will show up in Yahoo.com's 'Sponsor matches' area. You need to be sure you have paid enough at Overture to be listed top there, and then you'll show up on Yahoo. If you are listed second or third at Overture, then you'll be listed as the second or third sponsor match at Yahoo and so on, with the fourth and fifth highest ranking sites appearing in the 'more sponsor matches' area of Yahoo.

If you have a large budget it is therefore easy to get a high-profile listing at Yahoo; all you need to do is buy your ranking at Overture.

One important feature of the sponsor listings to note is that if surfers click on the 'next' button to see the second page of results, they will be presented with a new set of sponsor links, but this time they will be numbers six to ten from Overture. It is important, however, if you have the budget, to get listed on the first page. People usually find what they are looking for on the first page of the results in any search, and being a sponsored link will vastly improve your traffic.

If you want to be listed on the sponsor matches outside Yahoo.com – for example, on Yahoo.co.uk – you will need to target the search engine relevant for that country. Any user coming from the UK (Yahoo can detect this from your IP address) will be shown sponsor matches from Overture UK, so it's important to have a high listing on there as well. The process of where Yahoo gets its sponsor listings from gets quite complicated when you delve into it, but Table 3.1 shows basically where they will come from, depending on your location, if you visit Yahoo.com.

Table 3.1 Source of sponsor links according to search location

Search location	Source of sponsor links
United Kingdom	Overture UK
Australia	Looksmart Australia
America	Overture US

Table 3.2 Sponsor listings on country-specific sites

Search location	Local source of paid listings	Source of paid listings from Yahoo.com
America	Overture US	Overture US
United Kingdom& Ireland	Espotting UK	Overture UK
Australia	LookSmart Australia	LookSmart Australia
Germany	Espotting Germany	None
France	Espotting France	None
Spain	Espotting Spain	None
Italy	Espotting Italy	None

However, if you go through a country-specific Yahoo site, such as Yahoo.co.uk or Yahoo.fr, you will be shown sponsor links from different providers. Table 3.2 illustrates which sponsor listings searchers will see if they visit their regional Yahoo and do a search.

You therefore need to ensure that you have all the possible sources of results covered depending on which area you come from – so if you only want to attract traffic from the UK, you will need to cover Overture UK and Espotting UK.

Web matches

In October 2002, Yahoo made a revolutionary change in its search results screen. Before this the main results had always come from the Yahoo directory, with web results as a back-up to this if there was nothing listed or if the searcher wanted to find alternative sites. Now the main listings come from Google, with the directory listings taking second place. Your best bet for being found on a Yahoo search, therefore, is to rank highly in Google (see Chapter 2).

Yahoo does actually produce slightly different results from those listed if you were to perform the same search within Google, and this is to do with Yahoo's use of its directory information. When Google returns a listing, Yahoo automatically reviews it and checks whether it is listed in its own directory; if it is, then it will replace the Google listing with its own title and description. This is why results may appear differently. You can see this in Figure 3.3.

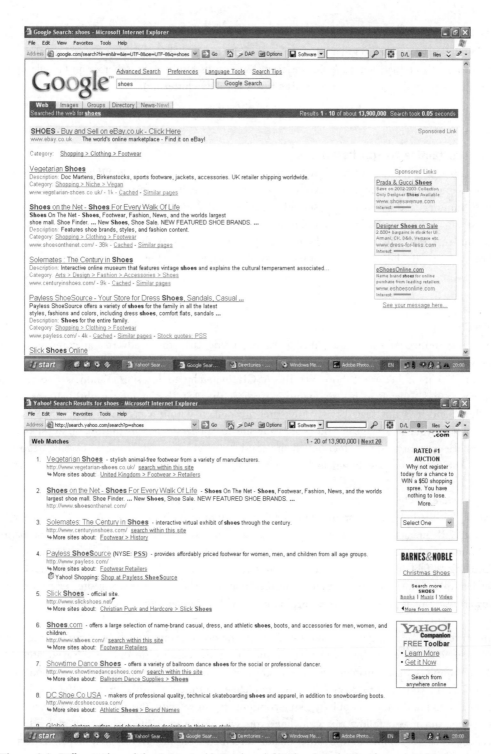

Figure 3.3 *Different titles and descriptions in (a) Google and (b) Yahoo (reproduced with permission)*

Any page that is also listed in Yahoo's directory will also get a 'more sites about' link, which appears below the page description that takes the user to the category home of that site. Yahoo also does not feature more than one page from each website on its results page, whereas on Google up to two pages from the same site may be listed (this is called clustering).

Special tactics to get listed

You can take advantage of the way Yahoo lists characters and letters; it indexes characters and word phrases rather than whole words, which means that if you search for 'run' you will also find 'running' and 'runner'. You should make sure that you use the longest variation of the most important keywords to describe your site. If you use the word 'runner', you can be certain that this will return results for 'runner' and 'run'; you should therefore think about how you can fit the longest variations of words possible into your site description.

ASCII

You may notice in some categories of Yahoo, particularly those advertising companies that provide search engine placement services, that many of the sites begin with a character such as '!' or ''. This is because Yahoo uses the ASCII hierarchy to list sites. Yahoo is essentially a database, and a database has to follow a pattern; the ASCII hierarchy is the pattern Yahoo follows, and it is this that dictates how sites are ranked within a particular category. You can use this to your advantage if you want your site to appear higher in the list of websites in a particular category, and, as mentioned previously, it is encouraged in some special categories. The ASCII hierarchy is shown in Table 3.3.

If you were to change your company website name to, for example, ' 1 sports shoes', then you would be listed above any sports shoes retailers beginning with the letter 'A', as ' ' is higher in the ASCII hierarchy. Yahoo has stated that as long as a website trades under the name submitted, whether it has ASCII characters in it or not, then it will accept the listing. Looking at Table 3.3 one tactic becomes immediately clear, and that is that capital letters rank higher than lower case ones. Yahoo specifies that you should write your site description in lower case, but it is worth at least beginning it with a capital letter.

In short, then, if you get your site listed in the Yahoo directory and have a high listing with Google, you will do well. If you have the budget, then a listing on one of the paid sites that feed Yahoo's sponsor matches is also a great way to get relevant results in a good page position. All you need to do is follow the guidelines outlined in this section and you will have a high ranking. Yahoo's popularity will continue to grow with the new portal services it is offering, and if you follow our guidelines you will also have a site description and title that can be used to submit to the other major directories on the Web – The Open Directory and LookSmart.

Table 3.3 The ASCII hierarchy

Position	Character	Position	Character	Position	Character
1	!	33	A	65	a
2	"	34	B	66	b
3		35	C	67	c
4	$	36	D	68	d
5	%	37	E	69	e
6	&	38	F	70	f
7	'	39	G	71	g
8	(	40	H	72	h
9	)	41	I	73	i
10	*	42	J	74	j
11	+	43	K	75	k
12	'	44	L	76	l
13	–	45	M	77	m
14	.	46	N	78	n
15	/	47	O	79	o
16	0	48	P	80	p
17	1	49	Q	81	q
18	2	50	R	82	r
19	3	51	S	83	s
20	4	52	T	84	t
21	5	53	U	85	u
22	6	54	V	86	v
23	7	55	W	87	w
24	8	56	X	88	x
25	9	57	Y	89	y
26	:	58	Z	90	z
27	;	59	[	91	{
28	<	60	\	92	|
29	=	61	]	93	}
30	>	62	^	94	~
31	?	63	_	95	DEL
32	@	64	'		

The Open Directory – http://dmoz.org

The Open Directory (Figure 3.4) is a human-compiled directory of websites. It works in the same way as Yahoo, meaning you find a category for your website, and then submit to it with a short description of your site. The Open Directory was set up in June 1998 by Rich Skrenta, and was originally called GnuHoo.

The idea was that editors would pick a topic that they were interested in and begin editing. It is now staffed by nearly 30 000 volunteer editors, who act in much the same way as Yahoo's editors, but the sheer number of them means that they can get through and list far more sites. The Open

Figure 3.4 *The Open Directory home page*

Directory sees itself as a part of the open source movement, and this is reflected in the fact that it is staffed by volunteers and that companies are free to use its search results. It actually provides search data to many other high-profile search engines, including AOL search, Netscape search and Lycos. The Open Directory says the following about its services:

> The web continues to grow at staggering rates. Automated search engines are increasingly unable to turn up useful results to search queries. The small paid editorial staffs at commercial directory sites can't keep up with submissions, and the quality and comprehensiveness of their directories has suffered. Link rot is setting in and they can't keep pace with the growth of the Internet.

> Instead of fighting the explosive growth of the Internet, the Open Directory provides the means for the Internet to organize itself. As the Internet grows, so do the number of net-citizens. These citizens can each organize a small portion of the web and present it back to the rest of the population, culling out the bad and useless and keeping only the best content.

This gives you a good idea of why the Open Directory was set up; it is essentially a search engine community of enthusiastic individuals, and because of this is the largest existing directory of websites on the Internet.

Search results

When you perform a search on the Open Directory you will see that the results are broken down into two sections, and the search page looks quite similar to that of Yahoo before it introduced its Web results in October 2002 (Figure 3.5).

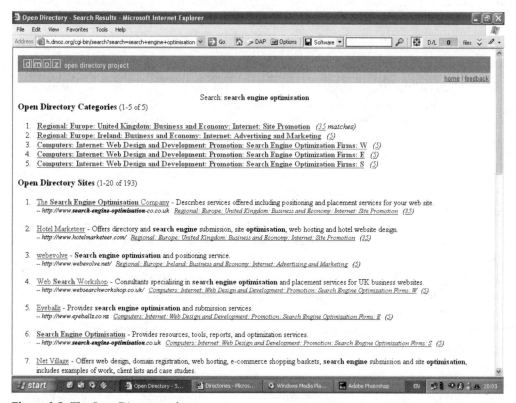

Figure 3.5 *The Open Directory results page*

The first section of the results is the Open Directory category matches; only the top five will be shown here. Below this are the web page matches, where individual websites are listed by their relevance.

Getting listed

As with Yahoo, you first need to find the right category to submit your site to, and again the easiest way to do this is to search for the key words that you would use to describe your site and pick the most appropriate category from those returned on the results page. If your search does not return any specific categories at the top of the page, look under each website that is returned and you will see the name of the category it has come from in italics next to the web address.

At the top of each category page you'll find an 'add URL' link; click on this to add your website to that particular category. If this is not at the top of the page you'll be in a top-level category, and will therefore need to go down another level in that category before you can submit. Submitting is done in much the same way as to Yahoo, and if you have already submitted to Yahoo you should already have a decent website with a relevant, targeted description to submit. Site descriptions for the Open Directory should not be longer than 25–30 words. It usually takes around four weeks to index your site, but it could take more or less time, depending on how many editors there are for the category you have submitted to and how efficient they are.

Submitting to multiple categories

The Open Directory does let you submit to more than one category, but you can't submit your site twice to the same directory. The directories that you choose have to be relevant. The best way to submit to multiple directories is first to submit your home page to the most relevant category you can find, and then submit other pages from your site to other relevant categories. If these pages are relevant and individual enough, they will be accepted into that particular category. It's worth coming up with a new description for each page you submit, summarizing each individually. The Open Directory editor responsible for the category you submit your home page to will decide if your home page should be submitted to multiple categories. You should be careful, however, when submitting to multiple categories, as if you are too insistent and forceful the editor may think you are spamming the directory and not list your site. One good tip is to spread your submissions out over a period of time, as submitting them all at once (if you have a lot) will create the wrong impression – it is even worth waiting until one page has been accepted before going on to submit the next. Do not submit doorway pages to the Open Directory, and make sure that everything you do submit is relevant; you need to ask yourself if the page you are submitting would actually hold your attention if you went to it from the Open Directory listings.

You should remember that individual editors of the Open Directory will each have their own rules about spamming, and if you are unsure about how many sites a particular editor will accept you should email and ask; in most cases editors will be happy to give you assistance. The category editors are listed at the bottom of each category page.

Resubmission

You can safely resubmit if your site has not been listed within about six weeks. Before you do so, it's worth emailing the category editor to find out why your site was not accepted. If the category you submitted to does not have an editor, then you should email the editor of the category directly above the one that you chose to submit to. Following this, resubmit your site to the category you originally selected, and if this still does not work submit your site to the category above the one you chose previously. If you still don't have any luck, try emailing staff@dmoz.org; this will put your request in front of an actual staff member of the Open Directory.

If your site listings disappear

If you have only lost your listings for one editor, then you have probably only offended that editor and the rest of your listings will be OK. However, if all your site listings disappear it's very likely that you have violated the Open Directory's submission policies and been banned from the Directory altogether. You can email the Open Directory at staff@dmoz.org to appeal, but if you have been banned altogether it is unlikely that you will be re-accepted. The main things to look out for are:

- Affiliate lists. Do not submit your site if it is a list of products that link to an affiliate site such as Amazon; the Open Directory editors do not like this, and you will not be accepted.
- Doorway pages. Do not try to submit doorway pages that simply redirect to another page on your site; you will be blacklisted for doing this. Some people also try to submit mirror sites to the Open Directory. These are sites that share the same content but have different URLs; the scam involves submitting each URL as an individual listing, and does not go down well at all with the editors.

Updating your listing

To update your listing if this is necessary to reflect new website content, you should visit the category that you site is listed in and select the 'Update URL' link that is found at the top of the page. You're not really supposed to update your listing if you are not happy with it, and Open Directory states that you should only apply to update it if you need to:

- Replace an old URL with a new URL when it has changed
- Correct spelling and grammatical errors in the site's title and description
- Suggest a new title when the title on the site has changed
- Suggest a new description when the scope of the site has changed.

A form will appear to fill in that asks you to enter your URL, and then to edit the title and description of the site. You will also have to explain to the editor why you are updating your listing. Updates usually take a while to be acted upon, and if you are merely editing your listings to improve your ranking the editor will not be happy. Be careful when you are using this function, and only use it to update your listing when you really need to. As with resubmission, if your listing is not updated as requested, you should email the category editor; if that fails, email the staff at the Open Directory.

Special tips to get listed

As for Yahoo, make sure your site is ready for submission. There should not be any broken links, and the content should be relevant and well presented. Remember, you are trying to impress the editor of a particular category.

It also helps to add a link to the Open Directory to your website. If you want to get extra bonus points, link this back to a particular category; this will make the editor of that category more responsive to your submission. Editors of the Open Directory feel a sense of ownership over their particular categories as it is a volunteer-based service, so anything you can do to raise the profile of their category will impress them and make them more inclined to list your site.

Another tip is to become an editor yourself. You can do this be going to the category that you would like to edit, and clicking on the 'become an editor' link at the bottom of the page. This will bring up an application form. You will need to explain your expertise and interest in the subject, and whether you have a business interest in the category. It is unlikely you will be able to become an editor of a category that is directly related to your business, and it is also unlikely you will be able to edit the top level of a category; you should start at the bottom of the hierarchy and work your way up. The most important part of applying is to add two or three URLs of websites, including a title and description, and you should take your time preparing this. If you have an interest in the performance of specific sites in a category, it is definitely worth becoming involved as an editor.

Useful links

Here are some useful links to help you find out more about the Open Directory:

- The Open Directory newsletter (http://dmoz.org/cgi-bin/newsletter/), which is primarily for editors of the Open Directory but can also be viewed by the public. This will give you a good idea of how editors view the Open Directory, and what they will look for when deciding whether to accept sites.
- The Open Directory Guidelines (http://dmoz.org/guidelines.html), which is again primarily for editors of the Open Directory, but will give you a good idea of the guidelines they are expected to follow. It outlines what is deemed as spam, the type of site editors like to accept, and how editors are selected or removed.
- The Open Directory Feedback Form (http://dmoz.org/cgi-bin/feedback.cgi?), which can be used to send feedback to Open Directory staff.

LookSmart – http://www.looksmart.com

The LookSmart service began in 1996, and today indexes over 2 million websites (Figure 3.6). It also offers a distinct listing service that allows webmasters to get listed in the directory for free.

LookSmart is targeted on a worldwide market, so your site will have to provide a worldwide service for it to be listed. It is important to realize that the focus of the LookSmart service is as a listings distribution service, and LookSmart is more interested in securing partners to display its results than in driving users through the main directory listings. One of LookSmart's most important partners is MSN Search. A good listing in the LookSmart directory can drive quality traffic to your website, and it is worth getting listed if you want LookSmart's partners to send you traffic. LookSmart's website states:

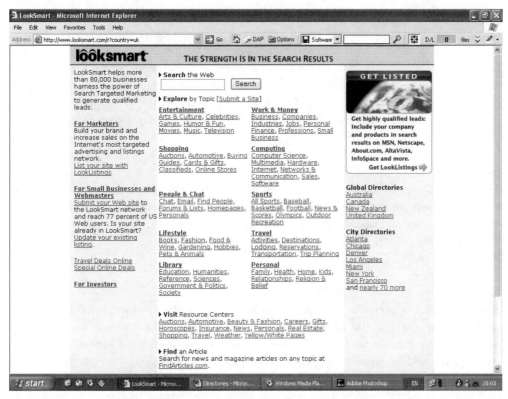

Figure 3.6 *The LookSmart home page (reproduced with permission)*

LookSmart helps businesses of all sizes harness the power of search marketing to generate cost-effective sales leads. LookSmart search listings enable businesses to reach 77 per cent or nearly four out of five US Internet users, through top portals and ISPs including Microsoft's MSN, About.com, AltaVista, Netscape Netcenter, CNN.com, Road Runner, Cox Interactive Media, InfoSpace (Excite, Dogpile, MetaCrawler, WebCrawler), CNET's Search.com and search services such as Inktomi. LookSmart is based in San Francisco, California, with offices in New York, Los Angeles, Detroit, Montreal, London, Melbourne and Sydney.

This shows why it is important to be listed with the service, and how getting listed with LookSmart can influence your listings in other important engines.

LookSmart results

As LookSmart's directory is human-edited, it can guarantee a quality results service and relies heavily on its database to provide results. Its directory results are supplemented by the Inktomi database when a search does not return any relevant results.

When you perform a search you will be presented with a page that features three different results panels. These different sections are 'Featured sponsors', 'Directory topics' and 'Reviewed websites'. The featured sponsors section is an area where sites can be listed by paying a fee for certain keywords. The directory topics section contains category listings from within the LookSmart database that are presented in order of keyword relevancy, and the number of results returned is dependent on the search terms used. The reviewed websites section returns direct listings to websites, with five displayed on the first page and a further ten displayed on the second.

Getting listed

The listing options for LookSmart are as a single listing, as multiple listings, non-commercial listings or crawler-based listings. This section will first deal with getting listed on looksmart.com, and then go on to discuss getting listed on looksmart.co.uk, which is an altogether simpler process.

Single listing

You should use this option if you want to get a single page of a commercial site listed on the service. When you visit the LookSmart home page, on the right you will see options for submitting your site. On the left of the page, follow the 'For small businesses and webmasters' link, and you will be taken to the 'Looklistings small business' program. To get listed on this program you have to pay a small non-refundable fee, and this will mean that your site will be reviewed by an editor – much in the same way as the Yahoo Express submission program. If an editor accepts your site, then you have to pay LookSmart a fee every time someone clicks on your website. This fee encompasses both the LookSmart service itself and any other site that uses LookSmart's results. There is a minimum spend requirement for your site every month; if you do not spend this much on clicks then you will automatically be charged the difference by LookSmart. You will also have to deposit money into your account, which is used to cover click payments, and you'll need to top this up when it runs out. This is refundable, so you can claim any excess back if you leave the service.

You should approach preparing your site for submission in the same way as for Yahoo. You should ensure that your site is fully working, has no broken links, and provides a worthwhile service. You need to remember that the site will be reviewed by human editors, not a piece of spidering software, so it is important to make sure it is fully working. The simpler you make the editor's role, the more likely you are to have your site listed. LookSmart also offer a service called 'Zeal', which should be used for those submitting a non-commercial site; it is also useful for small business site owners to see how to write a relevant site description for LookSmart that will not be edited too much.

When you enter the LookSmart submission form for small businesses, you will be asked for five key areas of information. You will need to specify your URL, the website's title (no more than 65 words), a website description (with a limit of 170 characters), ten relevancy keywords, and a category for submission. As with Yahoo and the Open Directory, you need to spend time preparing this information because it is very important for getting your site listed within both LookSmart and its partner sites.

Submitting your URL is quite straightforward; all you need to do is type the URL of your website. You should take care in coming up with a title for your site, as one of the key ways in which LookSmart rates sites is by how many of the search terms used rate in the site title. You also need to include your business name, so you should spend time creating a relevant title that will be accepted. Taking the Sport Shoes example, a title for your site could be 'www.sportsshoes.com – Shoes for running and sport'. Make sure the whole title is relevant, as otherwise the editor will change it.

You should approach your site description for LookSmart in the same way as for any other directory, and following the guidelines outlined for Yahoo in this chapter will provide you with a strong, relevant site description. The 'relevancy keywords' section allows you to specify ten keywords that you think will be most important to represent your listing. These are not as special as they sound, and all they do is provide extra words to be associated with your listing, but you should spend time choosing them and make sure you come up with some good ones. This section essentially provides you with space for extra keywords you could not work into your site description or title; the most important terms should be used in the description, and those that are less important in the keywords area. Your relevancy keywords can be single words or phrases up to three words long. If you have a word or phrase that is extremely important (in our example it would be 'sports shoes'), then it is worth including it in both the description and the keywords area to maximize its visibility.

Select your category for the final part of the submission process in the same way as for Yahoo or the Open Directory. Perform a few searches on your main keywords, and choose the most suitable category for your site. You can choose not to select a category and let LookSmart's editors make the selection for you, but it is better to choose yourself, as this increases your chances of being placed in a relevant category.

You will also be prompted to specify a monthly budget for your account, which is a projected click-through target. Once you have reached your limit your site will no longer be listed, so the budget is essentially a top level that you place on your account to stop you spending more than you want. You can update your budget at a later date.

You will hear whether your site has been accepted within five business days, and your actual listing will appear a few days after. The best way to check whether your site is listed is to search for it yourself. It may take longer for it to appear at the LookSmart partner sites.

Multiple listings

LookSmart's multiple listings program is for those who have a higher budget and who want more than one URL listed – you can have hundreds and thousands of URLs listed using this service.

When you apply for it online you are prompted to fill in an online form expressing your needs, and a LookSmart sales representative will reply to this with a custom package for your site.

Through this service LookSmart will do a deep categorization of your website, going through the site and linking every page they see as being relevant and each page you want to have listed. You can also pay to have your site featured in the 'Featured listings' section of the LookSmart results page in response to particular keyword searches. You achieve this by paying a fixed fee depending on which terms you want to appear in this section for – the more popular the term, the more money you will have to pay. It is worth remembering that this service is only for those who are managing large-scale websites, and is not for small-business site owners who want to increase their listings. You have to have a high budget to be able to use the service, but if you have this budget it is well worth taking advantage of.

Non-commercial listings

LookSmart owns a directory called Zeal, which is a volunteer-run directory similar to the Open Directory (Figure 3.7). The results for Zeal and LookSmart are combined, so when your site is listed with Zeal you will also appear in the LookSmart results, and will find that your site appears

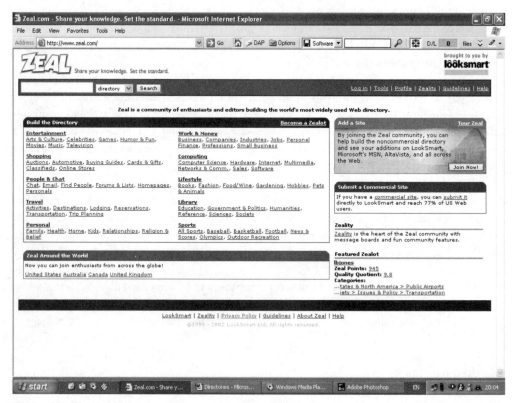

Figure 3.7 *The Zeal home page*

in LookSmart's partner results – such as MSN search. It is therefore well worth signing up at Zeal, but before you get your site accepted you have to pass a Zeal Member quiz. This is of value even if you are a commercial site webmaster, as it gives you a good idea of how websites are listed on LookSmart, and how you should best prepare site titles and descriptions in order to get your site listed. When you join Zeal you will be expected to help to contribute, and to add sites to the database, so passing this test is a must.

You can take the Zeal test as many times as you like, but because it becomes harder to pass every time you fail, it's in your interests to pass first time. By completing the test you will gain the knowledge to be able to submit in a way the editors like, and this in turn will enable you to get more submissions accepted. You will have the opportunity to see a 'corrected' version of your site description, which should give you an idea of where you have gone wrong and how to get around it. The test is essentially a way to make sure that the Zeal editors receive relevant websites from contributors and that the submissions are prepared in such a way as to be easy to process; it is a great tool.

When you submit to Zeal your submission will be considered by a Zeal or LookSmart editor, who will then either approve or reject it. If it is approved, it will be added to the directory. When you have earned enough points from being an active member of the community you can become a 'Zealot' of a category, which grants you certain administrative rights over that category. It is possible in this way to work your way up to category management status, in much the same way as in the Open Directory.

It is worth remembering that Zeal is ONLY for non-commercial sites, and you will not be able to add any sites to commercial categories. However, if you are interested in a topic it is a good way to become familiar with the submission process, and to work your way up to category management status. Zeal is only for non-commercial content. You can take advantage of this system and build pages that are non-commercial into your site to get a listing; however, be careful when you do this and try to make the non-commercial section actually fit in with the rest of your site's content. It is always worth using the paid submission program.

Getting rejected, or if your listing disappears

If your site is not accepted by LookSmart, you will be told why. You should make the necessary changes to your site and resubmit it. If you end up in a category that isn't right for your site, email LookSmart and explain the problem; the site editors will then make a decision whether to re-list it.

Submitting to LookSmart UK

Submission to LookSmart UK (Figure 3.8) is a much simpler process than to the .com version. In the UK LookSmart works in the same way as the paid submission service on the .com site, and you will get a response within five working days telling you whether your site has been listed. The

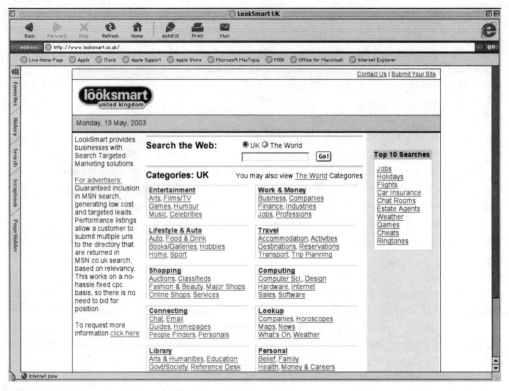

Figure 3.8 *Looksmart.co.uk (reproduced with permission)*

submission process is basically the same as on the .com site, except that you do not need to enter extra keywords and the description has to be no more than 500 characters in length. For UK submissions the description is only a guide for the LookSmart editors to write their own description of your site, so make sure it is clear and concise, and the chances are it will not be edited or changed too much. Submitting a site title is also different to when submitting to the .com site, as you have to submit your exact company name; bear this in mind when completing your submission to increase your chances of getting listed. The other significant point to remember is that you should only submit to the UK site if your site is targeted at the UK market; if this is not the case, your site will not be accepted.

Bidsmart

You need to register for Bidsmart on the Bidsmart home page at www.bidsmart.looksmart-.co.uk, and then you can place bids on a number of search terms and keywords. You only pay when a user clicks on your site in the 'Featured listings' window. It is worth concentrating your bids on a particular topic, as the aim is to be listed on the first page of any search.

Choose your most relevant keyword, and then place the maximum bid for this keyword. You will find that the bid is measured as a price per click-through, so it could be anything from £0.01 to £1.00, depending on the popularity of the term. Again your main aim is to be listed in the top four of the results for the keywords that you choose, so focus your bidding rather than spreading it. You need constantly to monitor how your site is doing in the featured listings, as it is a dynamic system and you can be outbid at any time. LookSmart UK also offers a full service package, which is similar to the multiple listings package offered by the .com site. The minimum cost of this package is £500 per month, so it is again not intended for small site owners. However, it is a good option for those with larger websites, as LookSmart will design a package to give your site maximum exposure across the LookSmart and Bidsmart networks. You also have the opportunity to download reports that monitor your progress, which is a useful tool for preparing site performance reports.

It is well worth getting listed with LookSmart, whether in the UK or on the .com site. The services it offers cover a wide range of submission budgets, and the results it provides are used by a number of high-profile search services. If you submit your site carefully, with attention to detail regarding your keywords and phrases, you stand an excellent chance of getting a good listing. If you are using the Bidsmart system in the UK, again make sure you concentrate your bids on your top keywords to achieve maximum exposure.

In conclusion

One of the best ways to start your SEO campaign is to get listed in the major directories. The main point here is that directory listings will make your site visible to many of the main spider engines as well as in the directories themselves.

Directory listings are reviewed and either accepted or rejected by human editors, and their content is organized into hierarchical categories.

The major web directories looked at here are Yahoo!, The Open Directory Project and LookSmart. You should start with Yahoo, and a Yahoo business category listing is essential for any serious business. The sign-up fee should not be a problem for most businesses, and represents great value for money when all is taken into consideration.

Next you should move on to the Open Directory, which is free, and will help your ranking in engines such as AOL Search, Google, HotBot, and Netscape. Remember that you can contact the Open Directory editors if you are having problems with getting your listing accepted.

A LookSmart listing is also important, and LookSmart feeds a number of high-profile search engine results. It costs money to be listed in LookSmart, so you need to consider whether it is worth the cost. If your site is non-commercial, then if you pass the Zeal test you can submit your site to the Zeal directory; through Zeal it will eventually end up in LookSmart.

Your submission will be reviewed and accepted or rejected by a human editor. The most important criteria for acceptance are the quality of your site, the category selected, and how well written your title and description are. Selection of the most appropriate category is very important.

When submitting your site, submit your homepage URL through the particular directory's 'add URL' page. You can submit your site through using just the online form, but make sure you have all the necessary information at hand before you submit.

You are presenting your site to another human, and therefore you should consider the process as the development of a relationship. Make sure you have read the submission guidelines outlined in this chapter, and be polite if you ever need to get in direct contact with an editor. Editors have the power to change your site title and description; if they decide to do this it will be for a good reason, but if you do not want it changed you must make sure that the copy is relevant and reflects your site's content accurately.

You need to select the right category to submit to, which requires a fair amount of work. Do a search on the directory for the keywords or phrases you would like to be found for, and see which categories return results. You then need to decide which is the most appropriate for your site. Check which other sites are in each category before deciding; if there are 100 sites in one and 20 in another you may be better off choosing the latter category, as your visibility will be higher. Most importantly, make sure the category is totally appropriate to your site. After you have chosen a category, submit your site.

Write your site title first. If the directory specifies that the title must be your site name then you must comply, but where there is scope to go beyond this make sure you include your main keyword at the start of your title.

Spend time writing your description, as it is very important – it is what a directory user sees when coming across your site in the directory. Make sure you keep within the specified word count for each directory, and that you weave your main keywords into the copy. Your description should be focused and read well, and not just be a list of keywords.

Chapter 4

Pay-per-click engines

In the past few years there has been a definite shift towards the acceptance of paid listings as being the best way to get listed on a search engine. Inktomi was the first major search engine to provide a paid listings service, and all the major search engines now offer this system, where payment of a fixed sum guarantees that your website will be spidered and listed on that engine. Paid submission to sites makes good sense, even if there are a few obvious loopholes and problems. However, real search optimization should not be neglected in the place of paid listings.

As well as paid listings there is pay-for-placement submission, which was touched on in Chapter 3. The engines allow webmasters to pay for their site to be listed under certain search terms and keywords. It is an efficient process, and one that can yield quality traffic to your site. Payment takes the form of a bidding process, and webmasters need to decide where in the ranking for the particular term chosen they would like to be and 'bid' the appropriate amount of money on that term. The nature of the bidding process dictates that there will always be high prices for particular terms, but if you are beaten by another webmaster you can then go back and raise your bid. Certain search terms have ridiculously high ceilings for their bids, and in some cases it does not seem worth paying that much money for a listing; however, this is an ongoing issue with this type of engine. If you place the highest bid, you will be placed at the top of the listings until someone outbids you. Bids are ranked in decreasing order of cost.

You should take care when submitting to pay-for-placement engines; it can be tempting to place high bids of lots of terms, but you will end up paying for this. If you follow the guidelines outlined here, you will be well prepared for bidding. The major advantage of pay-for-placement search engines is the amount of control you have. You can control your ranking and budget, and the keywords and search terms that you get listed for. You can really make the most of the budget you have available, and make sure that your listings are properly targeted.

There are generally two different payment systems involved with this type of service: click-through and fee-based. The click-through system means that for every click on a keyword that links to your website, you pay the amount that you had bid on that keyword. If you have placed a high bid, you can see how this can very quickly become expensive. The fee-based system means that you pay a set fee for your ranking, and this is not affected by the number of click-throughs on your site. When using the pay-per-click method you have to check regularly to see where your site is ranked, and in some cases you can request to have an automatic update put on your bid amount so that it increases as people bid against it.

Overture (formerly GoTo)

Overture is the main paid placement engine on the Web (Figure 4.1). As well as this it also supplies results to a wide range of other search engines, and it estimates that more than 95 per cent of its results are seen through their partner sites. As mentioned in Chapter 3, Overture provides the sponsored links for Yahoo.com, as well as links for AltaVista, Lycos, MSN, AOL Europe, Excite and Hotbot, amongst others. It is well worth getting your site listed on Overture, as it is a great way to get quality traffic to your site from a number of high-profile search engines.

Overture was started in late 1997, and was then known as GoTo. It was started in Pasadena, California, and there was a unique philosophy behind the service: that the sites listed would only

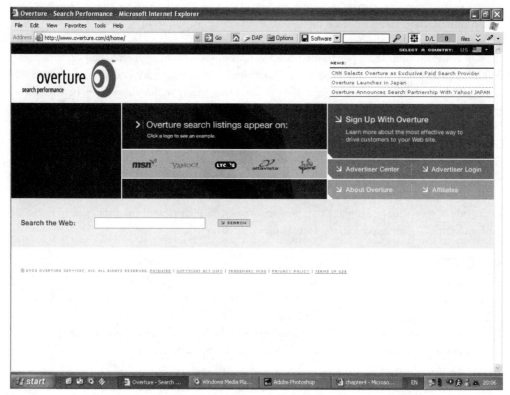

Figure 4.1 *The Overture website (reproduced with permission)*

pay for the keywords and search terms that were relevant to them. This would in turn produce a more relevant search engine than the other spider-based engines. Overture is essentially an advertising service, but with a twist, and is sort of a cross between Ebay and a search directory. You should see getting listed on Overture as a means of improving your visibility on the search engines it is partnered with, and it can work out to be a very effective tool – although the cost of using it can vary dramatically depending on the keywords you are targeting.

How Overture works

On Overture, webmasters bid against each other on certain terms and keywords. They are then charged the bid amount they specified every time someone clicks on the term. This amount is taken out of an account they have with Overture, which they have to keep funded. They essentially pay for each click they receive for their site. The amount they bid reflects their position in the search results – so, for example, if you were to place a bid on the term 'shoes' at 40p per click, and there were two higher bids on the term, 41p and 42p, your site would show up third on the list of search results for the term 'shoe' and every time someone clicked on your site from overture you would be charged 40p. In the case of a tie between two sites, the site that has been bidding on Overture for the longest will go highest. As it is a bidding system the cost per click can change quickly, and because you are constantly getting billed you can easily exhaust your budget. If this happens, sites below you automatically move up the ranking. To prevent this you should make sure that your account is always topped up.

Placing bids

In order to get your site listed on Overture you first of all need to open an account with them. This section of the chapter takes you through opening your account. There are two options for signing up to Overture, which you will see if you follow the 'Advertisers sign up' link from the home page of the site; these are 'Fast Track' and 'Self Serve'. The Fast Track system is a paid system, where you are given advice on which search terms, titles and descriptions to invest in, to meet with editorial approval. The Fast Track service will get your site listed, but it costs a fair amount to sign up, and the money could probably be better spent elsewhere. If you follow the techniques outlined in this section, you will not need to use the Fast Track service. We advise you to use the self-serve option on Overture; this gives you total control over your listing, and does not require any financial investment to set up. Once you have selected this option a sign-up form will appear, prompting you first to choose your target market, selecting one that is relevant to you, and then to fill in the personal details form that appears. This is a useful feature of the service, as it makes sure you are registered on the correct country-specific portal, and that your website reaches people from the right country. You will then be taken to the 'Add Listings' page (Figure 4.2) where you have to submit your website(s) and specify which words or phrases you are going to bid on.

Selecting your search term

Unless you have any search terms in mind its worth using the 'Search term suggestion' tool that Overture provide to help you select (Figure 4.3). This tool lets you enter a word, and then tells you

Figure 4.2 *The Overture Add Listings page (reproduced with permission)*

how popular that word is. Entering the phrase 'sports shoes' into the tool reveals that there are already 1088 searches in the last month for that term; it seems quite popular. However, if you try something else, like 'search engine optimization', it reveals that there are 4670 searches for that. Although volume and cost are not guaranteed to correlate, the popularity of the search term suggests that to rank on the top page for 'search engine optimization' will cost a fair amount of money per click. This tool also includes singular and plural forms of words, and covers variations on words as well, so it will give you the closest link to the words or terms that you are searching for. This also works when you are bidding, and means that if you have bid on the plural of a word (such as 'shoes' in the example above) the word 'shoe' will also be covered. You should take full advantage of the 'Search term suggestion' tool, as it is a very useful guide. Make sure you choose terms that are relevant to your site and title, and when you are happy with a term enter it in the box. You will be able to see how much you need to bid on it later.

Title and description

The next thing you need to do is specify a title and description for your website. This, much like submitting to a directory, provides the actual listing for your website. You can have up to

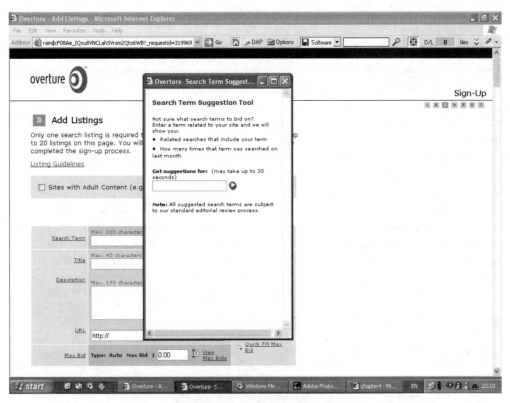

Figure 4.3 *The Overture search term suggestion tool (reproduced with permission)*

40 characters for your title and up to 190 characters for your description. It's worth taking your time over these, as they have to be appealing to someone who is looking at them, and you should include your search term in the title and description to maximize your click-through rate. If you have already prepared listings for Yahoo or the other directories covered in this book, it should be safe to use these; if not, follow the guidelines outlined in Chapter 3 to create a relevant title and description for your website. Next you need to provide a URL for each term you have specified. It is recommended that you use the home page of your website, but if you have chosen a specific term that relates to a specific section of your website then you can direct traffic to that page. Use your common sense when filling in the URL, and choose the page that will be the most relevant. For example, if we were bidding on the term 'web consultancy' for Sprite Interactive then this would be directed to the Sprite home page, as it is a fairly generic term that covers a wide range of disciplines. However, if the bid was on the term 'search engine optimization' then the user would be directed to the search engine optimization page of the Sprite Interactive website, as this is a more specialized discipline that has its own place within the 'web consultancy' umbrella, and its own section on the website.

Choosing a bid amount

All you need to do now is to specify a bid amount for each of the terms you have chosen. The price you specify is how much you will pay Overture for each person who clicks through to visit your site. Luckily, Overture has a tool that can tell you how much the highest bid is for each particular term. Click on the 'View max bids' link next to the box where you will specify your maximum bid, and a pop-up window will appear where you can type in a term and see its maximum bid. On the term 'search engine optimization', for example, the maximum listing was recently $7 per click, and it has no doubt gone up since this was written (Figure 4.4). This is a very high amount, and it means the company is paying $7 every time someone clicks on its link from Overture. This can clearly become a very expensive business.

When making your decision, you need to look at your budget and the amount you will have to pay for each click; this will indicate where you can afford to be listed on the results page. You may decide that being ranked second or third is good enough. Overture quotes a five-day turnaround time (for self serve) from when you submit your listing to when your site is actually listed; because of this there is a high probability that by the time your site has been entered into their listings you will have to change your bid amount, as someone may have bid higher than you. It is definitely

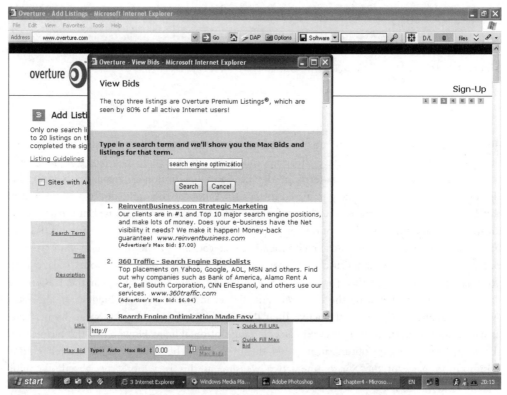

Figure 4.4 *The results for a search on 'search engine optimization' (reproduced with permission of Overture)*

worth checking where your site is listed as soon as is appears, and making any necessary adjustments to the bid amount.

What if two advertisers both have the same bid amount – who gets the highest listing? The site that was listed first will be listed highest. Overture rewards commitment to advertising, and you should therefore make sure that your listing does not go idle or get taken down as this will put you back at the bottom of the pile.

The overture payment plans

Once you have selected your search terms and the amount you would like to bid, you need to specify which payment plan you want to use. You can choose from the non-stop traffic plan, the fixed budget plan or the pre-payment plan. It's worth knowing that you will need a credit card to pay for the first two, but Overture will accept cheques for the pre-payment plan.

The non-stop traffic plan is for those who have a large budget and who do not want their listing to go offline. When you choose this you are telling Overture automatically to top up your account by a specified amount from your credit card any time your credit goes to zero. This is intended for those who can afford a constant stream of money from their account into Overture. It is useful because you will maintain your listing, but your card will be charged often if you have a popular website and this can become very expensive.

The fixed budget plan is for those who do not want to spend more than a certain amount on Overture every month. Here, you set a monthly budget (such as £100) and then if your click expenditure reaches that much before the end of the month your listing will be suspended until the start of the next month. At the start of the next month your card is again charged the fixed amount specified and your website is re-listed. If your expenditure does not reach the amount specified, then the credit is rolled over to the next month and your card is charged the amount you specified minus the amount rolled over. For example, if you specified a cap of £100 per month and you only ran up £70 worth of expenditure, then £30 would roll over onto the next month and your card would only be charged £70 to bring the total amount back up to £100. This plan is particularly useful for those on a budget, allowing you control over how much you spend each month on Overture.

With the pre-payment plan, you are left to manage your account personally. If the amount hits zero you have to top it up yourself, either by making a credit card payment or by sending a cheque to Overture. Overture warns you by email when your account is about to run out. This is a useful plan if you want to remain in total control of your expenditure, but as it is not automated it can prove annoying having constantly to update your account manually.

For all payment plans you have to put down a small initial deposit. This deposit does go towards covering the amount you are charged for bids, but you cannot get it back. There is also a monthly minimum spend for all payment plans when you register on the American Overture.

You should think carefully before choosing your payment plan. Overture recommends the non-stop traffic plan, but there are of course obvious advantages to Overture in this plan. If you have a large budget and do not want your site listing to be removed because your budget has run out, you should go for this plan because it will ensure constant traffic to your website.

If you are working to a fixed budget each month we recommend the fixed budget plan, as this allows you to stay in control of your account.

Making sure your submission is relevant

When you submit your site, it is reviewed by Overture and has to meet a number of guidelines for submission. You should pay close attention to these; if you do not meet them your site may be rejected and you will then have to resubmit your listing. The main reason for sites being rejected by Overture is that inappropriate search terms have been chosen. As mentioned above, it makes no sense to choose search terms that are not totally related to your site; this is another reason not to do this. If you choose inappropriate search terms, the chances are that your site will be rejected. Your site's content needs to reflect the search terms you have chosen and Overture will check this, so make sure you spend time choosing the terms that are right for you. Don't submit a website that simply links to another site, and do not provide misleading titles or descriptions for your pages, as Overture will check these too. In Overture's words, your site has to have 'substantial content that is clearly reflective of the search term', and 'The title and description must accurately describe why the website qualifies for the search term'; bear these points in mind when you submit.

Lesser issues highlighted by Overture include that your site has to be compatible with Internet Explorer 5 and Netscape 4 web browsers, and that you should not hinder the use of the Back button by a user of your site – meaning that users should easily be able to travel back to the search results page that they came from. For a more detailed run-down of the specific site requirements visit http://www.overture.com/d/USm/about/advertisers/relevancy.jhtml, which also covers submitting specific site types to Overture (e.g. gambling sites and adult sites).

One last point is that every time you bid on a new term for your site, it is reviewed for relevancy. Therefore, even if your site has been accepted for one term, there is no guarantee it will be accepted for another.

What happens next

After you have submitted your listing, Overture reviews it to make sure it fits in with the guidelines. This takes up to five days. Once your site has been approved, you will be notified by email and your listings will go live; you can then log into your account and manage it online. If your site is rejected, you can appeal against the decision. You should explain to Overture why the terms chosen are relevant to your website, and cover off any issues that Overture raises. If your site is still not accepted, choose new search terms and submit again.

You manage your account with Overture from the account management centre, which lets you look at your balance, see an estimate of your daily click-throughs and charges, and manage your bids. In managing your bids you are able to add and delete terms to bid on, and can also easily change your bid amounts. Because new terms have to go through the Overture approval process, adding a new term can take a further five days.

There are a number of bidding options that Overture provides to make managing your bid amounts a lot easier. The first is called 'Premium bidding', and this service means that Overture keeps your website listed in the top three positions on any search term. These are called 'Premium listings' by Overture, as they give your site maximum exposure in Overture's partner sites – on Yahoo, for example, you will be featured in the Sponsor matches section on the Yahoo results page if you rank in the top three results for any search term on Overture (see Chapter 3). There are also a number of bid management tools that have been created to manage your bids for you, and these can be downloaded; there is more on these in Chapter 7. Bear in mind that there are only certain bid management tools that Overture recommends (see Chapter 7); the others are not welcome by Overture because they do not comply with Overture's rules on frequency of bids. It is up to you how you manage your bids. It is worth using the 'Premium bidding' service if you want maximum exposure for your site, but as it raises the bid amount automatically you have to also make sure that your account budget is topped up to cope with it. The bid management software is useful and can help to streamline a bidding campaign, but if you want to remain in total control of your bids it is better to do it yourself even though this can be time consuming.

One particular area to be aware of is that at Overture 'bid gaps' can open up, where someone lowers a bid without you realizing it. For example, you may be bidding on a term to be number one at 90 pence per click, with the second place person at 89 pence. If things change and the second place person is now rated at 80 pence per click, you are paying 9 pence more than you need to; this is a 'bid gap'. This can be monitored by watching your account closely, or by using the bid management tools covered in Chapter 7.

How Overture distributes its results

Until the year 2000 the best way to see Overture's listings was to visit the site itself, but in 2000 Overture began distributing its results and listings to other major search engines. This was quick to catch on, and now Overture supplies results to a number of major engines and directories, including Yahoo, Lycos and MSN. This means that you can theoretically buy your way to the top of these search engines. If you get in the 'Premium listings' at Overture, you're going to be featured in the 'Sponsored listings' of major search engines. Where you will feature is covered in Table 4.1.

Being placed in the Premium listings (i.e. ranked 1–3) means that your site will attract considerably more traffic than if listed further down. If you have the budget we therefore advise you to go for Overture's Premium bidding service, because of the great exposure you will get. If you don't have such a large budget, aim for at least the top ten results, as these are distributed across a wide range

Table 4.1 Overture rankings and associated directories

Overture ranking	Where sites will appear
1 or 2	AltaVista, AOL, Ask, Direct Hit, Excite, Go, HotBot, iWon, Lycos, MSN, NBCi, Netscape & Yahoo
3	AltaVista, AOL, Ask, Direct Hit, Excite, Go, HotBot, iWon, Lycos, MSN, NBCi & Yahoo
4 or 5	AltaVista, Ask, Excite, Go, iWon, NBCi & Yahoo
6 to 8	AltaVista, Excite, Go, Won (6 or 7) & NBCi
9 or 10	Excite, Go & NBCi
11 to 15	Excite & Go

of other search engines. If your site is listed anywhere below the top then you will not receive the full benefits of the Overture service.

Top ten tips for Overture

1 *Bid into Premium listings.* Advertising in Overture Premium listings (i.e. being in the top three listings) is the best way to achieve maximum exposure for your website if you have the budget.

2 *Bid on multiple search terms.* If you have the budget to bid on a lot of search terms, you will experience the greatest success in reaching potential customers.

3 *Include the search term in the title and description.* You should create your website title and description so that it reflects the search terms you have chosen.

4 *Wait until your site is listed before setting your maximum bid value.* This will ensure that you are totally up to date with bidding amounts, as it takes up to five days to get your site listed.

5 *Make sure your search terms and listings are relevant.* This is probably the most important point. Make sure the terms you choose are relevant to the content they point to; if they are not they may not be accepted by Overture, and also you will not receive a high click-through rate.

6 *Don't let your account go idle.* Make sure your account is active so you keep your status when there is a tied bid.

7 *Be careful which payment plan you choose.* Its very tempting to go for the non-stop traffic plan, but bear in mind that this can be very expensive. You may be better off choosing the fixed budget plan.

8 *Write concise descriptions.* Make sure your descriptions are concise and to the point; users like to know quickly and easily what they are getting.

9 *Make sure your website is working.* Don't link to a site with any broken links, and make sure that your site is well designed and carries relevant content.

10 *Look out for 'bid gaps'.* You need to keep an eye on your bid amounts and those of your competitors to make sure that you are not bidding more than you have to.

It is clearly advantageous to be listed with Overture. You should make sure that you choose your search terms carefully and manage the bidding process in a way that fits in with your search engine optimization budget, as it is very easy for the amount bid to get out of control and for you to spend too much. The fact the Overture supplies premium results to a number of major engines means that if you have the budget to get listed in the top three results for your particular category, you're definitely going to receive a lot of quality traffic to your site.

Overture was the original pay-per-click service on the net, but it has now been joined by a number of other smaller, although still important, services; these are discussed below.

Espotting and targeting the UK and Europe

In Europe the major pay-per-click engine is Espotting, www.espotting.com (Figure 4.5). The only competitor for Overture in the USA is FindWhat, which is covered later, but in Europe Espotting has won a number of major accounts, including supplying results to Yahoo Europe.

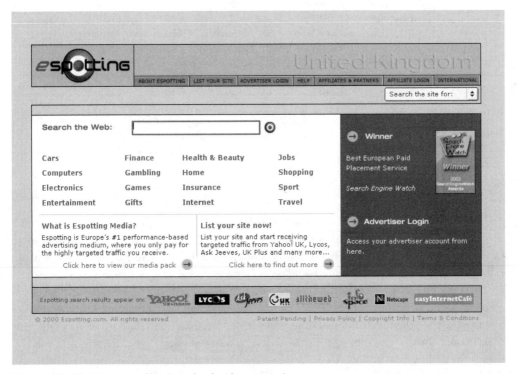

Figure 4.5 *The Espotting website (reproduced with permission)*

Therefore, for companies targeting Europe and the UK it is worth submitting to Espotting as well as Overture. If you submit to both you will be able to cover, among others, Yahoo and Lycos through Espotting, and AOL Europe and MSN UK through Overture. The major reason for the success of Espotting in Europe is the fact that the company was live across Europe at the time of signing the deal with Yahoo, whereas Overture was only live and serving ads in the UK. Table 4.2 illustrates the distribution of advertising across Europe.

Table 4.2 The distribution of advertising across Europe

Site	UK	Germany	France	Spain	Italy	Scandinavia
Overture	AltaVista	AOL (by 04/02)	AOL France (no date set)			
	Ask Jeeves Freeserve MSN	T-Online				
Espotting	Ask Jeeves FAST/ AlltheWeb	Ciao	AltaVista	AltaVista	AltaVista	
	Copernic	Copernic	EresMas	Ciao	Lycos	
	EasyInternet	FAST/ AlltheWeb	FAST/ AlltheWeb	FAST/ AlltheWeb	FAST/ AlltheWeb	Yahoo
	FAST/ AlltheWeb	Fireball	Lycos	Hispavista	Iltrovatore	
	Infospace	Freenet	Nomande.fr	Lycos	ilNuovo	
	Lycos	HotBot	Tiscali	Vizzavi	Lycos	
NetscapeLYCOS	Yahoo	Wanadoo	SuperEva			
Yahoo	Yahoo					

Table 4.2 is helpful in that it shows how the major search engines are served in Europe, but a couple of points must be borne in mind. First, you have to remember that in Europe many more users go to the Internet through their ISP page. Looking at Table 4.2, you will see that three major ISPs are listed – Freeserve, AOL and T-Online (a German provider) – and these are all covered by Overture, so people using these will be exposed to Overture's results. You also need to take into account the fact that many people in the UK and Europe still use the .com version of the websites listed and will see the results from an American perspective, although Yahoo automatically detects which country users are from and lists the relevant search results. If you are targeting the UK market it is therefore still worth advertising on Overture.com, because of its extensive ad distribution in the USA.

Getting listed on Espotting

Espotting offers three ways to sign up to its service: Gold, Silver and Bronze. The Gold service is a fully managed service where Espotting will set up your account and provide targeted listings for you; the team at Espotting contacts you to find out about your site, and then provides you with potential keywords for your site to be listed under. The team also analyses your website, providing a title and description of it for you, and deep links to relevant pages. All your keywords will be activated at the number one position when your site is listed, and Espotting then offers a bid management service in much the same way as Overture's. For the Silver service package you have to enter your own contact details and set up your own account, but Espotting then creates titles and descriptions, and provides deep links into your website using relevant keywords. It also provides an optional bid management service. The Bronze service is suitable for those on a tight budget; this service expects you to provide your own listing and decide yourself on what keywords to bid on.

If you have the necessary budget you can go for the Gold or Silver packages, but here we will talk through registering using the Bronze service. Registering on Espotting is much the same as registering on Overture; there is a 'Current bids' tool that tells you how much the top bid is for a particular term, and a quick search on 'search engine optimization' recently revealed that the maximum bid is £2.40. As on Overture, this is very high. There is also a 'Keyword generator' to give you guidance regarding which keywords to bid on, as it tells you how many searches have been made on a particular term or related terms in the last 30 days. It's worth paying close attention to the results of the 'Keyword generator' and bidding on a term that it recommends. As with Overture, you should make sure you only bid on words that are totally relevant to your website. Espotting's guidelines state that:

> An advertiser may only bid on keywords that are substantially relevant to their website. To be eligible to bid on individual keywords, the website must either sell or show information relevant to the desired keyword.

Espotting will also check that your keywords are relevant to the services you offer, and will reject your site if they are not. You have a maximum of 40 characters for your site title, and of 180 characters for your site description. Espotting has a strict style guide, which is covered in Appendix B. Like the Overture style guide listed earlier, this has been sourced from the Espotting website, so you should follow it carefully.

Espotting also gives you the opportunity to attach a logo to each listing; this appears next to your listing on the results page at Espotting and is well worth doing, as it gives your listings a more visual edge. Your logo must be 90×53 pixels and no more than 1000 bytes in size.

You have to make sure that all URLs are direct links to the relevant page, and that the page has relevant content. Choosing keywords should be done in exactly the same way as for Overture. As with Overture, bid amounts can go quite high so you have to be careful which keywords you chose and how much you set you bid level at. You can pay Espotting by either cheque or credit card. Once registered you can manage your bids in the same way as at Overture; at Espotting you select the number of keywords you would like managed, and then specify which position you would like your keywords to appear in and Espotting will manage your account for you. This service does come at a cost, however, which operates on a sliding scale depending on how many keywords you would like managed. You can find yourself finding a lot of money on clicks, but for those with large budgets and a lot of keywords to manage this can be a useful service.

Google AdWords

Google is another major search engine to have launched a pay-per-click service, called AdWords. You can access the AdWords service by visiting https://adwords.google.com/select/. The listings are those that appear on the Google results page on the left of the screen (Figure 4.6).

The service works in the same way as any other pay-per-click service, and the advantages are clear: your site will be listed on the most popular search engine in the world. However, some of the functionality of AdWords is different to that of other pay-per-click services. Adwords works out the position of an ad by multiplying the cost per click by the click-through rate of your site, and thus if your click-through rate is higher than that of your nearest competitor you only need pay

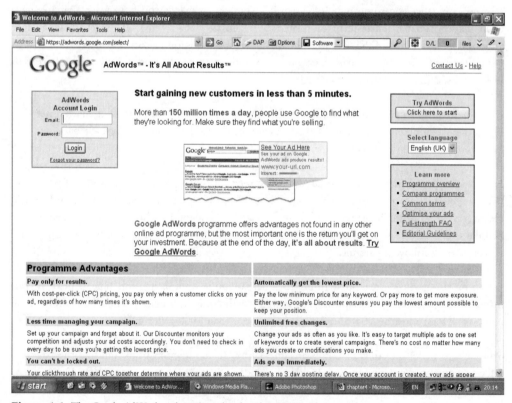

Figure 4.6 *The Google AdWords website (reproduced with permission)*

a penny more than that competitor to stay at the top, but if your click-through rate is low you will need to pay more to stay on top.

Google also has a service, called the Adwords discounter, which automatically lowers the bid amount for your keywords until it is as low as it needs to be for you to maintain a top position. The advantage of the ranking system is that if your site is highly relevant and receives lots of click-throughs, it can rank higher than another site that does not receive as many click-throughs but is willing to pay more. By creating this system Google is rewarding relevant and popular sites, but it does mean that you need to make sure that your site is totally relevant to the terms you have chosen. Another advantage of AdWords is that there is no minimum spend per month and Google does not charge up front; you are only billed when your site is clicked on, and there is only a very small start-up fee. Also, rather than having to register at different country-specific sites, Google lets you choose which sites your ad will appear on.

There are some downsides, however. Google actually sets higher minimum bid amounts for terms that it considers popular, ensuring that it gets the greatest return on any particular keyword. This is not so good for those placing ads with AdWords. If, for example, we were to set up an account bidding on the term 'sports shoes', which we have already seen that nobody is bidding on, and configure our account so that it only appears in the UK, then Google may return with a cost of around $0.25 per click. This is high, as Google has decided that its popularity warrants the fact that it should be $0.25 per click. Also, although the bidding system rewards sites that get high click-through rates, it can also be disadvantageous to webmasters because those paying more can be listed lower just because fewer people click on their listing. For example, if one company is bidding on the search term 'sports shoes' at $0.07 per click but receives only 2 per cent of all click-throughs, and another company is bidding at $0.05 per click but receives 4 per cent of all click-throughs, the result of the equation used by Google to work out where advertisers rank will be 14 for the first company and 20 for the second company, and therefore the second company will rank higher. You need to be aware of this when submitting your listing, and to keep an eye on the reports Google provides on your site's performance. Also, if your ad gets below 0.5 per cent of all clicks out of 1000, its listing will be removed. Google says that this is to 'protect the long term value of the ad area'. It is unlikely that your site will be removed if you submit a good listing, following the general guidelines outlined in the Overture section, but this is another area that you should bear in mind if your performance at Adwords is not going well. Basically, if you select bad keywords and provide a bad title and description for your site it will not last long on Google; this is the rule for your whole account, and the 0.5 per cent rule covers the total of all the keywords you are using for your sites in your account. Google will actually prompt you to reconsider your listings if your click-through rate falls below the 0.5 per cent minimum, and will suggest ways for you to improve your ranking. However, if you prepare your listing properly this should never happen.

Getting listed on AdWords

Getting listed on the AdWords system is much the same as for Overture and Espotting, and if you use the techniques already covered in this chapter you will be able to set up your account quickly and easily. When you get to advertise on AdWords you need to specify a 'headline' for your listing, which should be your website title; this must be a maximum of 25 characters. You can then enter up to two lines of text under the headline, and each line can have a maximum of 35 characters per line; think of these as the description of your site. You are more restricted in creating your listings than with Overture or Espotting, so take you previous description and cut it down to make it relevant but concise. You then need to add your target URL as displayed on your listings, followed by your destination URL, which is where users will be taken when they click on your listing. The website behind this URL, as with Overture and Espotting, has to have relevant content that is related to your keywords.

Once you have entered your listings, you need to specify keywords for your site. Google has a 'keyword suggestions' tool that provides you with a list of matches for any keyword you type in, and with alternatives. You should experiment with this tool, and choose keywords that will match with the most possible search terms in order to give you maximum exposure on Google. Unlike Overture, Google lets you use broad keywords that can link to more than one search term – so if we type in the term 'search engine', Google states that our ad will show up for 56 different searches, from 'search engine optimization' to 'best search engine'. In this case we may want to narrow our terms down to 'search engine optimization', which returns a narrower but more relevant list of 21 possible results. This amount is just about right. You should choose terms that are quite broad in their appeal but not too broad, as this will mean that your site ad will be shown in searches that are not relevant to you. After you have selected your terms, you can use the Traffic estimator tool to give you some idea of how much you will be paying each day for your listing.

It's worth setting a daily maximum payment, as this prevents you from going over budget. As with the other services, if you exceed your maximum your site will be taken down until the next day. In contrast to the other pay-per-click services, AdWords actually puts your site live immediately and then reviews it to see if it is relevant; there is the obvious implication here that the system can be abused, but if something abusive is posted Google will spot it quickly and take it down. Remember that Google will still review your listing, even though it goes live immediately.

Although AdWords is less straightforward than Overture, it is still well worth investing the time to get your ad listed properly. Google is the most popular crawler-based search engine, and having a well-placed ad on it can increase your traffic dramatically.

Inktomi Index Connect

Inktomi's Index Connect program is a bulk listings service for those who wish to list 1000 or more pages with the service (Figure 4.7). The usual Inktomi paid listing program uses a flat fee for listing, but this service uses pay-per-click. You can read more about Inktomi in Chapter 2. If you manage a very large website this service can work out to be more economical; it is well worth considering, as paying a flat fee for every URL out of 1000 pages submitted is, as you

Figure 4.7 *The Inktomi Index Connect website (reproduced with permission)*

can imagine, very expensive. We're not going to cover the service in great detail, as finding the right program for you is not a set science; you will have to contact Inktomi and also its partner providers to find out which offering is best for your company. Inktomi does not charge a set-up fee or a monthly payment, but if you decide to go through one of Inktomi's partner providers they may charge. You can expect your pages to go live within about 48 hours.

Index Connect offers a bonus in that it is free to charities, so if you are a large charity you have nothing to lose by registering. Inktomi also supports an XML feed, which means you can feed a list of URLs, their descriptions and keywords straight to Inktomi to reduce submission time. As mentioned above, Inktomi offers its services through a number of partner sites (Figure 4.8), and which one you choose will depend on your personal needs and requirements. Different partners offer different prices, so it is best to shop around and make sure you are getting the best deal to suit your requirements. Inktomi has more than 1000 Index Connect partners, including companies such as Amazon and the National Wildlife Federation. If you want ot find out more about Index Connect, visit http://www.inktomi.com/products/web_search/connect.html

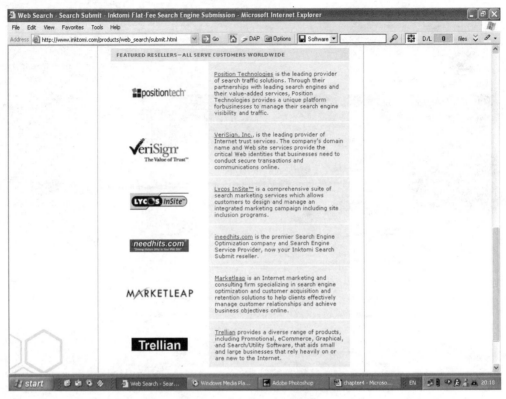

Figure 4.8 *Example Inktomi Connect partner resellers (reproduced with permission)*

FindWhat

FindWhat.com (Figure 4.9) was conceived as a new search engine offering better solutions both to web surfers trying to access specific information quickly, and to advertisers seeking to be found among the increasing clutter of results on other search engines. FindWhat's creators built the service as a 'lean and mean' engine, with no irrelevant sites and no redundant information. Their main aim was to provide fast searches with totally relevant results.

FindWhat.com uses pay-per-click, bid-for-position technology in a similar way to Overture, albeit with a different and smaller distribution network. However, it is still worth considering if your budget will stretch to it. The fact that FindWhat has lesser distribution may also be an advantage, in that it may bring you higher quality traffic at a lower cost. Moreover, the major search service to use FindWhat's results is Excite, so getting listed on FindWhat can get you listed quickly with Excite; FindWhat also supplies listings to Search.com, WebCrawler and News.com amongst others. However, getting listed with FindWhat is nowhere near as high a priority as getting listed with Overture. FindWhat is also an American service, so getting listed is more of a priority for American companies than for European companies.

Figure 4.9 *The FindWhat website*

Signing up for FindWhat is similar to signing up for other pay-per-click services; you need to enter your contact details and then whether you would like to pay by credit card or other methods (cheque, money order or bank transfer).

FindWhat requires a small initial deposit. However, there is no monthly minimum spend, so you may be able to stretch this money out for several months if you target your terms carefully. You can sign-up for FindWhat's paid listings at https://secure.findwhat.com/signup/signup.asp

Summary

Advertising in pay-per-click search engines is great for small business start-ups. Your listings are usually online in a day or two, and you can start with a minimum account and add funds as you need to, staying in total control of your SEO budget. Well-chosen keywords can lead to quality, targeted traffic, as you know your site will be listed for those words.

It is recommended that you start with Overture.com, as this is the biggest pay-per-click service and it is worth the cost for building a listing. If you are on a very tight budget you can go for

Findwhat.com, as this does not have a monthly minimum spend; however, it does not have the coverage offered by Overture. If you are based in the UK then Espotting comes highly recommended, as it supplies results to Yahoo UK, and Google AdWords also is a very worthwhile service – if only because you will be featured on the most widely used search engine in the world. If you do it right, listings in the pay-per-click search engines provide very cost-effective advertising. It takes quite a lot of work and research to get started, but after your accounts have been set up they won't need much upkeep unless you opt to keep them topped up with funds manually.

Keys to success

1 *Write a focused title and description that will appeal to your target audience.* Describe your product or service as clearly and succinctly as possible. You pay for each click, so you only want to encourage interested visitors. For some terms you can link to pages apart from your home page; remember that you are in complete control of your listing and of where site visitors go when they click the link. The more directly you take visitors to what they're seeking, the better. Include your main keyword in both the title and the description, as this will encourage more clicks.

2 *Bid on* relevant *words and phrases.* The more terms you can afford to bid on, the more often your listings will be seen. Use the keyword suggestion tools from each particular engine to research the terms you should be bidding on before you place your bid, and choose the most relevant, but also consider the cost. If you're bidding on a very competitive word, costs can mount up quickly. You can do your keyword selection 'by hand', checking keywords one by one in several search engines to see what sort of searches people have been conducting. It is important to consult the keyword suggestion tools at more than one search engine, because they are different and will sometimes produce varying results. Be aware that not all traffic is good traffic; you want your traffic to be relevant, especially if you're paying for it, and this takes careful consideration and research. If you find specialized words or phrases that are exactly on target for your product but have a low bid price, bid on them anyway. Bids on less busy terms are usually cheap, and visitors who find your site by specialized keywords are often the most targeted and of the highest quality.

3 *Bid aggressively, but be aware of your limits.* You need to be aware how much you are bidding on each term, and to have an idea of the value of each new visitor to your site. This should effectively be covered by the amount you have paid for each click-through. If you're just starting, you may need to make educated guesses here.

4 *Don't worry about being Number One.* When you bid for ranking, don't assume that being ranked first is best. You're more likely to get more clicks at Number One, but these are not necessarily more profitable. You may get just as many clicks at a lower position, which would be much more cost effective. You don't need to be ranked first, but do try to appear in the top ten. If you are not ranked in the top ten your listing won't be seen very often, let alone clicked on. If high ranking is too expensive, you should either take what you can or go for a different term. A lower ranking will send fewer visitors, but at least the traffic from that term will be cost-effective.

5 *Watch your bids.* Be careful using the automated bid boosting functions of some engines, which keep all your bids topped up to first place; if the phrases you are bidding on are very competitive then you can end up with bids that are too high realistically to be profitable for you. It is worth

adjusting your bids by hand, unless you have a very large budget. Watch that you don't get caught out by bid gaps, where you are paying more than you have to in order to be ranked in a particular position. This occurs when a large gap appears between bids and you are at the top of this gap; you could save yourself a few pence per click if you were at the bottom of the gap, so watch your bids.

Once your listings are in place, they are easy to look after. You do need to monitor them, as they will change regularly. Bear in mind that towards the end of the month advertisers on fixed budgets may drop out for a while, allowing you to push your site higher; however, this is only really worth it for expensive keywords.

You can see which keywords work and don't work for when you need to select keywords for your web pages. Pay-per-click engines can be a good source of information regarding your consumer's searching patterns.

Another tip is that many advertisers set their bidding limits at round numbers. Bidding an extra penny or two to get past them could significantly boost your traffic for that term, even if it does cut your profit margin a bit. Give it a go, as long as you stay within your safe spending range.

In conclusion

The pay-per-click search engines offer some well-targeted advertising programs. Many advertisers do get a good return on their investment by using pay-per-click engines, and the return on investment is much higher than for other forms of advertising – such as banner advertising.

Pay-per-click programs can greatly benefit your optimization campaign, with many of the pay-per-click search engines supplying results to other influential engines and services. You have to be careful and know what you are doing with these engines; you have the potential to bid on hundreds of different terms and phrases, but this needs to be carefully managed or account costs can end up spiralling out of control.

For most of the pay-per-click engines the rules and listing procedures are pretty straightforward – the highest bidder for a phrase gets top spot. Google AdWords is the exception, having extra criteria that affect the position of your placement on its search results pages.

Pay-per-click engines are becoming more and more commonplace in the market, and it is well worth learning how to get the most from them. You will be able to use the techniques learned on one on others. Most importantly, read the guidelines outlined here, and don't go mad with your bidding – this can cost you dearly!

Chapter 5
Linking strategies and free listings

So you've built a great site and you have great content; all you now need is an audience. However, there is a problem: there are around 100 million web pages out there and well over a million unique domains. Of these, the top 10 per cent receive around 90 per cent of the overall traffic. The Web is a very tough place for small sites to get exposure, particularly those without a large budget for promotion. In this chapter we'll look at how you can build a presence for your site and increase your traffic, even if you have little or no site promotion budget.

Free mass submission services – do they work?

There are only two ways to increase a website's traffic: you have to increase the number of new users coming to the site, or you need to get your current users to look at more pages when they are surfing your site. One of the main ways that the site is advertised is through the use of mass submission services. Many people have lost money on lower-priced, poor quality services that guaranteed top search engine placements. If they had taken more time and invested the little money they had in more relevant services, then they could have done a lot better.

The first method discussed here of getting your site listed for free is one that should be avoided, and one that is readily available across the Web. This is the mass submission service. There are a number of companies offering this; just type 'free search engine submission' into Google and this will become evident (Figure 5.1).

When you sign up for one of these services you will generally pay a low monthly fee and in return the company will submit your site to what they describe as 'thousands' of search engines. Don't be fooled! Some services even offer submission to as many as 250 000 engines, although there are not 250 000 search engines in existence. Many of these companies will take your money and then generate spam email, which will give you no benefit and clog up your

Figure 5.1 *The results of a search on Google for 'free search engine submission'; notice the sponsored links (reproduced with permission)*

in-box. You only need to concentrate on the top eight to ten search engines. Many of the top search engines will not accept automatic submission of this kind, and, even if your site does get listed, if it has not been optimized in the first place it is very unlikely that it will rank well. When you next come across a service that offers guaranteed top ten positions or submissions within a certain time (say ten or fifteen days), it is worth remembering a few things. First, let's take the previous example. If eleven people apply to get the guaranteed top ten positions, what will happen then? Logic dictates that it will be first come, first served, which is not very fair on the eleventh person, who has also been guaranteed top ten placement. Anyway, submitting your URL to search engines does not guarantee anything (see Chapter 2).

If you are going to use a mass submission tool, then use a recognized one such as Submit It. This engine is so good and came so highly recommended that Microsoft bought it, and it is now a part of their bCentral suite of site promotion tools. The service is not free, however, and there is a charge of £79 per URL per year to submit your site. For this, Submit It promises to get you a prominent listing on a number of top search engines. bCentral is a great suite of tools, and is covered further in Chapter 7.

Free submission to major search engines

Many of the major search engines still include a free submission section for their listings. Paid inclusion is always the faster choice, but if your budget is limited you may want to consider submitting and waiting the six to eight weeks (or more) that it often takes to see your listings show up. Bear in mind that if you have no budget it is still well worth submitting to the major search engines, as your site will be listed eventually.

Major search engines providing free submissions include:

● Google
● AltaVista
● AlltheWeb.

If your site is non-commercial, you can also submit to Yahoo for free (Figure 5.2).

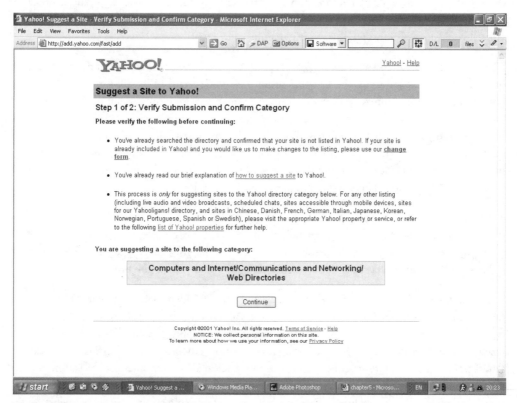

Figure 5.2 *Submitting a site to Yahoo for free (reproduced with permission)*

Building links

Another great way to get traffic to your site for free is to have other sites link to it. This is one of the most powerful tools you can use to promote your site. It's the online equivalent of word-of-mouth advertising and, just like word-of-mouth, it's the most effective way to get new business.

It's like one of your neighbours recommending a good plumber; a recommendation carries more weight than if a person just stumbles across your website using a search engine – and, for the purposes of this chapter, it can also be free or come at a very low cost. One of the best ways to find sites to approach to link to yours is use the search results for terms that are important for your site. Do a search at Google for phrases that you wish to be ranked first for, and then treat all the top listed sites as potential linking partners. Some of the sites listed may be competitors, and you will not realistically be able to trade links with them, but there should be a number of sites that do not sell competitor products to you – the only thing you are competing for being the same search terms. Now you need to visit the sites that are not competitors and see how it would be possible for your site to get a link from them. If they have a links page, this is an obvious place for your site to be linked from; if they have an ezine that users subscribe to then you could place a text link in this, maybe in return for promotion on your own site or a small fee. An example of this in action would be a nutritionist who has written a book on 'living better through healthy eating'; these words would therefore be very important to him on a search engine. Instead of trying to rank first for these results, he could try to exchange links with those sites listed first – which would mostly be stores advertising vitamins and nutritionist services.

The technique is a cost-effective way of getting your site to the top, and is known as 'piggybacking'. You are using the fact that some sites will be ranked highly for a specific search phrase, and will not compete with you. It can take you a very long time to get to these positions, especially if you have little or no budget, so the next best solution is clearly to have a link from their site onto yours. In time, if you have links from the top ten sites for a particular term or phrase you will receive a lot of traffic, as these sites will receive a lot of traffic anyway as a result of their high listing. However, it is not quite this easy, and you have to work out why these sites would want to give you a link. There are a number of possible options:

- You could make them an affiliate of yours if you sell products
- If you already have a number of high-ranking pages, then you could simply swap links between your sites in a mutual fashion – some sites actually have a reciprocal links page, in which case you'll have got lucky and will usually be able to place a link in return for a link from your site.

In any case, it's the research that goes into analysing sites and identifying how you can link from them in the first place that makes all the difference. You need to seek solutions where both parties win, and you can secure for your site a cheap and plentiful supply of valuable traffic. You need to take the time to visit any sites you are asking for links from, then find out who runs the sites and send a polite email – addressing them by name so it is clear that your email has not come from a piece of link generating software. Tell them your name and demonstrate that you have seen their site and taken the time to analyse it. Explain to them why you think a link exchange makes sense, and if they have a links page already, let them know you have been to see it and ask for a link from it. When you send another webmaster a link request or reciprocal linking offer, you should also state what you would like your link to say. It is suggested that you include a piece of HTML code in your email, such as the following:

```
<a href="http://www.yoursite.com">Your Keywords</a>
```

Finally, you should offer to talk by telephone. This may seem like a lot of effort, but it works – and is the only way that does. The goal is to leave zero doubt in the site owner's mind that you are a real person who has been to the site and taken the time to evaluate it and find out where a link can fit in.

Increasing your link factor

Linking from one website to another is, in essence, why the Internet was created. Researchers needed a way to link their documents together, and the Internet was how the academics were able to achieve this. This section of the chapter is about increasing the link factor of your site – both to make other sites link to yours more readily, and to give you the knowledge to be able to identify sites that are worth linking to.

A site's link factor is determined by having certain elements that will encourage other sites to want to link to it, and this in turn will inspire users to visit it more often and thus earn more overall coverage for the site. At the top end of the link-factor scale are sites such as the British Library website, which contains links throughout the site to vast amounts of data as well as a number of off-site links; there are also hundreds, possibly thousands, of websites that link into the British Library. This is because it has extremely rich content that is organized efficiently and with a lot of care. Sites with a low link factor include those that have little or no relevant content, or rely on databases or a lot of Flash content. This is not to say that Flash content or databases are a bad thing, but these do reduce a site's link factor. In the case of Flash content, the text in a movie is all pre-rendered and a movie exists under only one URL. Database-driven content constantly changes, so there are no static pages to link to and URLs in a database can change for every page load, which negates the power to link to these pages. In some cases a database may be absolutely necessary to organize a large amount of information, but when considering whether to implement one into your site you should bear this major factor in mind. For example, a magazine with a number of articles on the Web can have a very high link factor; however, if the articles have been organized as a database this link factor suddenly goes down because if a user wants to link to one a direct link will not work.

The main issue in increasing your link factor will always be the quality and relevancy of content, and the architecture to support it (see Chapter 6). For every website there are many other sites or venues (such as search engines, directories, web guides, discussion lists, online editors and so on) that will link to it, and your challenge is to identify these and contact them. As mentioned above, building links to your site can be a great free or low-cost exercise to increase your traffic and, as we will see below, your site's ranking.

A good way to get people to notice your site, and thus increasing its link factor, is to use guerrilla marketing techniques. There are a number of tactics and methods that can be used to increase the visibility of your website, but if you are operating on a small budget you need to remember one major factor when using these techniques: set realistic goals and keep to them. You can still achieve big results with a small budget, but this has to be done in a realistic and

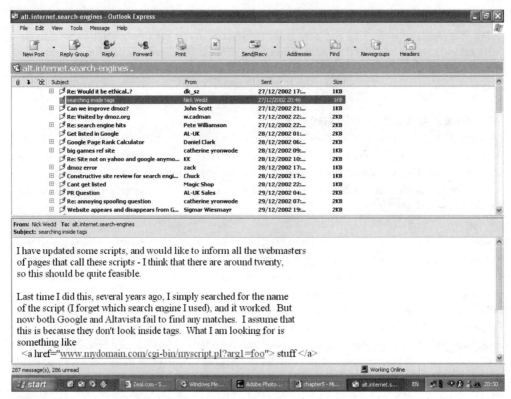

Figure 5.3 *A search engine optimization newsgroup*

clear manner, otherwise you can end up concentrating all your resources on one area only to find that it is not working. Make sure that you analyse the media related to your industry or trade, and learn about which trade shows to attend and who the respected figures are, etc.; you need to know all about your target audience, and this will give you the knowledge to create targeted campaigns that really appeal to them. One great guerrilla tactic for promoting your site is using newsgroups and chat forums. Most email clients now include a newsreader that will allow you to access thousands of newsgroups on a range of topics (Figure 5.3). You need to subscribe to these in order to contribute, and you can subscribe to as many different newsgroups as you wish.

You should be aware that each newsgroup is governed by a strict set of rules that generally apply to the posting of messages on the board and to members' conduct. You should make sure you read this before posting, as if you break the rules of a particular group you run the risk of being banned. Using newsgroups as a marketing tool is much the same as using a web forum (Figure 5.4), so you can take these lessons and use them elsewhere. The main aim is to attract more visitors to your site, and in turn more places that link to your site. The overall aim of this type of guerrilla marketing is to increase your site's link factor.

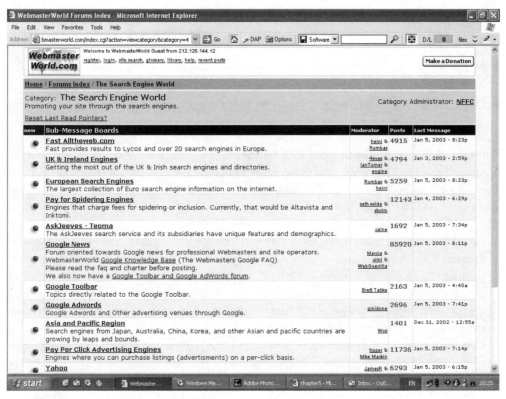

Figure 5.4 *A search engine optimization forum*

The first rule to remember when using newsgroups as a marketing tool is that you should never post 'in your face' postings or adverts, or any kind of classified sales adverts. You will almost certainly get 'flamed' for this – i.e. other users of the newsgroup will abuse you through posting. It may even get you banned. The way to approach newsgroup marketing is to get involved in the discussions, and gradually to become seen as an informative contributor. You should offer advice and tips on problems to the other contributors and become an accepted member of the group. If you offer well thought-out advice, then people will naturally want to find out more about you – which will involve visiting your website. Many newsgroups allow you to have a signature, which is usually a small graphic or message that you attach to the bottom of your posts; make sure you include your web address in here, and then any time you post people will see the link, and some of them may follow it.

Here are a few tips on conducting yourself in newsgroups and discussion forums:

- Before you post to a newsgroup, spend a bit of time reading others' posts so you can become comfortable with the posting style of the group.
- Read the rules before you begin to post.

- Never post 'in your face' postings or adverts, or any kind of classified sales adverts.
- Don't post the same message to multiple newsgroups; this will probably be noticed by somebody.
- Make sure you use a signature file if you are given the opportunity, and keep it short and to the point.
- Don't post messages that have nothing to do with the topic of the message.

Content that can increase your link factor

Here are a few ideas regarding basic site content that can increase your link factor. These are all free ways to promote your site, requiring only the time it takes to implement and integrate them.

1 *Email to a friend link*. Make it easy for people to send pages of your site to their friends. You need to make your site easily accessible by all, and by putting a link at the bottom of a page to recommend the page to a friend you can do this. You can take this one step further by having e-cards that are related to your product or website, which site users can send to a friend with a personalized message. You can also collect users' email addresses using this technique, and these can then be used to send out targeted ezines.

2 *Offer free tools*. You can try offering to your users a free trial version of your product if you are a software company, or perhaps free games or useful software for download. Make sure that whatever you offer is useful to your audience, and that it has links to your website contained within the software. You could perhaps create a high quality screensaver, featuring your company or products, for download. This has the extra benefit of advertising your site on the computer screen of whoever installs the screensaver.

3 *Newsletter/ezine*. Newsletters and ezines are great tools when used effectively. You need to offer an incentive for site users to subscribe, such as exclusive promotions and special offers, or the chance to be kept fully up to date with the latest site developments – make them think they will be the first to know. Your newsletter should be delivered to a subscribers' inbox regularly, and should always carry relevant, useful content. Make sure you provide a number of special offers and promotions relating to your products that the user cannot find anywhere else. To take part in the special offers from your ezine a user should have to visit a page on your website; this will increase hits to your site and essentially increase the number of links you have pointing to you. At Sprite we have integrated successful ezines into a number of our clients' sites, most notably TONI&GUY (Figure 5.5).

4 *Fresh content*. This is one of the most important considerations. Make sure that your site always offers relevant and fresh content, as this will encourage users to return to it. If the content you are offering is topical or exclusive news that they might not find anywhere else, such as breaking industry news, then this will encourage them further.

5 *Link page*. Create a page on your site that showcases or recommends your favourite websites, and offer reciprocal links to other webmasters from this page. It seems simple, but having a clear links page will make people far more likely to approach you for links, and in turn link to your site.

Figure 5.5 *Example of the TONI&GUY ezine*

Publishing an article

As regular contributors to Computer Arts and Computer Arts Special, as well as other top design magazines such as Create Online, we at Sprite know the power of an article to promote. This is true for printed articles, but is also particularly so for online articles. Identify magazines and other periodicals that relate to your product or service, and that feature articles on their websites. Articles also serve the purpose of increasing your credibility; if you or your company can be seen to be the authority on a certain topic, then people will visit your site to find out more about your subject. Allowing your articles to be freely published and submitting them to as many sources as possible means that they can potentially be viewed by literally thousands of web users.

Building links to improve your search engine ranking

Link popularity refers to the number and quality of the incoming links that are pointing to your site. In search engine optimization, 'off page' factors have become more and more important as they relate to rankings. If other sites consider your site important enough to link to, then so will the search engines. One of the most difficult areas of search engine optimization is building link popularity, because there are no easy ways to do this.

Building links to your site will improve your ranking in certain search engines. The main engine that does consider links to your site when working out rankings is Google, so there are clear advantages to building links – above and beyond the fact that they are a free way to promote your site. However, Google knows that not all links are equal, and that FFA (Free-For-All) links are worthless. Google actually measures the quality of links, taking into account each link's importance – so it's not only the amount of links to your site but also the relevancy of these links that is measured. Google actually lets you view the link popularity of any particular page, using its PageRank engine. To use this you have to download the Google toolbar and install it into your Internet Explorer; it can be found at http://toolbar.google.com/ (Figure 5.6).

Once the toolbar is installed, you will notice that there is a small green bar with the words 'PageRank' next to it. This is the PageRank meter, and it tells you how important Google considers a site to be. The PageRank actually refers to the current page you are viewing, and if you place your mouse over the meter you will be given a ranking of one to ten. This is a very useful tool in deciding whether a site (including your own) has a high link-factor. Sites with high PageRanks are the ones that you should approach to link to your site, as they will help increase your PageRank the most – which will in turn increase your ranking within Google. The PageRank is a useful tool, but it is not the only thing to be considered. You should also bear in mind that the site must hold relevant content, otherwise it is not worth being linked with in the first place. The key to ranking well on Google is not just the amount of links you have to and from your site, but also having content-rich pages in the first place.

Taking all the above information into account, here is a step-by-step guide to building free links to your website. All these steps are supported by the link planning charts and tables in Appendix C, which can be downloaded from Sprite Interactive (http://www.sprite.net/linkcharts).

Figure 5.6 *The Google toolbar (reproduced with permission)*

1 *Set yourself a goal and a schedule to keep to.* Set a goal for the number of links you want, as a way to stay motivated. Use a 'site link chart' (see Appendix C) to help you stay on top of the amount of sites you are linking to. You should set the amount of sites you are approaching at about three times the amount you hope to get. Some sites will not want to trade links, so you need to set yourself realistic targets to keep your motivation up. Put aside around 30–60 minutes for link building each day, so you work consistently on the project; it is easy to spend too much or too little time on it and to lose focus.

2 *Make your site worth it.* Your site needs to offer something of value to those sites you are hoping will link to it. You need to make sure you have a lot of linkable content. If all you do is sell products, then you need to have some content (such as articles, news, reviews or tips) that is exclusive to your site and that will be tempting for other sites to link to. Having this content on your site will increase your link factor. It will also improve the quality of your site, so it is worth doing anyway. If you create enough linkable content, then you will find that people will approach you to link to their sites. Make sure you write about something that you know about or, if you cannot write, add some kind of unique software tool or download.

3 *Work out which types of site you want to trade links with.* This will take you some thought. You are not actually finding the sites at this stage but are working out the types of site to contact, so

create a plan regarding which type of site to approach. For example, a site that sells tennis rackets might approach sites that sell tennis shoes and tennis clothes, but not tennis rackets. Once links from these sites have been accumulated, the tennis racket site can then develop a new section on playing tennis, and ask for links from sites that give tips on playing tennis. This will result in a significant number of links from sites related to the target market, and new pages of rich content for the website, to make the user experience more fulfilling.

4 *Locate quality link partners.* The best way to do this, as explained previously, is to type a search for the key terms or phrases you want to be listed for into Google, and choose your potential partners from there. The higher such potential partners are listed the better, as you do not want to be linking to sites that are not ranked highly by Google. You can extend your search to the other major search engines; Yahoo and the Open Directory are particularly good, as sites selected to be listed on these directories will already have been through a strict selection process (see Chapter 4).

5 *Evaluate.* You don't want to waste your time on link partners who are not relevant or who will not increase your search engine rankings, so you should use the Google PageRank software to evaluate your potential linking partners before you contact them. You should try to link up with sites that are ranked as highly or higher than your own.

6 *Organize your findings.* Use the charts in Appendix C to organize your findings. Keeping your findings organized is one of the most important things you can do when building links. Record:
- The full name of the site owner or webmaster
- The email address of the site owner or webmaster
- The home page URL of the link partner
- The URL of the page where you think your link belongs, and why you think it belongs there
- The PageRank of the page
- The date of the initial link request.

7 *Create a link exchange letter.* This letter requests a link exchange with your site, and should be directed to each of the sites you have noted in your list. Make sure you've come up with at least 50 good-quality content, non-competitive sites with a decent PageRank. Take great care in writing your reciprocal links letter, as this will be the most memorable point of contact. Make sure it's the best it can be before sending it out. Remember, you're asking for a favour, so be polite and respectful in your letter – otherwise you'll get nowhere fast.

8 *Contact the webmaster.* You now need to go through your list of websites and send a personalized email to each of the webmasters. Make sure you compliment their sites, refer to them by name, if you have it, and state which page you would like to be linked from and why. You should also include in the email some HTML that contains the link, so they can easily put it into their page. Always have a link already put on your own site before you ask for a link in return, and give the location of the link. It is harder for the other sites to say they will not link to you if you already have a link to them. When you do this, make sure you give them the exact link text to use; however, probably the most important thing is to make sure that they have some kind of linking policy or even a links page. Whatever information you give, make sure it's easy for them to link to you. If they have a big site

that's divided into sections, give them the exact URL of where your site would fit in and then provide the HTML for the link to your site.

9 *Follow up.* Check at each of the websites where you requested a link to see if your request has been fulfilled. If not, contact the webmaster concerned, asking why your offer has been rejected. Remember that these people are human and they may have simply forgotten to put your link in, so sometimes a polite reminder can work wonders. At Sprite, initial contact is always by telephone instead of email. More people are inclined to respond to your request when you introduce yourself by telephone and let them know that you have been visiting their site.

Linking campaigns never really end, so you will constantly need to update the above information and renegotiate deals. To do this well requires a lot of time. Chapter 7 provides advice on different types of software that can help you with this part of the process. It is difficult to manage this type of project if you're using an external agency, and the main problem is assessing performance. If you pay the agency on a per link basis, then you will probably get lots of poor links. Therefore, if you opt to pay based on the numbers of links generated, agree quality control standards up front and always reserve the right of approval for any link deals. You then need to police and assess the quality of these links. You will have to take control of your inbound-linking strategy and execution, because nobody cares about your site as much as you do.

Automated link-building software – beware

If you have ever received an email that looks like the one below, then you have been the target of a piece of automated link-building software:

> Hi, I was just looking at your website and think we should exchange links. Exchanging links will be a brilliant way to. . .

This email will have been generated by a piece of automated link-building software. This is another way to build your links, and can be free or inexpensive, but you should be very wary of using such software. Most of these pieces of software work in the same way: they prompt you to do a search at a specific search engine for a specific term, and then the software visits each site in the results and looks for email addresses in the HTML. It then sends every email address an automatically generated email like the one above. Automatic link generators are used by hundreds of novice webmasters who do not know what they are doing, but just from reading the description above you can see that the software is essentially flawed and most of the emails will be written off as spam. The most you can hope to achieve is a couple of worthless links and loads of spam in your inbox from the link generator provider. Link generators are a cheap and nasty way of doing a job that it should take you a couple of days to do properly. Finding a site to link to should be totally personalized, and most experienced webmasters will delete link requests as soon as they receive them – many of them will be insulted that you have used link-building software to attempt to link to their site. This software is totally indiscriminate, and contacts sites that are totally irrelevant or don't even have a links page in the first place. Also, a site may contain six different contact addresses and if those six people in the company received the same email, this would look a bit suspect.

Free-for-all links – a warning

Free-for-all links are another way by which webmasters can supposedly build up the amount of links going to their pages. You might also hear an FFA link page being referred to as a link farm. They have been in existence since around 1995, and are pages that anyone can drop a link onto – normally through using some kind of submission software or website. Novice webmasters are lured in by the promise of having their site submitted to 3000 FFA links; this may sound impressive but actually is not, and the links do not generate any real traffic. FFA links also ask you for an email address to confirm your entry; entering a valid address here will mean that you will get an inbox full of junk mail, generated by the FFA's autoresponders. This steady stream of junk mail can cause many people to have to close their email account because of the sheer quantity they are receiving. Another problem with FFA links is that they are temporary; they receive new links all the time, and your link will quickly be outdated by new submissions. If you plan to use FFA sites, resubmit often. Also consider submitting the URL of the FFA page containing your link to search engines to make sure the new link is indexed. If you are going to use FFA pages, you should also make sure you set up a dummy email account to catch all the junk mail you will undoubtedly receive. There is one minor benefit to FFA links, and that is that if your page stays on an FFA link for a bit your page will look a little more popular when you submit to search engines. However, some search engines, most notably Google, see FFA links as an artificial and illegitimate way to increase your link popularity – which they essentially are – and consider them spam. You run the risk of having your site banned from their listings for participating in an FFA scheme.

Business directories

If you are a small business, then a great way to get free listings is to seek out business directories to submit to – particularly those directly related to your business. Have a look in Yahoo and the Open Directory, and you should find directories relevant to your industry. For example, Sprite targets online SEO consultants' directories, getting the site listed in as many as possible (Figure 5.7).

Many people who are wanting to find out about your industry will tend to visit industry-wide sites first, and you will find that many of these hold targeted lists of suppliers. A number of them offer free listings, so getting your site listed is an economic way to get your site out to a targeted audience.

Get a link in an appropriate category from an About.com guidesite. The popularity of About and the extent of its quality links positions the network as an important stop in a marketing campaign. Look hard for industry association sites, as the amount of links you need to point to your site is invariably more than your competition. Look for themed directories. When you find a directory, make sure that it is already in Google, has a good PR, and doesn't use dynamic script in the address. Look out for directories, hubs, portals and vortals. Once you are listed, it's good to have a page on your site that you use to feed the spiders.

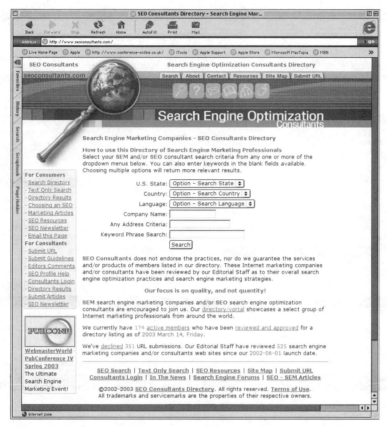

Figure 5.7 *An example SEO directory (reproduced with permission of SEO Consultants)*

Zeal

Another way to get your site listed for free on LookSmart is to use their Zeal service (Figure 5.8). This is only available to non-profit sites, but if your site falls into this category then you're in luck. You have to pass a test to be able to submit to the Zeal directory, but once you are through this (using the Zeal user guidelines to help, at http://www.zeal.com/guidelines/user/) you can submit your site to the directory. Your listing will eventually be carried by LookSmart, and will be featured on some of its affiliate sites – most notably MSN. You can read more about Zeal in Chapter 3.

Which method should I use?

Search engine optimization on a budget is not easy. You can of course submit to all the major search engines that still offer free submission; your site will be listed eventually, but it will take time. Since search engines are now discouraging the use of FFA sites and link-exchange programs, it is strongly suggested that you focus your efforts on contacting webmasters with link requests and on building up a network of free links to your website. Not only will this give you a number of new avenues for visitors to come to your site, it will also help to increase your ranking in Google and other search

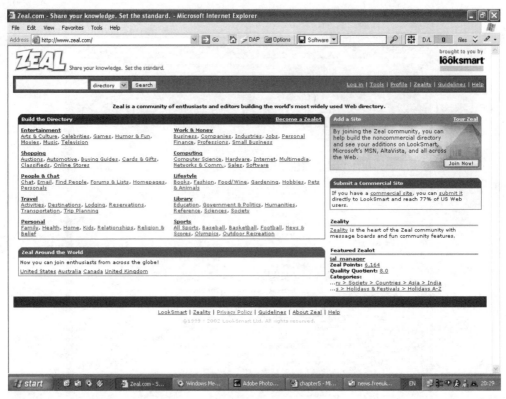

Figure 5.8 *The Zeal website (reproduced with permission)*

engines that measure link popularity. Building up links in related business websites will also help your site, and you should look into registering yourself on Zeal. Even though you have to pass a test to get listed with Zeal it is still worthwhile. You should invest time in reading the Zeal user guidelines, as they are a good source of information on best practice for submitting to directories and pay-per-click engines anyway, and reading them will teach you a lot. Although FFA sites may have been effective in the past, they are now considered to be 'spam' by some search engines, and it is not worth even dabbling in them because you run the risk of being banned from major search engines. As for mass submission tools, these are even worse than FFA sites and should be avoided. You can go some way to promoting your website with little or no budget, and still get quality traffic to it. The path is slightly more laborious and time consuming than with a large budget, but it is worth it, and many of the techniques outlined in the chapter – especially those for link building – are useful to any webmaster, whether they have a budget or not.

In conclusion

Getting your site listed for free is possible; however, it can be time consuming and you may not see the results for a number of months on the main search engines. If your website is non-profit making, you stand a much better chance of being able to get it listed for free or at least at a lower cost. Probably the main way to promote your site for free is by building up reciprocal links with other related sites.

Developing a link strategy

A link strategy is made up of three parts:

1 Linking to the directories, search engines and industry websites
2 Harnessing link suppliers, friends and associates
3 Creating mini sites.

Linking to the directories is what most people mean by linking. This entails finding the main web directories and paying to be in them. In addition to that you can focus on industry portals and offer them a free search optimization service for a particular engine in return for a link from their site for a period of time. You can also register your appropriate association site to all the web crawlers in return for a link. This is easy to do, and can increase both your stature in the industry and, most importantly, your link popularity.

The second part of the strategy is to create a list of all the people who fall into the categories of suppliers, friends and associates, and agree a link strategy and a links policy across the group. Once all the sites are fully linked, representatives of each site then register or subscribe (budget allowing) to all the directories and search engines they can in a given time. Over a short period of time, you will notice a continual improvement of search engine rankings.

Directories can help you to identify directories, informational sites and complementary businesses that may be interested in exchanging links with your website. Make use of directory listings as part of an ongoing link-building campaign. Yahoo has categories listing regional and topic directories, which are often willing to link to any website that submits information.

The third part of the strategy is to build mini sites around your service or product offering. When searching for information, people tend to start generally and get more specific as they narrow down their search. Therefore, if your first page has a lot of general links this should work better than a few very specific links. However, if each of your mini sites covers a product offering, you are creating a bigger target for the search engines.

Maintaining a links strategy is very important. Chances are, your site will not answer all the readers' questions off the front page. This means that your first page needs to be a good starting point for your readers to find what they need, because if they can't find a good starting place they'll leave immediately. This means that the links on all your landing pages should give your readers an excellent idea of what they will get if they click on them.

Link tips

● Review your search engine logs to see what people are looking for
● Make sure that your links are clear and that the appropriate landing pages go where you imply they will go

- Avoid cute links or links that are there just for the sake of a link
- Try to create links that go to content. Lists of links are useful, but the information that is the goal is usually found on content pages, and not on lists.

How to locate quality link partners

There are many ways of finding partners, but the easiest way to find quality link partners quickly is to start at Open Directory and Yahoo. You are really looking for two types of links from these directories: the first is one that is going to gain you popularity in the search engines stakes, and the other is going to drive business your way. The Open Directory and Yahoo are good places to start, as these directories are both so difficult to get listed in that each potential link partner found there is likely to be of a higher quality than those found elsewhere. Yahoo and the Open Directory greatly boost a site's link popularity when they list it, and your site will receive a little bit of that boost each time someone from one of those directories links to you. The links you build don't help your link popularity in the search engines unless the engines know about the link, and since the search engines crawl the sites listed in Yahoo and the Open Directory on a regular basis, you can be sure that the search engines will find you new links quickly.

Increasing link popularity is very much about building one step at a time. One good link is better that ten mediocre links. You are certainly going to get good links from your mini sites, so build them first and then start linking and promoting your site. Doing things this way will make a ten-fold difference to the success of your mission. The worst thing you can do is to start a campaign when the linking out is just not there.

Use the guerrilla marketing techniques outlined in this chapter to promote your site in related forums and newsgroups; you will find that you can attract a lot of traffic in this way. Writing articles and adding interesting, 'sticky' content to your site will also increase its link factor and make people more likely to return to it.

It's worth researching the various business directories that exist on the Web, and joining the directories and associations that are relevant to your industry. Zeal is a great way for non-profit sites to get listed on LookSmart, although this does take time; however, eventually such sites will be sifted through to LookSmart and its partner sites.

Avoid using any mass submission software, particularly free-for-all link farm pages. Search engines are wise to these techniques, and you may end up getting your site banned from major search engines for using them. These forms of site promotion will usually just leave you with a clogged inbox and no results.

In short, by using the techniques outlined above you can get your site noticed for free. This requires a bit more thought than merely submitting your website via paid submission programs, but for the webmaster who is on a tight budget it is very worthwhile.

Chapter 6
Placement tips and page architecture

A search request on a search engine turns up thousands or even millions of matching web pages. Most users never visit the pages beyond the ten 'most relevant' matches on the top page, so there is intense competition to be in the top ten. It's rare for users to visit the following pages of matches; being listed at eleven or beyond means that most people will miss your site. Some esoteric products or product names are more likely to be in the top ten; however, sometimes a large community in other industries shares the most ambiguous product labelling. This creates a problem not only for the search user but also for the search engines, which have to create millions of indexed pages to cater for this.

An interesting case study is a client of Sprite Interactive, EMB, an actuarial company that creates its own software and has a product called prisEMB. The last three characters happen to be EMB's name. Most people who know the product name will almost certainly know of the website; however, people who do not know the correct spelling of the product are going to have a problem. The following section will look at some solutions to this problem.

Site architecture can definitely impact your results with search engines. Most search engines don't know anything beyond two directory levels, but they'll index 40–50 files in those directories alphabetically. So you must place your most important pages at the first or second directory level, breaking them up into 50 files per directory. Be sure to name your files and directories with your keywords, and don't use the underscore to separate keywords – use hyphens instead.

Entry pages

These pages are sometimes known as landing pages, and are the pages that bring traffic to the site. Once you have decided what entry pages you need, you should optimize them and then submit each of these pages to the search engines. Treat these as stand-alone pages, just like your home page. When visitors land on one of your entry pages, will they know where they are? Who you are? What the page is about? Include full navigation on all entry pages, and make it obvious what the page and site is about. Don't assume that visitors will find the index page first.

Figure 6.1 *The Sprite Interactive Contact Us page*

If searchers land on your 'Contact us' page, for example, and all they see is your address and an input form, that doesn't tell them anything about your offering. You should always build global navigation into your site and treat all pages as potential landing pages. Figure 6.1 illustrates this point.

To help reinforce the relevance of the topic, name all your images after keywords, as image searches will pick these up. All your rich media and PDFs should also be named after your keywords.

Site map

It is always worth having a site map on your website. This can be a very important entry page. Correctly built site maps can fuel searches, especially if they have links to every single page that your visitors care about. Submit your index page and your site map. Put your site map at the root level, and name it after your keywords. Use global navigation on the site map. Add all your website descriptions of the company or services at the top of the page or in the left column before the links, and use keywords in your links as well. Avoid using graphics; keep to text and this page will work wonders for you on all search engines.

Good site architecture is when:

- The title of the page is relevant to its content
- The site has a consistent global navigation scheme
- Page layout is consistent and is based on a template
- Directories are set up in a structured manner consistent with the navigation.

Help your target audiences

Each website has two target audiences: the primary audience is the end user, while the secondary audience consists of the directory editors and search engine spiders. Your goal in search engine optimization is to receive regular traffic over time from both the search engines and the directories.

Search engines do three things: they index text, follow links, and measure popularity. Of these, the measure of popularity is the factor most influenced by end users.

Visible text

Search engines see text, so if you have to perform any kind of action to view text then almost certainly the search engine will not be able to see it. ALT text is not visible, so it's not as important to the search engines as visible text. However, you must include your keyword phrase in your ALT text. ALT tags can be used as text in logos, image maps, navigation elements, Flash movies, and photos. ALT text in a clear gif is considered spamming. You should always put width and height on image maps so the browser knows the size of the graphic; by doing this you are speeding up the process of having some content appear quickly on screen in particular text. The graphics will then follow.

Cascading style sheets

Cascading Style Sheets (CSS) are used to control web page design parameters, such as margins, font/typeface, link appearance, colours, and placement. CSS massively decreases download time, but style sheets themselves have no effect on the search engines. You should always make use of a robots exclusion file on sections of your site that the search engines have no interest in, such as your style sheets, CGI-BIN, and any pages under construction, to keep them from getting indexed. All search engines support this protocol – after all, the last thing you want is to drive traffic to your site and then present searchers with an incomplete landing page. There is always a period when you have kicked off your search optimization strategy but not quite finished the site build, and this is when these anomalies occur. The best thing you can do is present those pages that are finished and block the pages that are still work in progress.

META tags

The most valuable feature offered by META tags is the ability to control web pages for both searching and administration. META tags will help keep your pages more up to date, make them easier to find and even stop them from becoming framed, but they have never been a guaranteed way to gain a top ranking on crawler-based search engines. META tags can also help you provide keywords and descriptions on pages that for various reasons lack text – maybe because of image maps, large images, splash pages and frames pages. They might also boost your page's relevancy.

Simply including a META tag is not a guarantee that your page will suddenly leap to the top of every search engine listing. They are useful tools, but not a magic solution. They can be used to identify the creator of a page, its HTML specs, the keywords and description of the page, and the refresh parameter. Statistics show that only about 21 per cent of web pages use keyword and description META tags. If your competitor is using them and you aren't, he may have an advantage over you. META tags are something that visitors to your website are usually not aware of, but it was probably your META tags that enabled them to find you in the first place.

There are several META tags, but the most important for search engine indexing are the description and keywords tags. The description tag presents a description of the page in place of the summary the search engine creates, and the keywords tag provides keywords for the search engine to relate with your page.

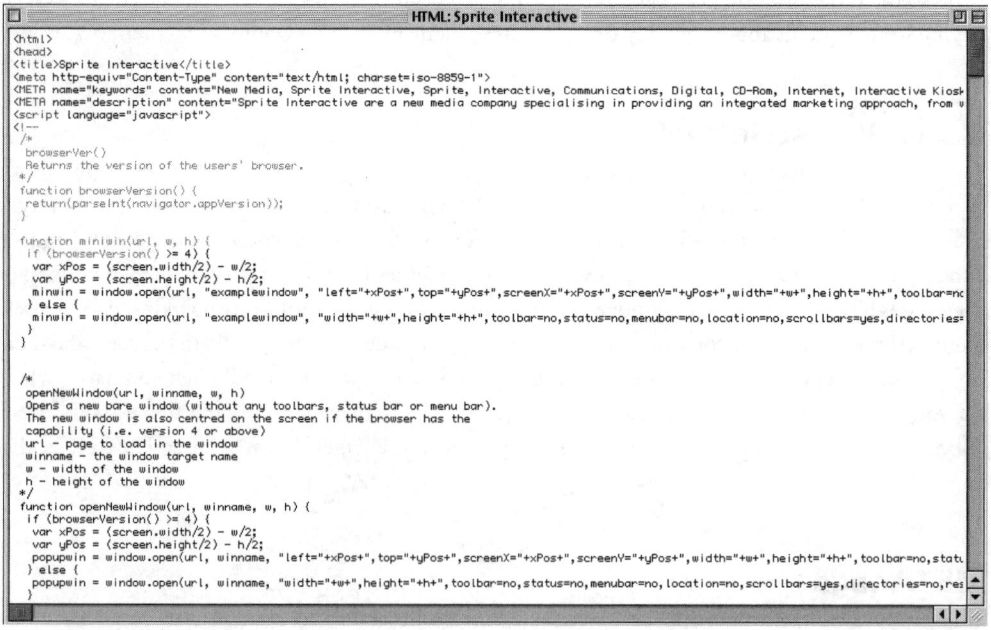

```
HTML: Sprite Interactive
<html>
<head>
<title>Sprite Interactive</title>
<meta http-equiv="Content-Type" content="text/html; charset=iso-8859-1">
<META name="keywords" content="New Media, Sprite Interactive, Sprite, Interactive, Communications, Digital, CD-Rom, Internet, Interactive Kiosk
<META name="description" content="Sprite Interactive are a new media company specialising in providing an integrated marketing approach, from w
<script language="javascript">
<!--
 /*
  browserVer()
  Returns the version of the users' browser.
 */
 function browserVersion() {
  return(parseInt(navigator.appVersion));
 }

 function miniwin(url, w, h) {
  if (browserVersion() >= 4) {
   var xPos = (screen.width/2) - w/2;
   var yPos = (screen.height/2) - h/2;
   minwin = window.open(url, "examplewindow", "left="+xPos+",top="+yPos+",screenX="+xPos+",screenY="+yPos+",width="+w+",height="+h+",toolbar=nc
  } else {
   minwin = window.open(url, "examplewindow", "width="+w+",height="+h+",toolbar=no,status=no,menubar=no,location=no,scrollbars=yes,directories=
  }
 }


 /*
  openNewWindow(url, winname, w, h)
  Opens a new bare window (without any toolbars, status bar or menu bar).
  The new window is also centred on the screen if the browser has the
  capability (i.e. version 4 or above)
  url - page to load in the window
  winname - the window target name
  w - width of the window
  h - height of the window
 */
 function openNewWindow(url, winname, w, h) {
  if (browserVersion() >= 4) {
   var xPos = (screen.width/2) - w/2;
   var yPos = (screen.height/2) - h/2;
   popupwin = window.open(url, winname, "left="+xPos+",top="+yPos+",screenX="+xPos+",screenY="+yPos+",width="+w+",height="+h+",toolbar=no,statu
  } else {
   popupwin = window.open(url, winname, "width="+w+",height="+h+",toolbar=no,status=no,menubar=no,location=no,scrollbars=yes,directories=no,res
  }
```

Figure 6.2 *HTML META tag in source mode*

Placement of META tags

META tags should always be placed at the head of the HTML document between <HEAD> tags and before the BODY tag. This is very important with framed pages, as missing out the tags on these pages loses them to the search engine. If you only use META tags on the frameset pages, you'll miss a large number of potential hits. The problem with frames is the inability of most search engines to understand whether a page is a content page or a navigation page. Figure 6.2 is a screen grab of an HTML META tag in source mode.

The example shows a title tag, then a META description tag, then a META keywords tag.

The title tag

The HTML title tag isn't really a META tag, but it's worth discussing in relation to them. Whatever text you place in the title tag (between the TITLE and /TITLE shown in Figure 6.2) will appear in the reverse arrow of a user's browser when he or she is viewing the web page. If you look at the reverse arrow in your browser, you should see that same text being used, similar to the screen grab in Figure 6.3.

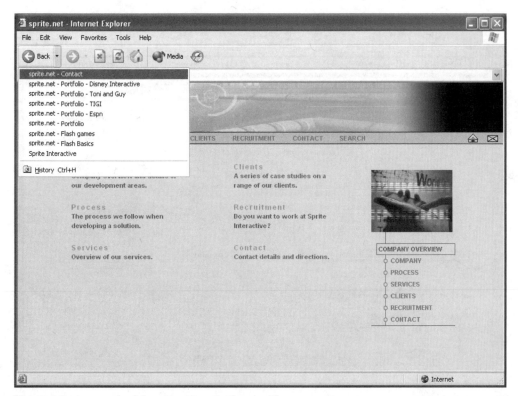

Figure 6.3 *An example of the reverse arrow showing site titles*

Some browsers will supplement whatever you put in the title tag by adding their own name, as you can see Microsoft's Internet Explorer doing in Figure 6.3.

The title tag is also used as the words to describe your page when someone adds it to their 'Favourites' or 'Bookmarks' lists.

The title tag is crucial for search engines. The text you use in the title tag is one of the most important factors in how a search engine may decide to rank your web page. In addition, all major crawlers will use the text of your title tag as the text for the title of your page in your listings. For example, Figure 6.4 shows how Teoma lists the Sprite web pages.

You can see that the text 'Sprite Interactive' is used as the hyperlinked title to the Sprite home page as listed in Teoma's results.

Think about the key terms you'd like your page to be found for in crawler-based search engines, then incorporate those terms into your title tag in a short, descriptive fashion. That text will be used as your title in those engines, as well as in bookmarks and in browser reverse bars.

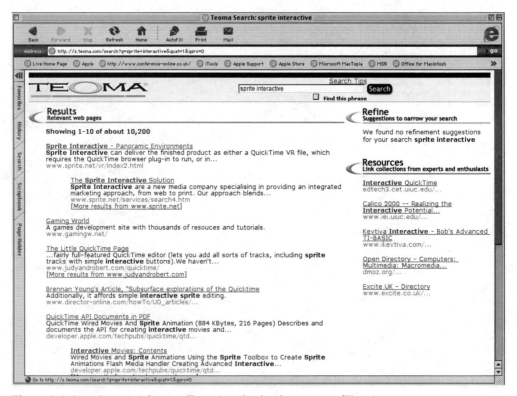

Figure 6.4 *Sprite Interactive's listing in Teoma (reproduced with permission of Teoma)*

The META description tag

The META description tag allows you to influence the description of your page in the crawlers that support the tag. In Figure 6.2 you can see a small description file.

Google ignores the META description tag and instead will automatically generate its own description for this page. Others may support it partially. You can see in Figure 6.4 that the first portion of the page's description comes from the META description tag, and the remaining portion is drawn from the body copy of the page itself. However, not all search engines work like Teoma.

It is worth using the META description tag for your pages, because it gives you some degree of control with various crawlers. An easy way to use the tag is to take the first sentence or two of body copy from your web page and use that for the META description content.

The META keywords tag

The META keywords tag allows you to provide additional text for crawler-based search engines to index along with your body copy. Generally, up to 1000 characters may be indexed. On the few crawlers that support it, it can be useful as a way of reinforcing the terms you think a page is important for. The text in the META keywords tag works in conjunction with the text in your body copy.

The META keywords tag is also sometimes useful as a way to help your pages rank for synonyms or unusual words that don't appear on the page itself. For instance, let's say you have a page all about the 'pre-press' design but you never actually mention the word 'origination' on this page. By having the word in your META keywords tag, you may help increase the odds of ranking if someone searches for 'pre-press and origination'. Of course the highest way of increasing the odds is by having the word 'origination' in the title and body copy of the page itself.

Avoid repeating a particular word too often in a META keywords tag, as this could actually harm your page's chances of ranking well. For clarity, keywords and multi-keyword phrases are separated by commas. You do not have to use commas in the tag. By leaving out commas or spaces, there is more room for words. Here is how the team at Sprite Interactive writes META tags:

```
<META name="keywords" content="keyword1, keyword2, keyword 3">
```

That's 29 characters, including spaces, between the quotes after *content=*. But sometimes you might need the additional space, so you can leave out the commas, like this:

```
<META name="keywords" content="keyword1 keyword2 keyword 3">
```

With the commas removed, the content portion of the tag is only 27 characters. If you have a lot of keywords, these small differences add up and become worthwhile.

An alternative method is to use commas but to leave out the spaces:

```
<META name="keywords" content="keyword1,keyword2,keyword 3">
```

This is still 27 characters, and is perfectly acceptable as it still retains the commas. The official specs say only that elements should be separated by commas. Most search engines say you don't need commas, so don't use them if you want to squeeze in every last keyword that you find in your thesaurus.

Quite a few search optimization companies don't bother with commas. This is in order to increase the chance of matching a string of words or a phrase that someone may enter. If your web page is about search optimization, having the keyword *optimization* in your META tag is not suddenly going make it come up when people search for *Search*. In contrast, adding some extra words like *service* or *consulting*, if they don't appear on the page already, may help you to appear when someone searches for *optimization service* or *search consulting*.

The META tag should always reflect the keywords that are on the page already, especially those that are unique. A few synonyms may be added, but overall the tag should be kept tightly focused.

How big can the tags be?

There is no common size for either the keyword or the description META tags. Commonly, search engines accept about 1000 characters for the keywords tag and 200 characters for the description tag. They can be longer, and going over the limit does not mean that your tag will be thrown out; it just means that the search engines will not use the excess material beyond their own respective limits.

When search engines warn against repetition, they generally mean spamming attempts such as this:

```
<META name="keywords" content="Search Optimization, Search Optimization,
    Search Optimization, Search Optimization, Search Optimization, Search
    Optimization, Search Optimization">
```

There's no good reason for the words *Search Optimization* to appear so many times. In contrast, the tag below is not a spamming attempt:

```
<META name="keywords" content=" Search Optimization, Search consulting,
    Search services, Searching, Surf Searching">
```

The word *Search* is repeated so many times in order to preserve phrases, the objective being that the words should appear in the tags exactly as someone might enter them into a search box.

As a note of warning, the repetition may still be too much for some search engines, which may downgrade a page the more often a word is repeated in a tag. Some pages can do perfectly well with multiple repetitions of a word, but it makes sense to repeat as little as possible. None of the search engines have published standards or specifications on this. Most search engines will see phrases as phrases, so if you think searchers are going to search for a particular string of words, include phrases into your keywords tag. However, always make sure that each page within your website has tags that match its content. Only a page that deals with eMarketing promotions should include that phrase in its tag. Never 'overload' your tags.

The major search engines do not expect the title tag to come first, or the META tags to appear in any particular position. There are many reasons why a page may not rank well, and changing the order of your tags alone will not result in any improvement. Stick with what works for you.

META robots tag

Crawlers will try to index all your web pages, and to follow links from one page to another. This tag lets you specify that a page should not be indexed by a search engine. Simply add the opt-out text between your head tags on each of the pages you don't want indexed. Most major search engines support the META robots tag. However, the robots.txt convention of blocking indexing is more efficient, as you don't have to manage the opting out on a page level. If you do use a robots.txt file to block indexing, there is no need also to use META robots tags.

The robots.txt standard is a text file placed in the root server's HTML directory. If, for example, we did not want the entire Sprite.net site to be indexed, we would make a file that would be found under the URL http://www.sprite.net/robots.txt. An engine respecting the standard would ask for the file before trying to index any page within the site. To exclude the entire site, the file would say:

```
User-agent: *
Disallow: /
```

The *user-agent* portion lets you specify engines or browsers; more than likely you will want to specify all the engines and browsers, and the * is specifying everything.

The *disallow portion* is where you specify directories or file names. In the example above, the * is used to protect everything within the site. You can also be more specific and block particular directories or pages:

```
User-agent: *
Disallow: /Search/
Disallow: /contactUs/
Disallow: /portfolio/
Disallow: /clients/disney.htm
```

Now the engines respecting the standard will not index anything in the site with the addresses:

http://www.sprite.net/Search/
http:/www.sprite.net/contactUs/
http:/www.sprite.net/portfolio/

This page is also blocked:

http://www.sprite.net/clients/disney.htm

Because the robots.txt file must go in the server's root directory, many of those using free web space will not be able to use it.

Security and robots.txt

Not every search engine respects the robots.txt convention, although all the major ones do. Other web users may take advantage of the file. All they have to do is enter the address to your robots.txt file, and they can then read the contents in their web browser. This may contain data that is off limits to other users. If you don't want the robots.txt file to be a roadmap to sensitive areas on your server, keep those sensitive areas off the Web or password-protect them.

Other META tags

There are many other META tags; those listed here are just some of the more useful ones.

META tags have two attributes:

```
<META HTTP-EQUIV="name" CONTENT="content">
```

and

```
<META NAME="name" CONTENT="content">
```

HTTP-EQUIV

META HTTP-EQUIV tags are the equivalent of HTTP headers. HTTP headers are how your web browser requests a document from a web server. When you click on a link, the web server receives your browser's request via HTTP. The web server has to make sure that the page you've requested is there, and then it generates an HTTP response. That response is called the 'HTTP header block'. The header tells the web browser information about displaying the document.

META HTTP-EQUIV tags usually control or direct the actions of web browsers, and are used to refine the information that is provided by the actual headers. They are tags that are designed to work with web browsers as normal headers. Some web servers may translate META HTTP-EQUIV tags into actual HTTP so that web browsers see them as normal headers; others, such as Apache and CERN httpd, use a separate text file that contains META-data.

NAME

META tags with a NAME attribute are used for META types that do not correspond to normal HTTP headers. For example:

1 *Expires.*

```
<META HTTP-EQUIV="expires" CONTENT="Thur, 20 Jan 2003 08:11:57 GMT">
```

This means that that document will expire on Thursday, 20 January 2003 08:11:57 GMT. Web robots delete expired documents from a search engine, or, in some cases, schedule a revisit.

2 *Content-Type.*

```
<META HTTP-EQUIV="Content-Type" CONTENT="text/html;
    charset=ISO-2022-JP">
```

The HTTP content type may be extended to give the character set. It is recommended that you always use this tag, even with the previously default charset ISO-8859–1. Failure to do so can cause display problems where the document uses UTF-8 punctuation characters but is displayed in ISO or ASCII charsets.

3 *Content-Script-Type.*

```
<META HTTP-EQUIV="Content-Script-Type" CONTENT="text/javascript">
```

This specifies the default scripting language in a document (see MIMETYPES for applicable values).

4 *Content-Style-Type.*

```
<META HTTP-EQUIV="Content-Style-Type" CONTENT="text/css">
```

This specifies the default style sheet language for a document.

5 *Content-Language.*

```
<META HTTP-EQUIV="Content-Language" CONTENT="en-GB">
```

This may be used to declare the natural language of the document. It is used by robots to categorize by language.

6 *Refresh.*

```
<META HTTP-EQUIV="Refresh"
    CONTENT="3;URL=http://www.sprite.net/contact.html">
```

This specifies a delay in seconds before the browser automatically reloads the document, which can result in the loading of an alternative URL.

7 *Window-target.*

```
<META HTTP-EQUIV="Window-target" CONTENT="_top">
```

This specifies the named window of the current page, and can be used to stop a page appearing in somebody else's frameset – i.e. it prevents another site from hijacking your pages.

8 *Ext-cache.*

```
<META HTTP-EQUIV="Ext-cache" CONTENT="name=/jobs/path/index.db;
    instructions=Help pages">
```

This defines the name of an alternate cache to Netscape Navigator.

9 *Vary.*

```
<META HTTP-EQUIV="Vary" CONTENT="Content-language">
```

This implies that if a header Accept-Language is sent, an alternative form may be selected.

10 *Robots.*

```
<META NAME="ROBOTS" CONTENT="NOINDEX,FOLLOW">
```

This stops robots indexing on a per page basis, but will allow it to follow links from this page. Robots include:

NOINDEX – this prevents indexing
NOFOLLOW – this stops the crawler from following the links on this page
NOIMAGEINDEX – this stops images on the page from being indexed, but allows all the text to be indexed
NOIMAGECLICK – this stops direct links to the images; instead there will only be a link to the page
NOARCHIVE – this stops Google from caching pages.

11 *Description.* For example:

```
<META NAME="description" CONTENT=" Sprite Interactive is a new media
    company specializing in providing an integrated marketing approach,
    from web to print. Our approach blends traditional design experience
    with new media development, our service is focused on consultancy,
```

```
digital marketing and promotions, search optimization, online games
and e-magazines.">
```

This gives a short description of your site, and is used by search engines to describe your web page. It is particularly important if your page has very little text, is a frameset, or has extensive scripts at the top.

12 *Keywords.*

```
<META NAME="keywords" CONTENT=" New Media, Sprite Interactive, Sprite,
    Interactive, Communications, Digital, CD-Rom, Internet,
    Interactive Kiosks, Intranet, Extranet, Screen Saver, Cross Media,
    Cross Media Solutions, Internet, Brochures, Corporate Literature,
    Presentations, Interactive Presentations, Search Optimization,
    Digital Marketing, Online Promotions, Consultancy, Games,
    E-magazines, Games Library, Print Media, Fetcham Park, Integrated
    Marketing, Design, Web Design, Information Architecture,
    Copywriting, Multimedia, CD Business Cards, Technology, WAP,
    Integrated Magazines">
```

These are keywords used by search engines to index your document, in addition to words from the title and document body. Typically, keywords are synonyms and alternates of title words.

Sprite has built a META tag builder and it is freely available from http://www.sprite.net/ METABuilder. This form allows you to create very complicated META tags using much more than the keywords and description tags, if you wish. Sprite will be credited with a commented credit line in the tag. Figure 6.5 shows you the interface for this.

The law

There are several legal issues concerning the use of tags on your website. There have so far been five key legal suits that focused on sites that utilized someone else's keywords within their META tags. The largest of these suits brought a settlement of $3 million.

Usually, the misuse of META tags becomes an issue because people believe that you are using their investment in their brand by 'hijacking' their traffic. This happens when your website comes up when someone searches for your competitor or a big brand name. So far, most defendants have lost on this issue. You need to ask yourself if there is a legitimate reason for using someone else's brand name, or whether you are trying to deceive users. Using a competitor's term in your tags is no guarantee that you'll do well, especially if your competitor's site has been properly optimized.

Within a competitive environment, the temptation to spam people is great. You do this by repeating a brand name over and over with the intention that you get past the filters and make

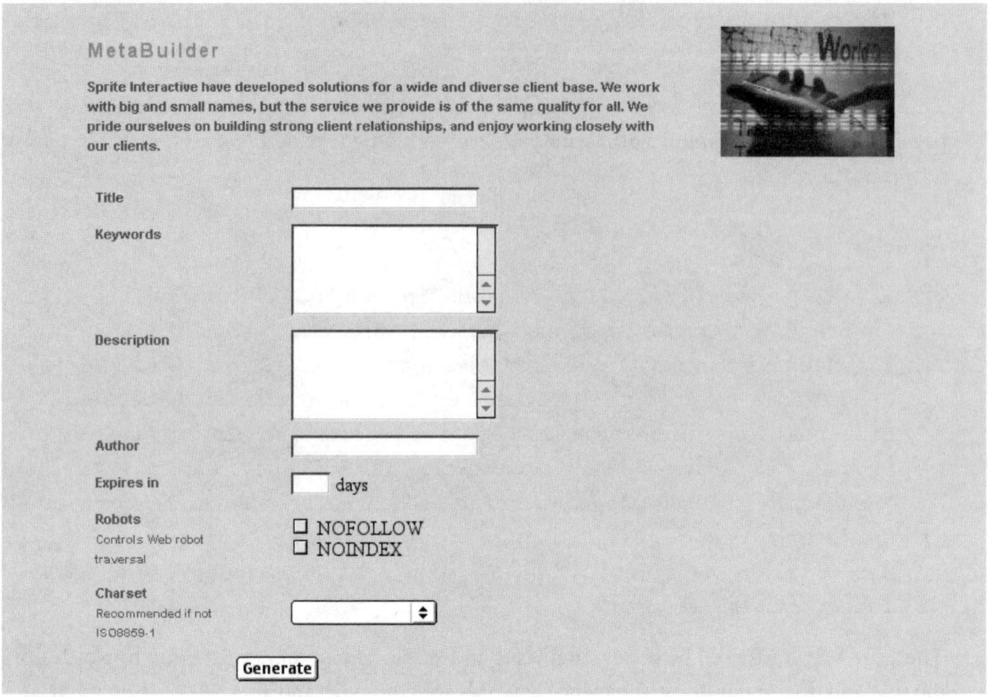

Figure 6.5 *The Sprite Interactive META builder*

it to the top of the rankings, but it's hard to prove to a judge that this tactic is not deceptive or misleading.

Is it ever legitimate?

There may sometimes be a case for the right to use brand names or a competitor's terms in your META tags. For example, a book retailer might argue that people looking for 'Cinderella' are doing a generic search for anything on Cinderella, and thus the retailer needs to include the term 'Disney' to ensure that his site is properly indexed, so he can draw the traffic to the Disney section of his site. Furthermore, the retailer might want to create a page comparing Disney's Cinderella to another publisher's version. He has every right to use the word Cinderella on that page. Furthermore, he would have every right to use the word Cinderella in his META tags in order to classify the page properly. The key to all of this is not to overuse a term in a META tag. The issue is whether a company is being deceptive and trying to fool people into coming to a site that appears to be something else.

What if someone uses your own trademark?

A company that tags its own pages properly should have a higher ranking for its trademarked terms, mainly because they have many, many pages relevant to those terms, which are reinforced by the META tagging, the URL and the title of the page. Tagging your own pages will make you so dominant that the people attempting to hijack your traffic will not be ranked. This is a great way of solving the problem without resorting to expensive legal action.

If you do decide to use trademarks in your tags, you might consider using the following guidelines in order to limit potential problems. The guidelines can help site owners to avoid problems or defend themselves should someone suggest that they are infringing trademarks. They are not legal guidelines.

1 Use a brand name in the META keywords tag only if you mention it on the page
2 Avoid repeating the brand name more than once
3 Brand names should only be used in the title tag when they are a prominent feature of the page's content.

META tag lawsuits

The five key lawsuits that have focused on the use of someone else's keywords with a site's META tags are described briefly here.

1 The first known case dealing with the issue of misleading META tags was the Oppedahl & Larson action. The defendants had no clear reason for using the name of Oppedahl & Larson, which is a law firm that has dealt in domain name disputes. It was believed that the defendants hoped to capture traffic that would gain them domain name registration fees or website hosting clients. The court banned them through a permanent injunction from using the name without authorization. Oppedahl & Larson's complaint can be read on http://www.patents.com/ac/
2 On 27 August 1997, Insituform sued National Envirotech for using its name in its META tags. It was alleged that some slogans and images from Insituform were also used. META tags were central to the case, as the words only appeared in the META tags and not on the screen. The judge decided that the only plausible reason for these registered trademarks to be in the META tags was to misdirect people to the National Envirotech website. National Envirotech removed the disputed material. The parties reached a settlement, but the judge also issued a permanent injunction. You can read more about this case on http://www.cll.com/keyword.htm
3 In Playboy vs AsiaFocus and Internet Promotions – Civ. No. C-97–3204 (N.D. Cal., Sept. 8, 1997), Playboy sued two adult website operators who spammed their pages with the word Playboy and Playmate hundreds of times in the site names, the domain names and in their slogans. This helped them rise to the top of some search engine results for a search on 'Playboy'. The San Francisco federal judge issued a preliminary injunction against the operators, deciding that trademark infringement and false representation could be proven.
4 In Playboy vs Terri Welles – Civ. No. C-97–3204 (N.D. Cal., Sept. 8, 1997), a judge refused to grant an injunction against Terri Welles, Playboy's 1981 Playmate of the Year, to prevent her from

using terms such as 'Playmate' and 'Playboy' on her web pages and within her META tags. He gave the reason that Welles had a legitimate reason to use them in order to describe herself, and to catalogue her website properly with search engines. The judge also noted that Welles was not using the terms in an attempt to mislead users into believing they were at a Playboy site. You can read more on this and the Appeal in Welles Case at http://caselaw.lp.findlaw.com/data2/circs/9th/0055009p.pdf (US Court of Appeals, For the Ninth Circuit, Feb. 1, 2002), and on Terri Welles' counterclaim case at http://www.terriwelles.com/legal/counterclaim.html

5   In Brookfield Communications Inc. *vs* West Coast Entertainment Corp, West Coast won the first time round after using Brookfield's 'MovieBuff' trademark in its META tags. However, this was reversed on appeal and the case was sent back with a grant of preliminary injunction. The appeal found that the use of the trademark in the META tag created 'initial interest confusion', because users visited the West Coast site first. You can learn more about this case if you do a VerdictSearch for Brookfield Communications Inc. *vs* West Coast Entertainment Corp on http://www.lawnewsnetwork.com

JavaScript

Most search engines weight the text that appears at the top of your pages more heavily than that which appears further down. They assume that the first paragraph of the article tells you all the main points. Using JavaScript at the top of your documents may impact your pages' relevancy, as some search engines may put the biggest priority on scripting code rather than on your opening paragraphs.

Using a META description tag can help to solve the listing issue, but won't keep the JavaScript from still being indexed and possibly degrading relevancy. If you surround the code with a comment tag, this should stop most engines from seeing the code. What is supposed to happen is that nothing between <!– and –> is indexed by a search engine that ignores comments. However, remember that code strings can contain the > character ?.

You may use .js files, which are 'external' files that contain your JavaScript code. You call to them from within your page, and the JavaScript code is then only loaded by browsers that understand JavaScript. Since most search engines don't read JavaScript, you start to tackle a key stumbling block of most search engines.

Make your site useful

You can spend a large amount of time trying to get good search engine rankings and lots of visitors. However, when visitors arrive at the site they may still find a poorly designed, badly written website with content that bears no relevance to either the keywords or the title tag. Success is not about how many page views you get but about how many sales you get, and it is amazing how many people miss this simple concept. Making your pages 'people friendly' is as important as making them 'search-engine' friendly. It is much easier to triple your sales effectiveness and conversions to your site than to double your traffic.

Use keyphrases, not keywords

It is difficult if not impossible to get high rankings based on keywords. Instead, you need to consider using keyphrases. The way to do this is ask yourself what users trying to find the site would type in when searching. Make a list of these phrases, and test them out on the search engines. See if you can find your type or product or services. Think about variations on the keyphrases and write them down. Two great resources for finding out which keyphrases are the most effective are the Overture.com Search Suggestions Page, and WordTracker. On Overture's search suggestion page, type in a very general keyphrase (like 'New Media') and it will tell you all of the more specific keyphrases that relate to that keyphrase, and how many hits they get. This is a great way of finding out what your keyphrases actually are.

The art of the <TITLE> tag

So many websites have titles that are good for people but abysmal for the search engines. This is a big mistake. A title like 'Alex Michael – Animating in Flash MX' is a disaster! The golden rule is that the most important keyphrases should be in the TITLE tag. So what you do is look at your keyphrases, make a list of all the important words, and create a title tag that uses the top one or two. Also, keep in mind that browsers only display the first few words of a title tag (whatever fits into the title bar of the window). So while the first sentence of your title tag should be 'human readable', the rest can be just a list of keyphrases.

There is some debate as to whether a very long title tag is a good thing or a bad thing when it comes to search engines. Some people are concerned that a very long title tag might result in the search engines deciding the page is a 'spam page'. Our advice is to keep the title between 15 and 20 words. However, you might want to try longer title tags on some of your pages, just to see what happens! So Alex Michael might have a title that looks like this:

```
<TITLE> Alex Michael – Animating in Flash MX, Storyboarding, Games</TITLE>
```

The reason for this is that the three most important places to have keyphrases and phrases are in your title tag, your META tags, and your first paragraph. You want them to all contain the same important words, as this increases your keyphrase density and improves your rankings.

The first paragraph

The first paragraph of your page should expand upon everything in your title and META tags. You need to have all the keyphrases in it. However, since this is going to be read by people, it needs to be written with them in mind. This is where you introduce yourself to your guests, so you want to make a good impression.

Try to put this first paragraph as close to the <BODY> tag as possible. Avoid putting graphics or other HTML in front of your first paragraph as much as you can. Also, use the <H1> or <H2> tag to emphasize your opening sentence.

Do not put up spam pages or anything that looks like spam! Keyphrases should not appear too many times, because that might make the search engines think your page is a spam page trying to rank highly for a particular phrase. So, how much is too much? This varies from search engine to search engine. Google likes pages with less than thirteen repeats of a keyphrase, for example. The best advice is to try to keep the number of repeats of important phrases down to ten or less in all instances – in the title, META tags, and the text of the page.

The major search engines are actively penalizing/banning sites that employ the following techniques:

- Machine-generated pages
- Pages that contain hidden text and hidden links
- Large volumes of text pages
- Link farming and link spamming, all free-for-all (FFA) links
- Cloaking – a practice in which the search engine and the end user do not view the same page
- Sites with numerous unnecessary host names
- Excessive cross-linking of sites to inflate a site's apparent popularity artificially – affiliate spam.

Make sure your domain name reflects your service or product. This is the best investment you'll ever make. There are three major reasons for getting your own domain name:

1 Some search engines won't list you unless you do
2 People are more likely to buy if you have your own domain name – what looks better to you, 'http://www.alex.com/' or 'http://members.aol.com/alex123/'?
3 You can change your webhosting service without messing up all of your search engine listings.

There is no benefit in having a long domain name. A domain name with lots of keywords in it (e.g. seo-url-promotion-website-Designsite-alex.com) will not get a higher ranking in the search engines. NONE of the major search engines will significantly boost your rankings based on keywords in your URL. So the added benefit of keywords in the URL is insignificant. Don't waste your money. Go for a short, memorable domain name, either one word or two words combined, or with an i, e, i- or e- prefix.

Avoid search engine tricks

Some 'experts' advise trying to trick search engines by, for example, putting keyphrases in comments or putting them in text that is the same colour as your background, and so on. Do not try this, as most of these methods don't work and if they do they may stop working at any minute, as the search engines are constantly trying to detect them. You should help search engines by making it as easy as possible for them to get a good idea of what your page is about. That way, as search engines get better and better at rating the contents of sites, your rankings will improve over time with no effort from you.

Check your HTML

Almost all websites have HTML errors – even those that appear to display nicely on your browser. Browsers are very tolerant of errors, but it's a good idea to make sure your HTML is as perfect as possible because this increases the chance that your website will display the way you want it to on as many browsers as possible.

Have HTML links

Often, web designers only create image map links from the home page to inside pages. A search engine that can't follow these links won't be able to get 'inside' the site, and unfortunately the most descriptive and relevant pages are often within inside pages rather than the home page.

To solve this problem, all you need do is add some HTML hyperlinks to the home page that lead to major inside pages or sections of your website. Put them at the bottom of the page, and search engines will find them and follow them. A site map page with text links to everything in your website will help the search engines to locate pages within your website. You must do a good job of linking internally between your pages. If you naturally point to different pages from within your site, you increase the odds that search engines will follow the links and find more of your website.

Frames can be a big problem, as some of the major search engines cannot follow frame links. Make sure there is an alternative means by which they can enter and index your site, either through META tags or smart design.

Search engines and dynamic pages

Crawler-based search engines have problems indexing web pages that are delivered via database programs, as this makes the site virtually invisible to them. This is because the page is dynamically delivered. An additional problem is that many dynamic delivery mechanisms make use of the ? symbol. Most search engines will not read past the ? in that URL; it acts as a stop sign to them and kills the indexing for that site. Other symbols that are often used include &, %, +, $ and reference to the CGI bin directory. You can see an example of this problem in Figure 6.6, where the site is fraught with the searchability issues – check it out on www.rawstyle.co.uk. If your database program uses these, then you need to look at alternative ways of naming your content.

Many major websites may not have a single page listed, because none of the search engines can crawl them. It's worth the time to see if your dynamic delivery problem has any easy solutions. There are workarounds that will let you create search engine-friendly URLs and still take

Figure 6.6 *The RawStyle website*

advantage of a dynamically generated site. Look for these. One site made this simple change and gained over 600 visitors a day from a particular search engine, simply because its content could now be listed.

The following suggestions may help:

1 *Active Server Pages (ASP).* These pages usually end in .asp. They are delivered by Microsoft's server software, and most of the major search engines will index these pages. Just avoid using the ? symbol.
2 *Apache.* Apache has a special 'rewrite' module that will allow you to translate URLs containing symbols. It is not compiled into the software by default, but many hosting companies add it anyway. You can find more about this by visiting http://www.apache.org/docs/mod/mod_rewrite.html
3 *Cold Fusion.* These files end in .cfm. Normally the database will use a ? symbol to retrieve pages, but there are workarounds to this that will make your pages accessible. Cold Fusion can be reconfigured to use URLs without the troublesome symbols. To learn more, visit the Cold Fusion site at www.macromedia.com.

4 *Direct submit/paid inclusion*. Directly submitting specific dynamic URLs to AltaVista increases the chance that they will be picked up by that search engine. Also Google began increased finding of dynamic URLs as part of its normal crawls toward the end of 2000. Several search engines offer 'paid inclusion' programs where, for a fee, you are guaranteed to have the pages you want listed. These programs can usually handle dynamic URLs with no problem. The downside, of course, is that you have to pay.

5 *Server Side Includes* (SSI). The major search engines have no problems indexing pages that are built in part with SSI content. Search engines generally don't mind how your files end – in other words, even if your pages don't end in .html or .htm they'll probably still get indexed, assuming you've solved the ? symbol problem. However, Northern Light is rather picky. It will index any page ending in these extensions: .html .htm .shtml .stm .asp .phtml .cfm .php3 .php .jsp .jhtml .asc .text .txt. It will not index pages ending in .cgi. However, there may be a problem if the pages use the cgi-bin path in their URLs.

6 *The ultimate solution: static pages*. If the database is simply used as a page creation tool, you can use it to create static pages — especially for sections of your site that don't change often. Alternatively, consider creating a mirror of your dynamic content in static pages that the search engines can spider, and then linking these pages to content within your database. These pages are known as 'landing pages'. You need to create mirror pages on your server that search engines can crawl. E-commerce sites where information about prices and product availability can be stripped out of the databases and mirrored as non-dynamic pages provide good examples of the use of landing pages. It is quite possible for a user, having landed on your pages, to be diverted to any part of your database.

Rich media

AlltheWeb, FAST's search technology showcase and one of the world's largest search engines, is the first major search engine enabling users to perform searches in Macromedia Flash content and applications. Users of AlltheWeb can refine their searches in Macromedia Flash content and applications through the use of the site's Advanced Features functions at www.alltheweb.com/advanced. This functionality will automatically be made available to FAST's portal partners, such as InfoSpace, Lycos, T-Online and Tiscali, as well as to the millions of people who perform their searches through these portals. More and more rich media is becoming searchable, but on the whole the results are not good and are a poor alternative to a full description alt tag.

In conclusion

Search engines see the Web in the same way as someone using a very old browser might. They do not read image maps, and they may not read frames. So anticipate these problems, or a search engine may not index any of your web pages.

Of all the META tags you may come across, the META description and META keywords tags are probably the most important. However, remember to make sure your pages have visible text. Give the spiders a link architecture to help them find visible text. Use the Robots Exclusion Protocol to exclude information that you do not want to be visible to search crawlers, and keep the most important pages in the top-level directory on your server.

Content needs to be relevant to users who are searching. Make sure the page architecture helps that search, and that the landing page has a clear navigation system.

If you have a legitimate reason to use trademarked terms in your META tags, then you can certainly do so. However, you may be facing a suit regardless of the correctness of your action. If you push the keywords terms to extremes, such as by spamming, you will probably not get onto most of the search engines.

To find quality links manually, search for websites that have the same theme as your own. When requesting a link, be sure to highlight what your site has to offer their visitors and why they should link to it. A compelling case will increase your chance of success.

Link quality simply means how well positioned the pages are that link to you. If you are linked to by a spammy link farm, you get a penalty; conversely, if you are linked to by a directory like Yahoo, LookSmart or Dmoz you get a boost. What about the hundreds of free directories? Yes, they all help. Take a few days and submit your site *manually* to every directory that will take it. There may be local directories, and regional directories can often supply plenty of incoming links. Every relevant link helps.

Chapter 7
Software toolbox

It's not enough simply to optimize your website and hope for high traffic; you need to use tools and techniques to achieve success. A search optimization strategy is made up of three parts (see Figure 7.1):

1 Subscription to commercial registrations
2 Page architecture and structure of your website
3 Links popularity.

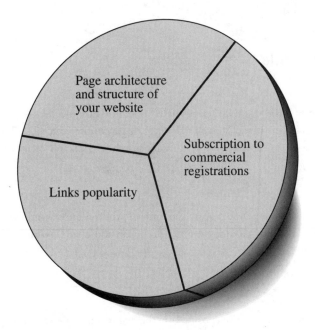

Figure 7.1 *The SEO pie chart*

Each one of these parts has a number of tools on the market that help to automate the processes, but before you can use these tools you need to have defined goals for your strategy. Even if the campaign just establishes name recognition, this is an admirable goal. Search engine marketing is no different from any other advertising or marketing campaign; all your goals have to be defined. Several types of data are needed to measure the success of the search engine marketing campaign, including:

- Search engine submission and ranking reports
- Click-through reports
- Monthly traffic reports, indicating unique visitors, search phrases with engines detail, entrance and exit pages
- Site administrative reports indicating number of users viewing
- Monthly sales data.

When you are working with a site that has a large number of new or changing pages, it would be ideal to have a tool that could do a deep submit to the various search engines, according to their different limits. You also need some page analysis tools, to help the service go beyond its submission roots. In an ideal world, your application would submit multiple pages from your site to the major crawler-based search engines and then measure the results.

If a user tries to find you and you're listed, but not within the first 10–30 matches, the listing is almost worthless – no matter how many engines you submitted your site to. Ranking well on the major search engines is the ultimate goal. To help you to do this you need software tools, and some of these are described here.

Tools of the trade

Page generator
You need to create HTML 'doorway' pages based on keywords and details you enter about your business. This will give you a head start in reaching the top of the search list. These pages will also act as alternative entrances to your website, giving searchers a greater chance of finding you.

Submission tool
You must be able to submit any pages you choose to the most important search engines. Resubmitting can sometimes provide an extra bump up the charts, so the Submitter should be scheduled to resubmit regularly.

Reporter
This should be able to check your site's positions in the major search engines. You must be able to find out how you rank on every keyword or phrase that is important to you, on all the major engines.

Scheduler

You must be able to activate the Reporter daily, weekly or monthly to check your website's positions automatically. You should be close enough to know immediately if your site stays on top, falls in rank, or falls out of the index altogether. This allows you to release a new doorway page or re-optimize an existing one before sales start dropping. Submitting can also be automated by most schedulers on the market.

Traffic analyser

This tracks your visitors and where they came from automatically. It should be able to answer questions such as 'What keywords are people searching for to find my site?' or 'Which referring site sends me the most traffic?'.

Identifying your best content

If you have a large site, you'll have the issue of not being able actively to submit all the pages you have within the submission limits of the major search engines. Search engines can and do crawl independently of what they receive via their Add URL pages. Submitting to Add URL pages is absolutely *no* guarantee that your pages will actually get listed. However, submission generally doesn't hurt, and can at least help to ensure that the search engines know about the pages you consider to be important. This is where good analysis tools can help you to understand which of your pages deserve priority in the submission stream. A good analysis chart will show you at a glance the 'index values' for each of your pages. You can think of this as a content quality rating, and you should be able to examine the location, frequency and uniqueness of the terms on the page.

Table 7.1 gives the latest time estimates of how long it takes to see results.

There are a number of doorway page-checking services that will analyse your existing content to see if it can be improved. The problem with all of these services is that there are no actual rules

Table 7.1 How long does it take to see results?

Free inclusion:		Paid inclusion	
Direct Hit	5–6 months	Inktomi and its 125 partners	48 hours
Google	8–10 weeks	Yahoo	7 days
Northern Light	6–8 weeks	NBCi	5 days
Lycos	3–4 months	Google	1 hour
AltaVista	3–4 weeks	GoTo	3–5 days
Inktomi and its 125 partners	8–10 weeks	DMOZ	3 weeks
Excite	6 months	LookSmart	2 days
		Direct Hit/AskJeeves	3–5 days

for them to follow. One checker may say that a page is great, while another reports serious problems. You may, for example, find that your checker is counting words and thinks that there are too many in your title tag, although there are no particular limits published by the search engines regarding words or characters in a title tag. You should write a title of about five to thirteen words in length, which uses some of your key terms and entices people to visit your site but at the same time isn't misleading as to your site's content. If the checker queries this, you need to make a qualified decision – either to overlook this result or to try another checker.

If a checker does like your META keywords tag, then it has probably found that you do have the correct tag and that it is formatted correctly. Unfortunately, that is as accurate as the process gets. The rules are very few, and any enhancements on them are usually unique to a particular checker. The checker tries to guess what words you're trying to feature in your META tag by looking for phrases between commas in the META keywords tag. Unfortunately, commas are not required and can be detrimental to search engine ranking. As a result the checker gets confused, thinking, for instance, that you're trying to feature 'search optimization and checkers'. As it also can't find that phrase in the body copy, it reports that there are not enough keyword matches, which can result in a lower search engine ranking.

META tag checkers

META tag checking tools are less ambitious than page checking tools, and are much more widespread. They essentially look to see if you have a title, a META description tag and a META keywords tag. They also check to see that these are formatted correctly and, finally, that the lengths don't exceed general standards. For the record, most search engines that support the two major META tags allow a description of 200–250 characters and a keywords element of 1000 characters. Character length checking software will tell you if your tags use too many words. You need to be able to limit these word counts, as there are no rules and you can only base your decisions on experience. There are certainly no official rules regarding how many words META tags can have, although working to a count of 1000 characters appears to give the most flexibility across all the search engines.

Keyword density analysers

These are tools that tell you how frequently a term is being used in relation to other words in your documents. Imagine, for example, you have a website with 50 or 80 existing pages. You need software that can import all the files at once for analysis. You can then enter a search phrase, for the 'whole phrase', and you'll quickly be able to see which of your pages already use that search phrase with some frequency. These pages are the pages that you'll want to optimize for that phrase. Ensure that you use the search phrase as part of your page title and within your META tags. If you find that none of your pages actually use the search phrases you want to be found for, start reworking your body text to include these terms. A good density analyser can see the top three keywords or search phrases that each of your pages appears targeted toward, and by revising your page copy you can push up the values of particular words. Just use the page analyser again after making changes, to see how the scores have been changed.

It would be helpful to be able to choose what information you want to have displayed for each page – such as the page title and META tags. This information is usually available in other ways, but not in a unified table that can be downloaded. You should be able to tag pages that have been optimized in case you want to see only the pages in your site that are NOT optimized. The ability to sort by URL could also help if you want to find a variety of pages quickly, instead of having to locate them individually.

Rules for a perfect SEO strategy

People frequently ask questions about what 'rules' should be followed to construct the perfect page for each crawler-based search engine. How many times should a phrase appear on a page for top ranking? How often should a term be repeated in a META tag? How are spam penalties administered? The truth is that these statistics are not available, but from constantly search optimizing sites, analysing results and preparing strategies for the next approach it is possible to gain an idea of what achieves results. There are always exceptions to perfect page formulas.

In this chapter we are trying to help you to identify the tools that plug into your site's natural traffic. After all, if you do not have an audience for your website, nothing you do in the long run will work. We are not suggesting that you go out and try to build perfect pages with these tools, but the opposite – we want you do everything possible to tap into your 'natural' traffic. So if you have already done the work on your content and site architecture, then the tools described here will be of great help.

A number of search engines dislike the automated submission that software allows you. Google in particular appears to have an extremely strong stance against automated software, and it is strongly recommended that you do not include Google in any ranking missions you perform. In the past, Google has banned the IP addresses of heavy users of such software. Instead, select Yahoo pages. This will reveal your positions in the web page matches of Yahoo, fed by Google, which gives a fairly accurate representation of how you rank on Google anyway. You can then submit to Google manually at http://www.google.com/addurl.html

If you choose to use automated submission software, try to do so responsibly by scheduling your Reporter missions, not over-submitting your URLs, avoiding the creation of hundreds of doorway pages, and not running Reporter on Google and any other anti-querying software. In fact, using any type of software that runs automatic queries on Google is against their terms of service, and so you run the risk of your IP address and/or site being banned. Remember that if you bombard the search engines, it is NOT going to help you achieve high rankings.

Before we discuss various software solutions, consider the fact that this book presents the concepts and approach of search engine marketing. As a discipline it is continually evolving, so never assume you know everything – this discipline can only be mastered through a continual culture of learning. Start each campaign by analysing the previous one, and in this way you will evolve the next solution as a step forward in your eStrategy. It is only when you have made hundreds of these steps that you will have achieved something significant.

Software exposed

Automated software has always had its fan club, and although management information software that both analyses and manages your campaigns can be very good, some submission software can have a devastating effect on your results. These autosubmit tools that claim to submit your website to 'thousands of search engines' turn out to be failures at attracting visitors, but excel at getting you thousands of pieces of unsolicited email. For $100 or more, they claim to be able to advertise to 100 000 or more engines. As you will see from the list in Appendix E, most of these engines or directories are specialist industry engines – which is great if you are a restaurateur searching on a catering engine for new furniture, but not so good if you're not. The top fifteen search engines will produce 95 per cent of the traffic for your site, so that's where you should be investing your money. In reality there aren't thousands of relevant search engines, and the majority of web surfers around the world use only a handful of portals for all their searches. Nearly three-quarters of all search-engine referrals come from the top four services – Yahoo, Google, MSN and AOL Search.

So what about the other 'thousands' of search engines that autosubmission tools promote? These are mainly a way of collecting email addresses from naive owners of new websites. These 'hot' addresses are then sold as prime prospects to spammers, and can receive two to three thousand unsolicited emails. The 'hundreds of thousands' of search engines don't in fact exist, and instead many submission programs count entries they submit to 'free-for-all' (FFA) listings. These unedited sites accept anyone who submits a listing, but attract no visitors. Being listed in FFA sites may actually damage your ranking – if your site is new and you submit to a free-for-all engine, and then Google finds a thousand free-for-all links, it'll hurt you.

Experience has shown that most submission tools aren't necessary to get a website into the major search engines. Optimizing a site so it contains relevant search terms is a better use of your time than trying to get into 100 000 places.

To research appropriate keywords you can visit Wordtracker, which offers a free trial service (see http://wordtracker.com/). Pick three or four words that you want people to associate with your site, and then make sure these words appear where search engines look for them.

The following pages feature PositionWeaver, PositionPro, WebPositionGold and bruceclay.com, because these are tools that we regularly use. We also highlight tools that we have appraised and feel are of merit and should be mentioned in a book on search optimization. The list of tools is broken up in to eight areas:

1 *Deep submission tools.* These tools are designed to submit many pages from your site to crawler-based search engines. They may also have other capabilities, such as page analysis features, but on the whole their main focus is on deep submission.
2 *Multisubmission tools.* Multisubmission tools are designed to submit your website to hundreds of crawler-based search engines and human-powered directories at the same time. These tools should be reserved for targeting the many minor search engines that aren't worth the time required to do a manual submit. Free-for-all sites are likely to end up sending you a lot of spam,

so use a temporary email address or one different from your main address for submission purposes. Most marketers prefer manual submission, and think that it is more effective.

3 *Position checking/tracking tools*. With these tools you can see how your pages are ranked on different search engines. A better way to measure search engine performance is through log analysis, which shows you the way in which people have come to your website. Position checking tools can place a burden on search engines, which is one reason why Northern Light blocks them. Google also may block some usage.

4 *Page analysers/'perfect page' tools*. These are tools designed to help you produce the 'perfect page' for crawler-based services. Unfortunately, there is no guarantee that these perfect pages will actually rank well.

5 *Keyword density analysers*. Many 'perfect page' tools provide keyword density analysis. These tools tell you how frequently a term is being used in relation to other words in your documents. Achieving the 'perfect' keyword density is no guarantee of ranking success.

6 *META tag checkers*. These tools are designed primarily to determine whether your META tag coding is correct. There are no official rules for META tags that the search engines follow; each search engine has its own set of unreleased filters to watch for excess repetition.

7 *Bidding managers*. These tools are designed to help you research and optimize paid listings with search engines like Overture.

8 *Link and support software*. So you want to create Yahoo-like listings of websites, or categorize information within your own site? This section describes some leading packages.

Deep submission tools

PositionPro

PositionPro (Figure 7.2) is a tool for search engine marketing experts to use. Not all sites are accepted to use the service; the criterion seems to be that if you have problems placing your site with LookSmart or Yahoo, then Position Pro will not accept it. As part of the sale, clients learn about the software through an account manager who is assigned to them. The account manager initially reviews the site, then discusses some immediate optimization suggestions and ways to move forward with optimizing the site in an orderly fashion over time. In some instances it could be over a period of six months. The initial aim is to get clients to make basic changes to their existing pages rather than creating highly optimized doorway pages. Altering page titles and improving body copy can bring noticeable results in a short period of time (eight weeks). Account managers make contact with clients at least once a month, although they monitor status reports twice monthly.

This is not a tool for beginners, but a lot of help is given through the account managers, who support clients as they learn to use the system. A version of PositionPro with training material for the novice user was recently released. Called Submit Director, the annual service is exclusively for sites of 50 pages or less. Unlike PositionPro, you'll find plenty of help files and tutorials, yet you'll still have access to virtually the same analysis and submission tools that the normal PositionPro service offers.

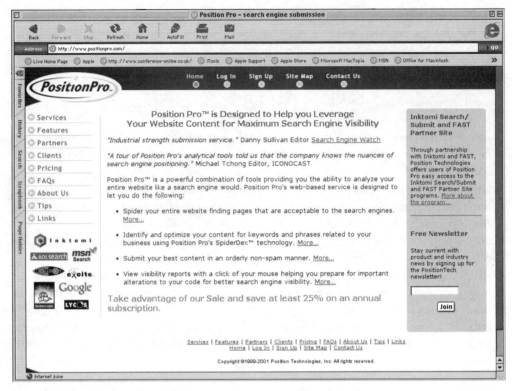

Figure 7.2 *http://www.positionpro.com/*

META tag generator

PositionPro offers an automatic META tag generating tool, which allows you to create some generic META tags for that URL. When you select the META tag link, the URL is retrieved in real time and META tags are created for it automatically, based on the content of the page. The keywords tag is created by using software to analyse the page for unique terms. Since this analysis isn't perfect, PositionPro does a second run with slightly different parameters. This creates longer version of the META keywords tag as a second choice. It is best to look at both versions of the META keywords tag generated, and choose the one that you think best reflects the content of the page. If your page is short, you should use the short version; a long page deserves a longer version of the META tag. PositionPro also advises that the page's HTML title should be reviewed to reflect what you think the page should be targeted toward before running the META tag generator.

The META description tag is the first significant sentences from the body. While it is preferable to create distinct tags for each of your pages manually, it is better to use automatically created custom tags than not to have them at all. Having the tags created for you is a good start; you should then tweak them to suit your requirements before you install them on your pages.

PositionPro and dynamic content

As an extra service, PositionPro can also spider sites with dynamic content. It creates mirror pages on the client's server that can be crawled by search engines. This is great for shopping and any transactional sites, where information about prices and product availability could be stripped out of the dynamic pages and replaced with links on non-dynamic pages that retrieve the latest information.

PositionPro is owned by Position Technologies, which is one of Inktomi's paid inclusion partners. If you are a PositionPro user, the Inktomi paid inclusion is integrated into the service. You can view a special report on the site analysis page that lists all of your pages ranked by index value. Using check boxes, you can then order that any of these pages be added to the Inktomi paid inclusion system. This makes it easy to focus on pages that may have the most luck in bringing traffic. Inktomi gives PositionPro a powerful combination role as a search engine optimization tool.

PositionPro has a an index system for measuring, but experience shows that in no way should a page's index value be taken as a guarantee of top scoring with the search engines themselves. One interesting observation is that a top-ranking page with an average index value has an average word count of 200 to 300 words per page. It's important to note that the index value is linked to the three top keywords or key phrases for each page. These keywords are determined automatically by PositionPro's algorithm, which looks to see what terms the page appears to be targeting, paying attention to the all-important words appearing in the page's title tag. PositionPro works with clients to encourage them at least to make title tag changes before running an analysis to choose which pages to target with further optimization work.

Once you've made your choices and your account is fully active, PositionPro goes to work. Pages will be submitted daily, but never in excess of the different limits allowed by each search engine. In fact, less than the maximum amount may be submitted for smaller sites, in order to avoid any possible spam concerns or connection problems. Overall, PositionPro follows the 'if it ain't broke, don't fix it' rule – which means don't resubmit unless you see a particular and continuing problem with a search engine.

eLuminator

The worst roadblock that can stop spiders in their tracks is having the content password-protected. If you place your pages in an area that can only be accessed by registered users, search engines will never find them. You might have an incredibly content-rich site in registered areas, which the general public might also like to discover. The eLuminator system (Figure 7.3) will duplicate protected content in a way that makes it accessible to search engines without dropping any restrictions required for human visitors. For example, if you have a website with 1000 pages hidden behind a registration system, eLuminator will read those pages and automatically make a search-engine friendly doorway page version of each one of them.

Figure 7.3 *http://www.inceptor.com/*

Although especially designed to deliver tailored content to spiders, eLuminator can also handle ordinary content for deep submission. The eLuminator service is especially designed to submit password-protected content in a way that makes it accessible to search engines without dropping any restrictions required for human visitors before they are allowed to view it. Inceptor also owns the Excedia package; this is software for maximizing your company's visibility, creating thousands of referral points for your site at major Internet portals for both 'invisible' and 'deep' content.

WebPositionGold

If you're listed but don't appear within the first two or three pages of results, you lose – no matter how many engines you have submitted your site to. There are three ways to resolve this problem:

1 You need to know the many techniques that will move you into a top ten position
2 You need to build your pages so they are optimized
3 Once you have learned how to achieve a top ten search position, you have to monitor your progress.

Figure 7.4 *www.webpositiongold.com/ (reproduced with permission)*

WebPositionGold (Figure 7.4) is one of a few products to combine all the following features:

- It generates HTML pages designed to rank near the top of the search results
- It analyses your existing web pages
- It has a built-in HTML editor for fast and easy changes
- It uploads your new and changed pages
- It submits your pages to the major search engines
- It reports your positions on each search engine for each keyword you are targeting
- It tracks the number of visitors to your site, where they came from, and what keywords they used to find you.

The real genius to WebPosition is that it walks you through the process of building doorway pages from scratch. The software's 'Page generator' module asks you to select a search engine to target, enter the term you want to be found for, provide the name of your company or website, and add some body copy text. If you then hit the 'Generate' button, a doorway page will be made for that term, and for that search engine.

In order to differentiate your pages from each other, the 'Page critic' module should be used. This will inspect each page and compare it with what it finds to be the average for top-ranking pages at particular search engines. You are also shown how your page places, so that you can constantly improve your page ranking.

The team at First Place Software is constantly supporting and downloading top-ranking pages for a variety of terms, and in particular for terms that are not especially popular as well as more popular ones. That's essential, because the more popular the term, the more likely it is that off-the-page criteria may be causing the page to rank well. As the software itself advises, the numbers it provides are intended as a 'starting point' rather than an exact recipe to perfect a site.

WebPosition has an incredible knowledge base, so this is definitely a first stop for keeping up to date. It is an important asset, providing in-depth information and suggestions for upgrading pages.

It is recommended that you archive all your old web pages so that you can maintain all links to those pages.

PrioritySubmit

This is a web-based system that allows you to submit your pages via paid inclusion programs to major search engines offering such services (see Figure 7.5). The same company also offers a software multisubmission tool, SubmitWolfPro, with paid inclusion capabilities.

Figure 7.5 *http://www.prioritysubmit.com/*

It provides a guaranteed and convenient one-step process to submit your URL(s) to the various priority inclusion services, all through a single interface. There is no need to fill out multiple search engines forms; it is claimed that the service will do everything.

To provide the solution, PrioritySubmit has partnered with the major engines to offer a priority listing service. A priority listing *guarantees* that your URL is added within 48 hours on most engines, or so it is claimed.

Search Mechanics

Search Mechanics (Figure 7.6) gives you 'your own spider', which communicates with you and can alert you to problems that affect your search engine listings. It behaves just like a search engine spider, but will crawl dynamic sites and help you to get listed. It provides you with an overall analysis of how search-engine friendly a site is. You can use this before and after your search engine optimization efforts in order to judge the success of your efforts. The site-wide analysis of every page that a search engine robot might index is good; you can use this to make decisions about which pages to promote and which ones not to promote. The report includes all page titles and descriptions, which are often used by search engines in their results listings.

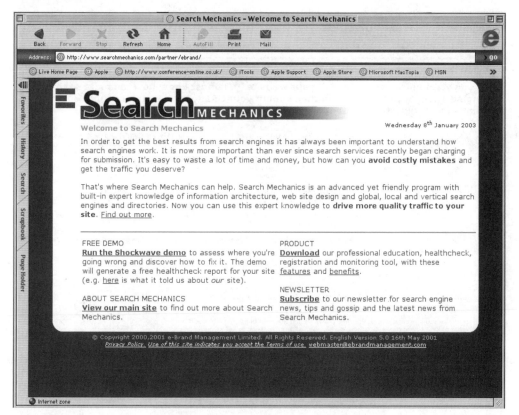

Figure 7.6 *http://www.searchmechanics.com/partner/ebrand/ (reproduced with permission)*

Search Mechanics builds a web page that lists all the pages you want to be registered with search engines. This can be used to preview your potential results listings. This then becomes an information console that you can use to inform search engines of changes to your site. Search Mechanics automatically builds a robots.txt file that contains all the pages you do not want to appear in search engine results listings. You can use this combination with a search engine map to control where spiders go on your site.

The submission tool is clear and easy to use. It confirms and records every submission visually to ensure that the task is done properly.

Multisubmission tools

SelfPromotion.com

SelfPromotion.com (Figure 7.7) has a shareware site philosophy that lets you submit to a large number of search engines. Like Submit It, this is primarily an automated site promotion service; the difference is that Submit It and other services like it usually only allow free submission to a limited number of sites. SelfPromotion will accept voluntary subscription, and those paying from $10 upward are rewarded with extra benefits.

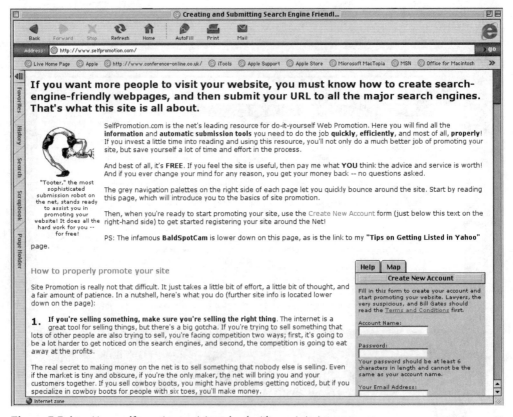

Figure 7.7 *http://www.selfpromotion.com/ (reproduced with permission)*

Among the benefits is the Rankulator form, which allows you to enter three search terms, and then it will search to see if you are listed for those exact terms and combinations of them. The 'Rankulator' is a basic position checker. It can't hold its own against a more dedicated tool, such as Position Agent or WebPosition, but as an extra benefit it's not bad. It tells you what pages you are listed on for AltaVista, Excite, Infoseek and Lycos.

'Keyword diffuser' is a great search engine tool. It is a META tag builder, but it allows you vary the META tags; this will given you a better chance of striking the right combination to increase relevancy. Also, with some search engines short pages with the same tags will be considered as duplicates and automatically excluded.

Addweb website promoter

Addweb (Figure 7.8) submits your site, analyses your pages for position-boosting content, builds position-boosting content on your pages, tracks traffic on your website, checks and reports your ranking on major engines, manages link trading with other sites – and much, much more.

Addweb's PageAdvisor will look at your web pages from the perspective of a search engine. It analyses every element of your pages, and generates a search-engine positioning scorecard report.

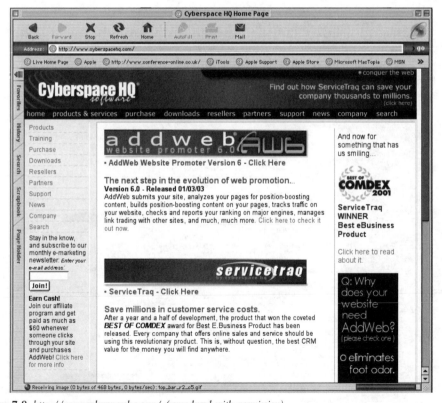

Figure 7.8 *http://www.cyberspacehq.com/ (reproduced with permission)*

This report tells you everything you need to do to help to boost your site's position on search engines. It will even score your page against your competitor's web pages! If you have the Platinum or Professional editions of Addweb, PageAdvisor will use live data mining to compare your pages to the top-ranking pages on the keywords you choose.

The PageBuilder feature allows you easily to implement the advice received from PageAdvisor. All key elements of a web page can be easily manipulated through PageBuilder. Many elements of a web page that affect the ability of a spider to understand the contents are not easy to edit with a standard HTML editor. PageBuilder helps you overcome this problem, and saves hours of tedious work.

Dynamic Submission 2000

Dynamic Submission 2000 (Figure 7.9) is a multi-award-winning web promotion and search engine submission piece of software. Dynamic Submission 2000 is the most important Internet marketing tool today. It has been developed to offer website owners the ability to promote their websites through submission to the ever-increasing number of search engines on the Internet without any hassles or complications. It will help you to submit your website to hundreds of major search engines with just a few button 'clicks', and will drive a large volume of guaranteed traffic

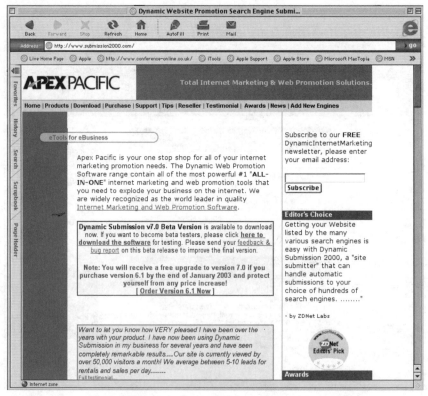

Figure 7.9 *http://www.submission2000.com/ (reproduced with permission of Apex Pacific)*

to your website. Simply enter your website details and press a button. This incredible program will automatically submit all your websites to 1000+ major search engines within minutes, and also provides you with all the tools to get your website listed in the top positions.

Easy to use and user friendly . . .

With the new Window Explorer-style interface, creating your web project and site file is now even easier. You can organize and navigate all your website files in one screen. You can now select all major search engines with one button, saving time. History submission files will help you track your submission task for analysis or resubmission. You can also export your engine list with one button click.

Yahoo and Open Directory (dmoz.org)

You can now submit to Yahoo and dmoz (the Open Directory) automatically with their 'Real Time Category Selection' technology. dmoz Open Directory will support AOL, MSN, Netscape, Lycos, HotBot and many other major search engines.

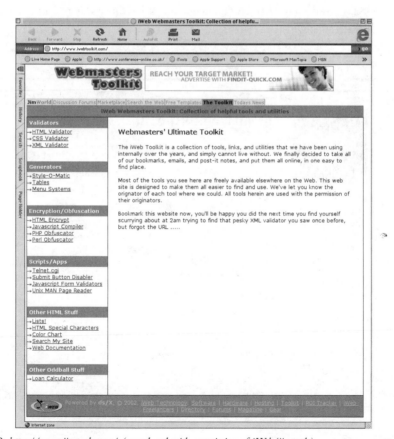

Figure 7.10 *http://www.jimtools.com/ (reproduced with permission of iWeb/jimtools)*

URL verification and link popularity checking is a smart search function to check your URL verification and link popularity.

JimTools.com

This website (Figure 7.10, page 145) has several useful resources and tools, including an HTML validator. This will check the HTML of any web page you ask it to, generating a report that will advise you on how to correct it. This can be very useful. There are also Cascading style sheet and XML validators, which work in the same way. In addition there is a style sheet generator, a table generator and menu generators, which produce quite impressive results but could be done just as easily in an application such as Dreamweaver. There are a number of encryption tools and various scripts that you can integrate into your web pages, as well as a lot of reference material. This site has some very useful content and is clearly presented; both amateurs and experienced webmasters can learn a lot here.

SubmitWolf Pro

SubmitWolf Pro (Figure 7.11) is a useful package that contains a URL rank feature (which tracks where your URL is listed) and a META tags generator. It has the ability to customize the engines

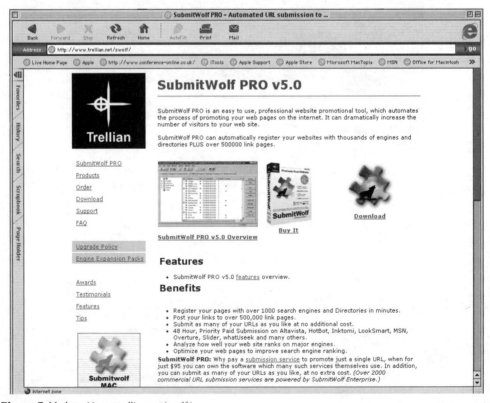

Figure 7.11 *http://www.trellian.net/swolf/*

it works with, and provides free program updates and detailed reports, which are very clear and contain a wealth of information. It is a useful program, with perhaps slightly limited functionality.

VSE Be Found

VSE Be Found (Figure 7.12) is a multisubmission tool for Mac users. Very few of these tools exist, and this is by far the most popular. The program has a built-in META tag generator, which is the most comprehensive bid manager available for the Macintosh. It lets you analyse your web pages in real time, and there is also a built-in ftp client. The built-in submission tool lets you submit your site to around 150 search engines, and the rank checker can then follow your progress in the top engines. One particularly notable feature is that the software contains a built-in link popularity checker, which will check the popularity of your pages at a number of major sites; this will also check the link popularity of your competitors. Overall this is the best submission tool for the Mac, and is well worth investing in if you are a Mac owner.

Figure 7.12 *http://vse-online.com/submit-website/ (reproduced with permission)*

Position checking/tracking tools

AgentWebRanking

AgentWebRanking (Figure 7.13) is designed for webmasters, webmarketers and search engine consultants. It enables you to compare how your site is ranking with your competitors, and when used effectively can help you to gain a higher ranking. The program lets you check keywords against URLs, and also specify how deep you would like the results to go. Results are presented in a clear browser window, which lets you link out to the actual search engine result you are viewing. The browser window provides several links to a range of online services for improving your visibility. Included in these tools and services are links to submit your site to search engines manually, a link validation tool, and a keyword analyser. Engines include Teoma and WiseNut, and a number of regional search engines. The program produces concise reports; these can feature your company logo and can be produced in a range of different languages, including German, French and Spanish.

This is a very good program for producing ranking reports as part of a site analysis. The reports are fully customizable, and clear; however, the software is very expensive and the 'lite' version is limited.

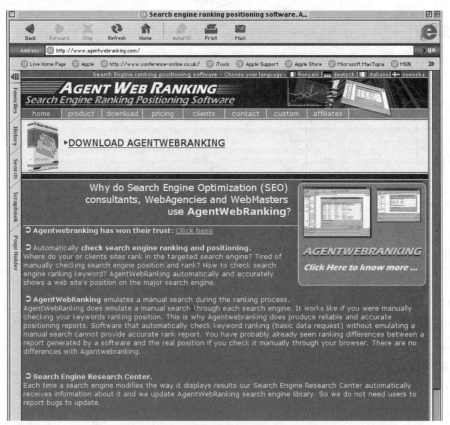

Figure 7.13 *http://www.aadsoft.com/ (reproduced with permission of Agent Web ranking)*

BeOnTop

BeOnTop (Figure 7.14) lets you check where your site appears in the search results of the major search engines. The software then compares your standing in the search engines with your competitor's. This can help you to identify any ranking patterns. The software checks all the major search engines, including Teoma and Google. The reports it generates are in clear English, and it also suggests ways for you to optimize your site META tags. Another useful feature is that you can download free script updates through the software, which means you are always up to date with the latest search engine ranking scripts and techniques. This is a good piece of software, at a fair price.

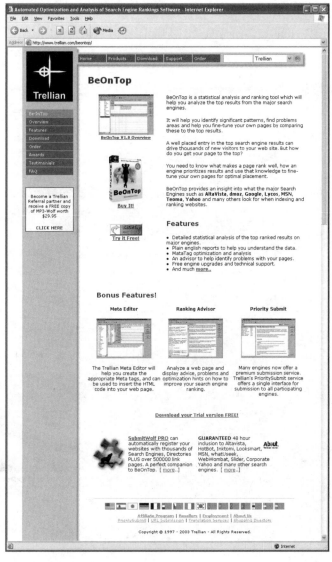

Figure 7.14 *http://www.trellian.com/beontop/*

Rocket Rank

Rocket Rank (Figure 7.15) is an online-based keyword rank checking tool. The free version only allows you to check for one term or phrase, but the results are accurate and it does search the main engines and directories – including Yahoo, Teoma, Google, Excite and AltaVista. The 'Advanced' version lets you, for a small fee, check for rankings on a number of different keywords or phrases, and also generates reports that are emailed to you every week to help you check your site's progress. This is a good site that is useful for a webmaster who wants to keep track of a site's performance on the major engines, but who does not want to invest a lot in a more expensive piece of tracking software.

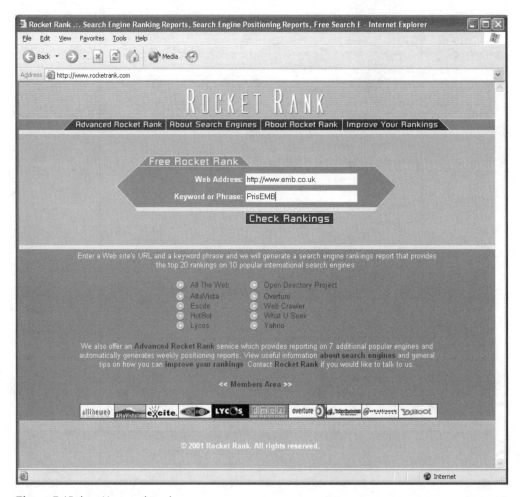

Figure 7.15 *http://www.rocketrank.com*

Submit It (PositionAgent)

As part of the Microsoft bCentral package of site marketing tools, Submit It (Figure 7.16) is a great tool for managing your search engine optimization. Submit It will spider your website and make sure that it is complete, with no broken links, and is ready for submission. It will also suggest the best keywords for you to use for your site when submitting it to search engines. The submitting tool manages your submissions to a number of major sites, and will resubmit your site if it has not been listed within a certain timescale. You can then easily monitor your performance on the engines your site has been submitted to, and the software will generate reports outlining your search engine performance. The report will also tell you which keywords web users are using to find your site. This is a great system, at a reasonable price, and comes highly recommended.

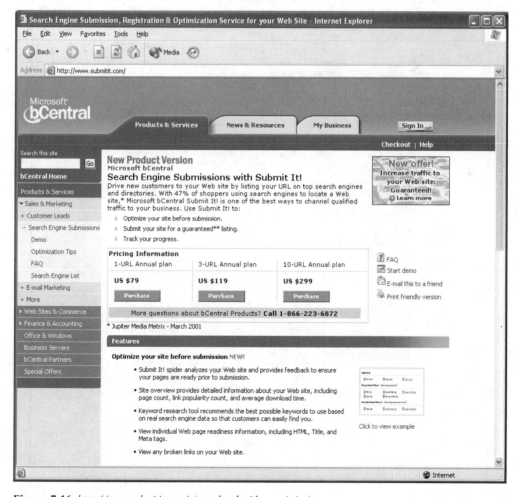

Figure 7.16 *http://www.submitit.com/ (reproduced with permission)*

Search Engine Power Pack

Search Engine Power Pack (Figure 7.17) contains a variety of tools and utilities that have been put together to improve your search engine ranking. First, there is a keyword popularity tool to select the best keywords for your site; however, this merely pulls data from Overture, which you could do yourself by visiting the Overture website. There's also a META tag generator, called META Mechanic, which generates and places META tags onto your site. The third tool is a 'Page primer', which looks at your web pages and offers basic advice on how to improve them to rank higher in the listings. Alongside these there is a submission tool to submit your site to a number of search engines at once, and a position tracking tool so you can manage your submissions. This is a fairly complete package at a reasonable price, and will suit the novice webmaster looking for an all-round package to help improve site rankings.

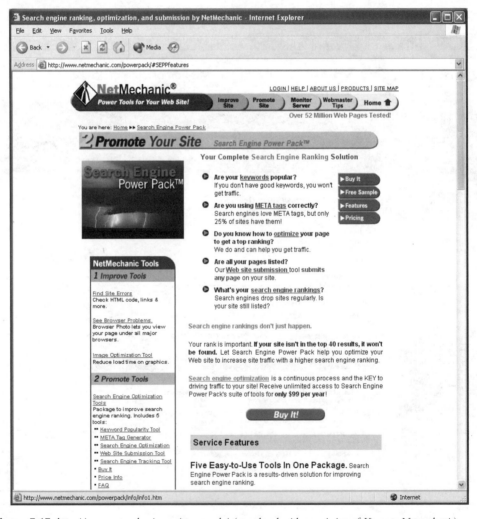

Figure 7.17 *http://www.netmechanic.com/powerpack/ (reproduced with permission of Keynote Netmechanic)*

SiteSnare

SiteSnare (Figure 7.18) is a free online rank checking tool. SiteSnare works in a web browser, and provides three areas of reporting. First, it lets you generate reports for a single keyword or phrase across search engines such as AltaVista, AOL, DirectHit, Google and the other major search engines. This provides a ranking score across all the engines, and allows you to perform competitor analysis quickly and easily. SiteSnare also lets you set up 'projects', and then performs automatic queries against these projects to keep up to date with your search engine ranking. Finally, it has an 'indexer reporting' function, which essentially tracks your site's position across the thirteen top search engines for certain keywords and phrases. The software produces concise reports, and as it is free it comes recommended.

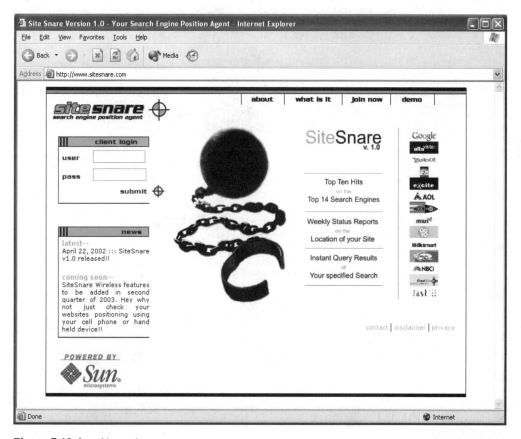

Figure 7.18 *http://www.sitesnare.com*

TopDog Pro

TopDog Pro (Figure 7.19) is a good search engine positioning and site submission software package. Managing submissions is easy through an intuitive interface, and the package lets you track your listing through the major search engines. The drawbacks are that it is quite a slow engine, there is no scheduling tool, and there is no feature to check how many of your pages have been indexed by any particular engine. However, it is a good all-round package, and allows you to submit to a wide range of engines – including international ones. The only problem is the price; it is quite expensive for the features of the package.

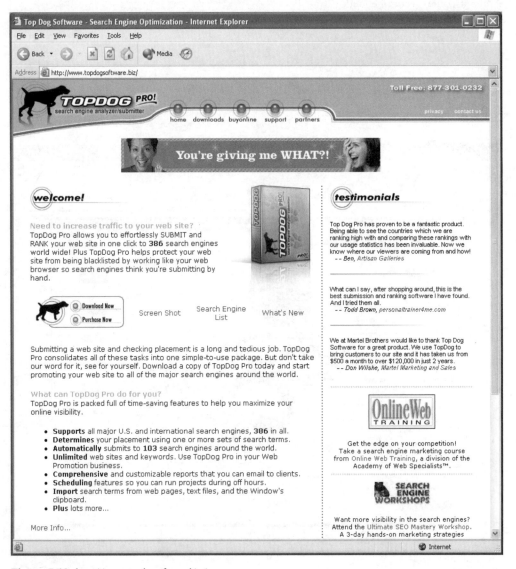

Figure 7.19 *http://www.topdogsoftware.biz/*

Search Engine Commando

Search Engine Commando (Figure 7.20) is a high-end submission tracking tool that submits pages and tracks results. It is presented with a simple and tasteful interface, and the reports that it generates are concise and easy to read. It uses 'trickle submission technology' to spread submission to sites over a certain time period, making sure they do not see the submissions as spam, and performs an in-depth ranking analysis on a set of user-specified queries and search engines. All in all this is a comprehensive package, with a range of features that will be found on other high-end position checking tools. The overall performance of the package is only marred by its high price.

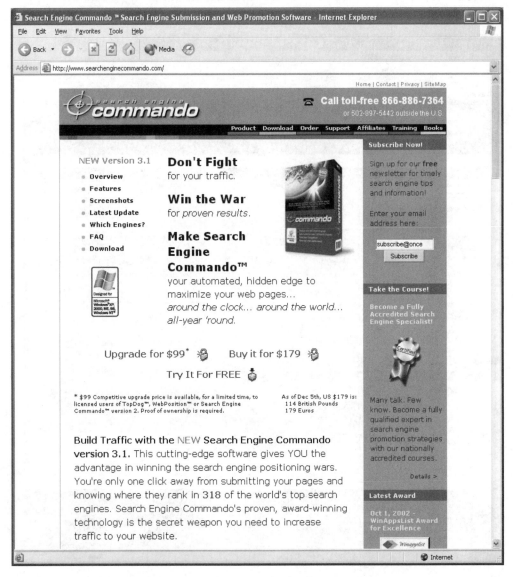

Figure 7.20 *http://www.searchenginecommando.com (reproduced with permission)*

Web Ranking Reports

Web Ranking Reports (Figure 7.21) is a real-time, web-based search engine that monitors your website's position across a number of major search engines. You sign up and pay a fee depending on how many reports you would like produced, which does give the user a certain amount of flexibility. You can then check up to 50 keywords, and specify how deep the reporting should go into the search engine. The software will then generate reports for you. One useful feature is the ability to generate reports that compare two or more reports with another, and another advantage is that it is web-based, so you don't need to download anything. This is a good piece of software if you need a clear report on how your website or your competitors' websites are doing, and the pricing model means you are more in control than if you were investing a lot of money in a large software package.

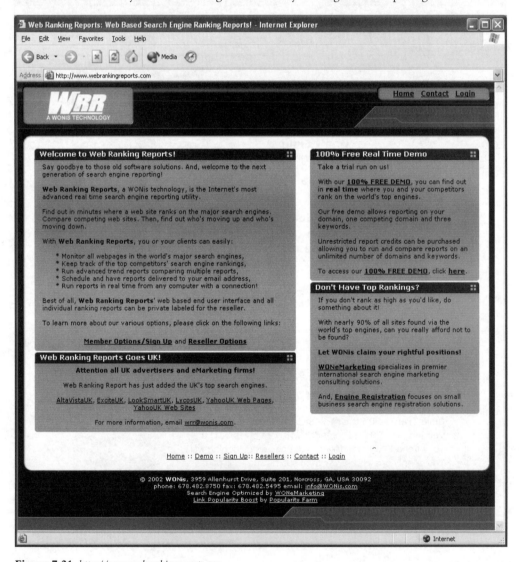

Figure 7.21 *http://www.webrankingreports.com*

Webrank

Webrank (Figure 7.22) is an online-based rank checking service that lets you check your web ranking against certain keywords. It also identifies your main competitors as well as possible link partners or affiliates, which is a unique feature. There is a suggested keyword generator and the option to view raw reports from individual search engines, which can be quite useful if you want to track your performance on a specific engine. The actual process is quite slow, but the reports that are generated are quite clear, and present all the relevant information on one web page. There are also quite useful hints and tips on increasing your web ranking, which will be useful to novice webmasters. There is a free trail of the system, so there is no harm in trying it out; however, the actual package is fairly expensive, and is provided on a subscription basis.

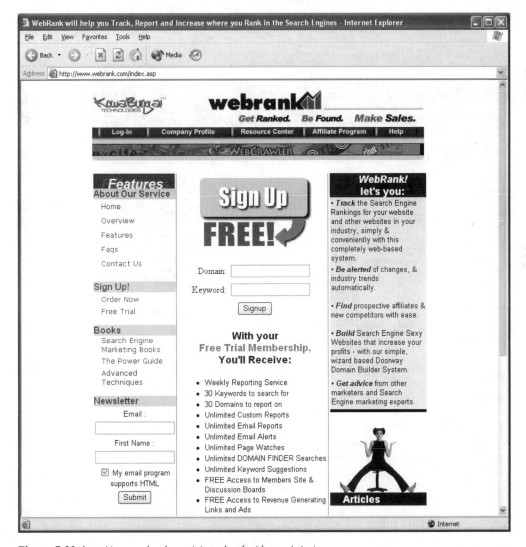

Figure 7.22 *http://www.webrank.com/ (reproduced with permission)*

Addweb webSite promoter

Addweb (Figure 7.23) is a user-friendly piece of software that automatically submits your URL(s) to the top search engines and directories. The software is well presented and easy to navigate, and lets you choose which engines to submit to. The submission process does not take long. The software also lets you check your ranking on the major search engines. It has a useful PageAnalyser built into it, which identifies content that can affect your ranking; it also lets you make changes to your pages through using a simple editor, although the extent of this is limited. This is a useful package, with many features that are all implemented well. The price of the professional package is quite high, but this does reflect its quality. Overall, it is a good package.

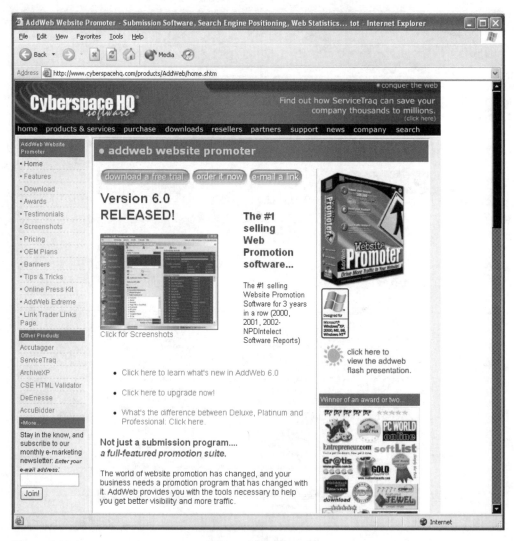

Figure 7.23 *http://www.cyberspacehq.com/ (reproduced with permission)*

Page analysers/'perfect page' tools

bruceclay.com SEOToolSet

This product (Figure 7.24) is available on a subscription basis only, and is priced per calendar quarter per site (domain). Further sites may be added and managed. Both the doorway page and META tag checker/keyword density analyser can be found here. The keyword density analyser reports show frequency, density and information used for single words and phrases in each selected web page. This tool will list the top keywords, plus all words used in your META tags. It presents the density for each word in the various categories: META title, META description, META keywords, ALT tags, comments, heading levels, and two categories for body copy. These reports should be reviewed to see what you need to change in or add to your pages. A useful feature is the ability to compare two web pages for a single phrase. A weakness of the keyword density analyser is that you can't specify particular terms to check in either the free or fee-based versions.

A free doorway page generator is just part of the search engine optimization toolset that consultant Bruce Clay offers via his website. Like the previous tools mentioned, you enter terms, select options, then generate a page that is meant to be optimized for search engines.

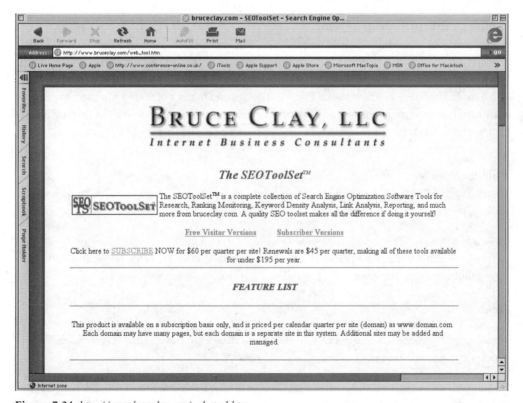

Figure 7.24 *http://www.bruceclay.com/web_tool.htm*

The search engine submission recommendations program produces a report for each web page in your site that is listed for any of your keywords, retaining the best-ranking page for any keywords for each search engine. It is designed to show where the pages are not ranked in any positions for any keywords, as test of viability for submission.

The search-engine ranking monitor is designed to query the major search engines and produce reports on the rankings of various pages from your site. If you specify your site URL, any of your pages appearing in the top positions will be reported for each engine. The output from this tool may be analysed in the ranking reports. In tables, each keyword phrase ranking is compared across each search engine for each domain.

The paid version of the doorway generator offers a slick 'envelope' option, which we've always privately termed 'poor man's cloaking'. It creates your doorway page code within a frames page. The user sees the main page of your website (or whatever page you submit to the doorway generator), while the search engine reads the optimized code in the no-frames area. This gives you one of the best benefits of cloaking, which is to hide the ugly doorway page text from visitors, without the disadvantage of using special software to feed the spiders' optimized code. However, it doesn't provide the other benefit of cloaking, which is to hide your code from the prying eyes of competitors.

Azooq Doorway Page generator

Azooq Doorway Page Professional (Figure 7.25) is an easy-to-use doorway page creation tool. It builds relevant doorway pages and will identify weak links, making it one of the best doorway page generators in the market. It lets users make changes to doorway pages and generate them, and will generate and optimize description and title META tags, and more. There are a number of templates for you to base your pages on, and all the doorway page optimization options can be user-defined. If you need help in creating and optimizing your doorway pages, this is a useful product.

PositionWeaver

PositionWeaver (Figure 7.26) is an HTML doorway page generator that allows you to increase the ranking of your website on search engine results.

Doorway pages are HTML pages designed specifically to rank highly on search engine results for a particular search engine and a particular phrase or keyword. They are easily found and noticed by large numbers of search engine users, given their high rank on search results (see Chapter 2).

All doorways include a Robots tag, which keeps the search engines automatically returning to check for the latest versions. They also possess a visitor recapture feature, which automatically launches your website in a new window if the visitor decides to leave your doorway page without proceeding to your website.

PositionWeaver lets you create doorway pages for five URLs; set doorway background, text, and link colors; and include banners and background images. It also generates all the HTML code. This

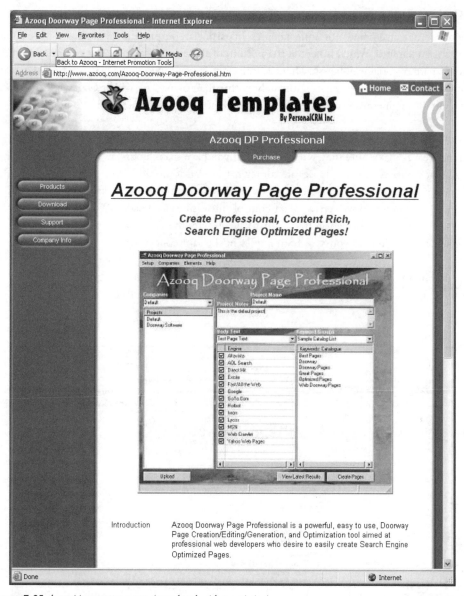

Figure 7.25 *http://www.azooq.com (reproduced with permission)*

function in WebPosition is a lot of work; you have constantly to tweak your basic doorway page to please its Page Critic suggestions. In PositionWeaver, the process of getting the perfect page is painless.

As with WebPosition, you enter some basic information, and then PositionWeaver creates doorway pages for various search engines, based on what they like. Once generated, you have a series of very different pages for each major search engine.

The pages will need to be enhanced, as they look very ugly as they come out of the system – they are designed for search engines, not human beings. In particular, the program generates body text that is recurring and absurd, which is kept at the bottom of the page because search engines do not like pages that are essentially gibberish. There is nothing to suggest it doesn't work. It is probably safe to assume that users who are using it legitimately, within their own topic, will be OK, while those using it to spam the engines using unrelated keywords will be penalized if caught.

It is always a concern with automated doorway pages that keywords may appear too often. PositionWeaver makes sure they will not. Even if you have many doorway or information frames, one for each phrase, and the phrases are somewhat similar, it should not be a problem. Difficulties only occur if you have too many doorway or information frames for the exact same phrase, as this would be spamming. However, you can control this easily, and PositionWeaver will also replace any old doorway or information frames that have exactly the same phrase as a new one that you are generating, as long as you save both copies in the same directory.

In addition, the program specifically covers AltaVista, Excite, HotBot, InfoSeek, Lycos, and Northern Light, and integrates and works through Microsoft FrontPage.

Figure 7.26 *www.positionweaver.com*

Search Engine Optimizer

This package (Figure 7.27) was created by search engine specialist Robin Nobles, who is a well-known figure in search engine optimization. The software is really simple to use; all you need to do is tell it what pages you want to it to look at, and it will tell you how well these pages will rank. You can then edit your site template pages for search engines in general, before fine-tuning your pages to work and rank well on specific search engines. These small changes are easy to implement, and the program guides you through making them in a clear fashion. There are also detailed suggestions and warnings of why certain page factors will cause your pages to rank badly. You will

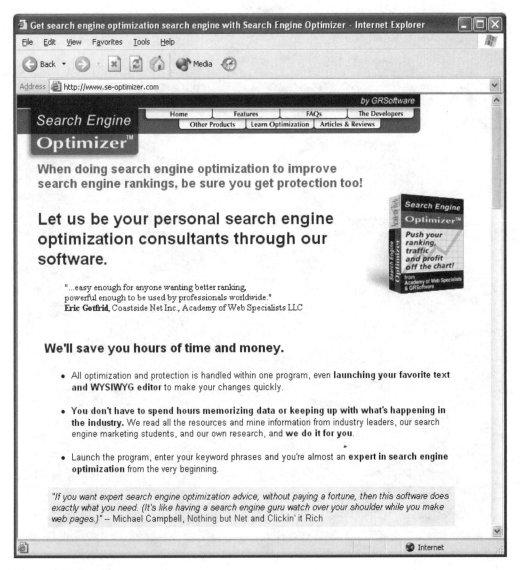

Figure 7.27 *http://www.se-optimizer.com*

learn a lot from using this program, and the price is reasonable for the amount of information it contains. If you want to build perfectly optimized pages, this application comes recommended.

Search Mechanics

Search Mechanics (Figure 7.28) is an advanced program that scans and analyses your site and suggests ways for you to improve its search engine ranking. Some elements of the service are free (e.g. the summary report and marketing information), but more detailed information is only

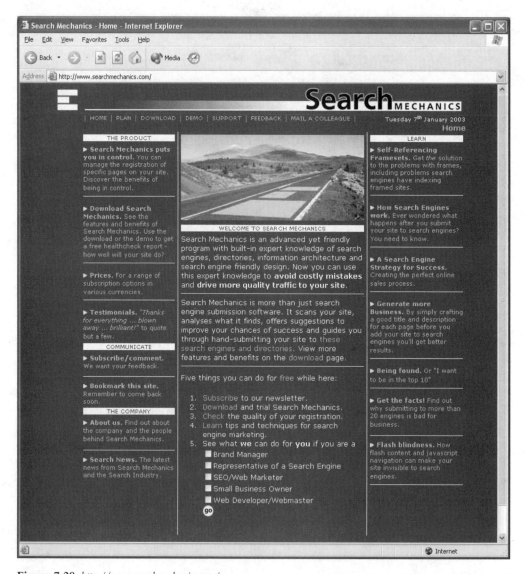

Figure 7.28 *http://www.searchmechanics.com/*

available to subscribing customers. The software 'spider' that it provides will also analyse dynamic database sites. The package will give you a page-by-page breakdown of every indexable page in your site, giving you information such as whether it has a title and META tags, and whether there are links from the page. This is a very useful way to see a complete overview of your site on one page and to identify any possible issues. The software also gives you a preview of how each page in your site will rank on search engines. Another useful feature of the package is that it can automatically generate a robots.txt META file for your site (saving you from having to do this), which will control where spiders can and can't go on your site. The software can then submit your site and track your submissions to the top search engines. This is free, and is a very useful tool and a great learning resource.

Keyword density analyser

The GRSoftware keyword density analyser (Figure 7.29) is a word analysis program designed to check keyword density throughout your HTML files. The software goes through your site and tells you how your keyword density will affect your ranking on search engines; it also takes into consideration the fact that if keyword density is too high, you can be penalized. The software strikes a good balance between too many and too few keywords, and there are various options that

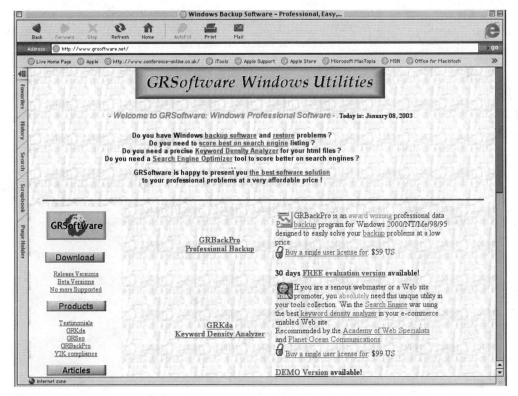

Figure 7.29 *http://www.grsoftware.net/ (reproduced with permission)*

you can choose from to customize the analysis. If you want to perform an in-depth keyword analysis on your site this is the program to use; however, the functionality is a bit limited for the price. There is a free demo version available from the website.

KeywordDensity.com

KeywordDensity.com (Figure 7.30) is a free web-based service that allows you to perform comparative keyword analysis on two web pages. All you need to do is type in your URLs and the keyword you would like to check, and it will return the results in an easy-to-read and understandable table. It recommends that keyword density should be around 1–7 per cent. As a free tool this service can be very useful; the website does not offer much more than this tool, but it is accurate and fast and well worthwhile checking out.

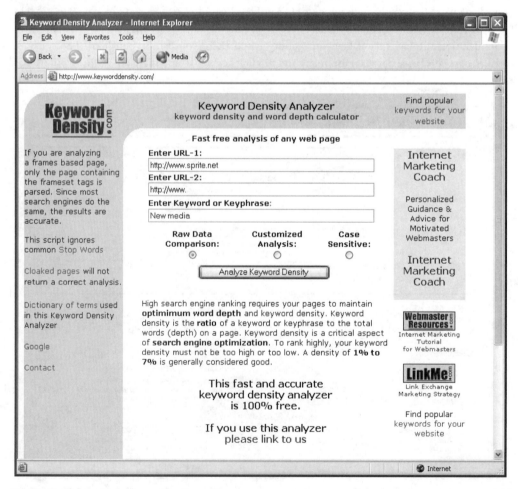

Figure 7.30 *http://www.keyworddensity.com/*

PageSneaker

PageSneaker (Figure 7.31) is an online resource that allows you to pull up a page and see its contents divided into different elements, such as body copy and header information. It is helpful for pages that do fast refreshes. You can also do a keyword density analysis in different areas. If checking on the home page of a site be sure to use a slash at the end of the domain, or the program doesn't work properly – in other words, input http://www.site.com/ rather than http://www.site.com.

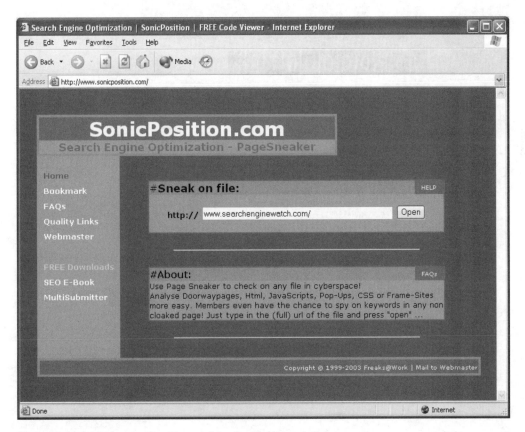

Figure 7.31 *http://www.sonicposition.com (reproduced with permission)*

WordCounter

This free web service (Figure 7.32) allows you to paste a paragraph or page of text into a box on the page; it will then look at this text and tell you which word you are overusing. This is a very simple service, but it is useful for putting in a large amount of text that you can't easily check yourself.

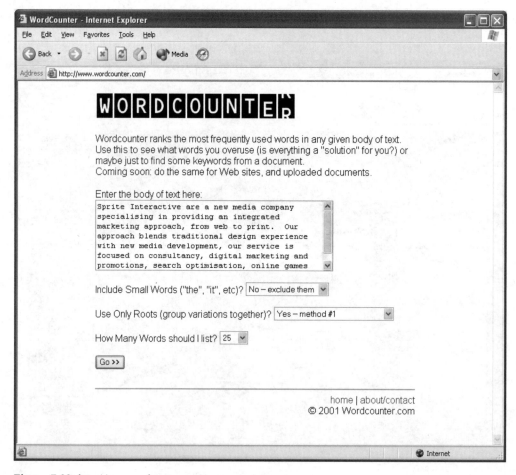

Figure 7.32 *http://www.wordcounter.com/*

META tag checkers

idesignbusiness META tag generator

This is a simple, free, online-based META tag generating tool (Figure 7.33). It is recommended that you use a title of 65 characters or less (about ten words). Do not worry about it becoming too long – search engines will simply cut off the end if this is the case, so just make sure that the most important information is at the top of your word count.

Start with the title tag. Search engines use the words in your title to match search terms. For example, if someone searches for '*search optimization*', the majority of site results will have the term '*search optimization*' in their title.

Your site's title will also be displayed on the top of your web page (see Figure 7.33). Create a title that describes your page; this should reflect the desired search term for the page. Your site's title will be the first thing seen by searchers, and it needs to grab their attention.

Figure 7.33 *http://www.idesignbusiness.com/META_tag_generator.htm*

Advanced META tag generator

This site (Figure 7.34) has to be as good as the META generator at www.sprite.net/metbuilder, which covers all the META tags – especially those beyond the keywords and description tags supported by major search engines. You can use the page or the JavaScript code to make an offline version. Using these META tags means that you are focusing on AltaVista and Inktomi; the other major search engines either ignore these tags or provide only limited support.

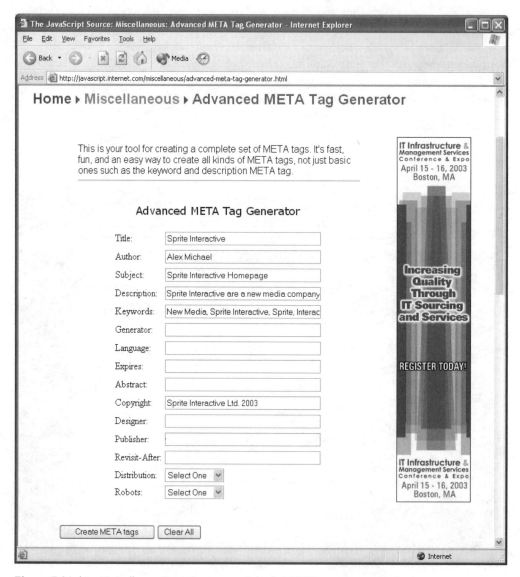

Figure 7.34 *http://miscellaneous.javascriptsource.com/advanced-META-tag-generator.html*

HitBox Doctor

If you just type your URL into HitBox Doctor (Figure 7.35), you can find out everything about your web page – how long does it takes to download? How easy it is for visitors to find your site? Are there any broken links or misspelled words? The HitBox Doctor provides valuable information that it would take hours to find if you were doing it manually. This tool helps you to improve your web page.

Figure 7.35 *http://resources.hitbox.com/cgi-bin/page.cgi?tools/doc*

Metty

Metty (Figure 7.36) is a freeware META tag maker. Having invested your time in building a website, you'll want the right people to locate your site via search engines like Looksmart or MSN Search. These search engines send out spiders and crawlers that 'crawl' the Internet for web pages. They look at HTML META tags to index information about web pages by subject matter, type of content and author.

META tags are neither fun to read nor easy to remember. Metty presents you with simple forms that allow you to input the information you want, then generate all of your META tags. Once generated, you can copy and paste the META tags into one of your HTML files or insert them into a new or imported HTML file. No knowledge of META tags is necessary to use Metty. It will create 33 HTML META tags by filling in simple form fields. Import an existing HTML file from your hard drive or the Web, insert the generated META tags into the HTML file, and save it. These saved tags can be used as a template. Metty also supports the mysterious Dublin Core META tags.

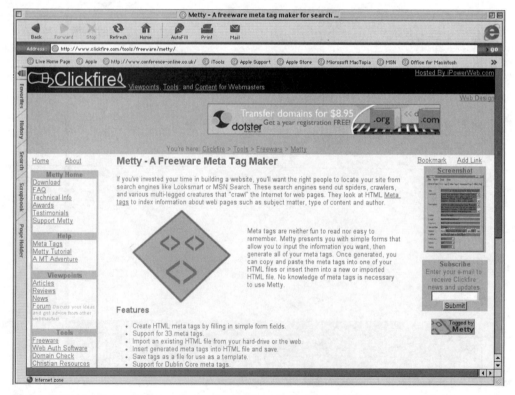

Figure 7.36 *http://www.clickfire.com/freeware/metty/ (reproduced with permission)*

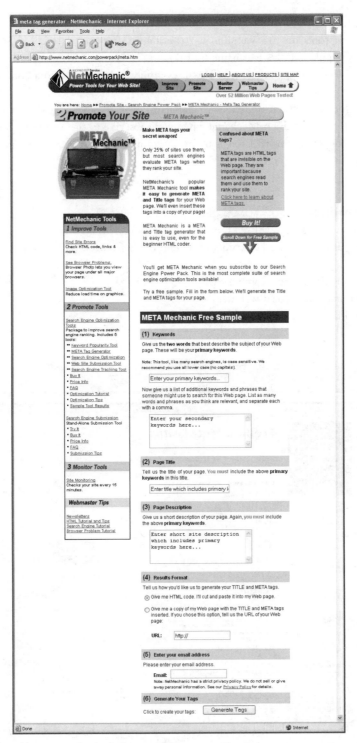

Figure 7.37 *http://www.netmechanic.com/powerpack/*

Search Engine Power Pack

There are lots of tools on this website, but a particular favourite is the META tag checker. NetMechanic's popular META Mechanic tool (Figure 7.37, page 173) makes it easy to generate META and title tags for your web page. It will even insert these tags into a copy of your page!

META Mechanic is a META and title tag generator that is easy to use, even for the novice HTML coder. You'll get META Mechanic when you subscribe to the Search Engine Power Pack package. NetMechanic claims that this is the most complete suite of search engine optimization tools available!

Trellian MetaEditor

Trellian MetaEditor (Figure 7.38) is a free tool that imports META tags from an existing HTML page and offers drag-and-drop keyword sorting and other features. Its features include:

- Importation of META tags from an existing HTML page
- Easy navigation of your local website
- Easy retrieval of pre-set default values

Figure 7.38 *http://www.trellian.com/META/*

- An intuitive interface
- A source code preview.

It can optimize your web pages to improve search engine ranking. The predefined default values will save you time, as you do not need to retype duplicate information on every page, and it manages META tag information with ease through a simple, intuitive interface.

Sprite MetaBuilder

Sprite MetaBuilder (Figure 7.39) is a reliable free tool that has been much used by professional SEO consultants, and is now available to the general public. It is good, solid, and it works – all that for free.

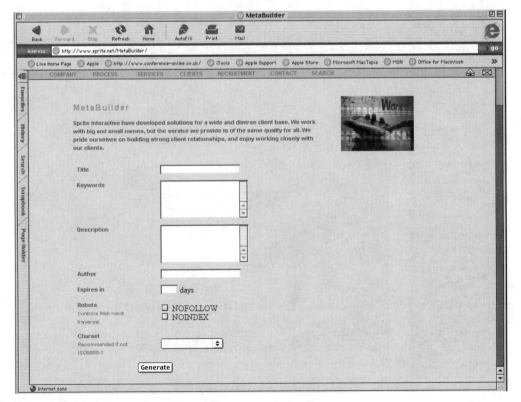

Figure 7.39 *http://www.sprite.net/MetaBuilder*

Bidding managers

BidRank

BidRank (Figure 7.40) has to be installed on your computer. It allows you to customize a rank range, a target ranking and a maximum bid for each keyword you have listed on the pay-per-click engine you are using. BidRank will push your bid up or down, depending on the settings you give it, and it will do all this automatically. It uses 'gap surfing' technology to close bid gaps, so that your bids always remained optimized. This is an authorized Overture bid management tool, and the 'plus' version has support for FindWhat, Kanoodle, Ah-ha, Espotting, BrainFox, SearchFeed, Sprinks, and Zuppa. This package has been voted the top pay-per-click management software by a number of industry sources, and is the first choice if you need bid management software.

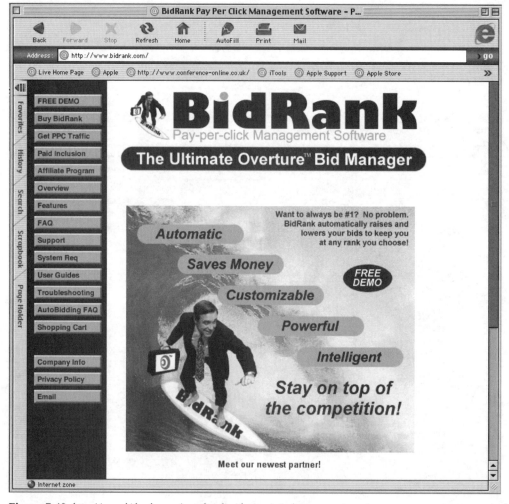

Figure 7.40 *http://www.bidrank.com (reproduced with permission)*

GO TOAST

GO TOAST (Figure 7.41) is also authorized by Overture, and the package works with other pay-per-click engines, including FindWhat, Kanoodle, and Espotting throughout Europe. The software also features support for Google AdWords. The keyword management features are strong, and it lets you set scheduling for updates to your bid amounts at up to every 30 minutes. There are a number of interesting features, such as timed rank (which will change your ranking depending on the time of day) and a bidding war eliminator. The package also includes ROI tracking, allowing you to see which keywords and engines are producing sales. The software sends you detailed email reports, and is presented through a clear and easy to understand interface. This is a very good piece of bid management software, and is cheaper than BidRank; there is a free trial version available from www.gotoast.com, so check it out.

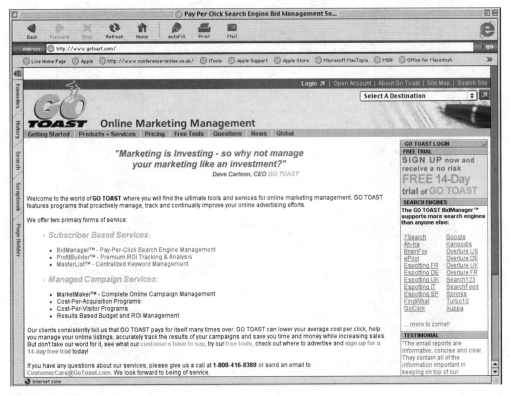

Figure 7.41 *http://www.gotoast.com*

PPCBidTracker

PPC BidTracker (Figure 7.42) is a solution that's worth considering if tracking isn't needed and listing positions are known. Bidding rules that you can implement include BidSaver, which looks at bid gaps and makes sure your site has not fallen into one. The software also enables management of multiple accounts. This is a solid package, but is not as comprehensive as GO TOAST or BidRank.

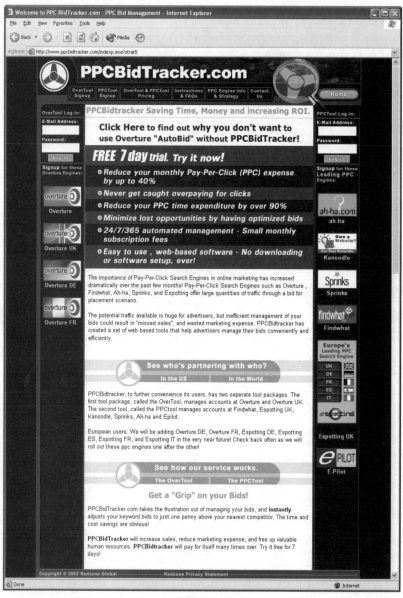

Figure 7.42 *http://www.ppcbidtracker.com/ (reproduced with permission)*

Compare Your Clicks

Compare Your Clicks (Figure 7.43) is a free tool that lets you track top bids for a keyword or phrase across the top five pay-per-click engines. It is useful for a quick bit of research.

CPC Manager

CPC Manager (Figure 7.44) is a bid management tool that automatically manages bids placed with the major pay-per-click engines. It will also track the performance of any URL, which lets you check the ROI of your bids; the program performs cost-per-visitor and cost-per-conversion calculations, but the package is very expensive. It provides trend analysis reports and is aware of bid gaps to prevent you overspending. The package is a high-end solution and comes at a price, but for those with the budget it may be worth looking into.

Keyword Bid Optimizer

Keyword Bid Optimizer (Figure 7.45) is a bid analyser tool for Overture, FindWhat, Ah-ha and ePilot. It identifies bid gaps and informs you of where you can save money in your bidding.

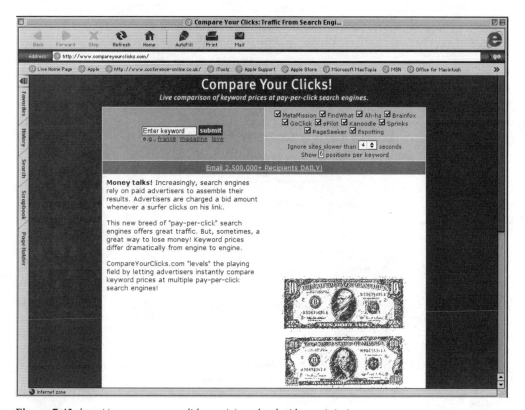

Figure 7.43 *http://www.compareyourclicks.com/ (reproduced with permission)*

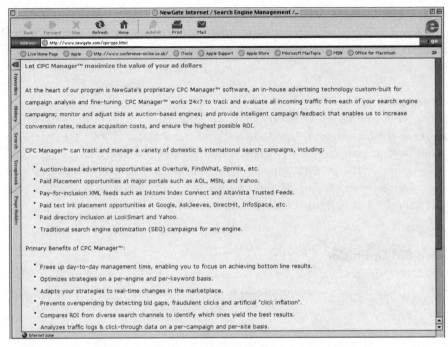

Figure 7.44 *http://www.newgate.com/cpc-ppc.html (reproduced with permission)*

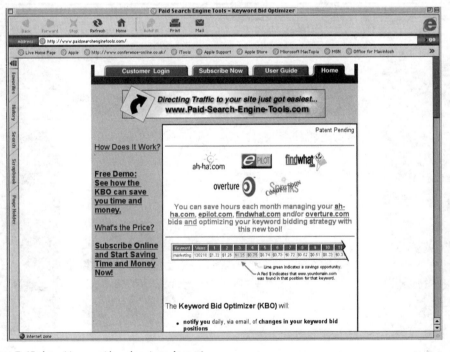

Figure 7.45 *http://www.paidsearchenginetools.com/*

PPC Bid Cap Calculator

PPC Bid Cap Calculator (Figure 7.46) is a free service that works out how much you can afford for each particular bid. There is a conversion calculator that works out your sales conversion rate, and this is then used in the Bid Cap Calculator to work out your maximum bid amounts. The service is clearly laid out with comprehensive instructions. As the service is free it is well worth checking to see how much you can afford for your bids.

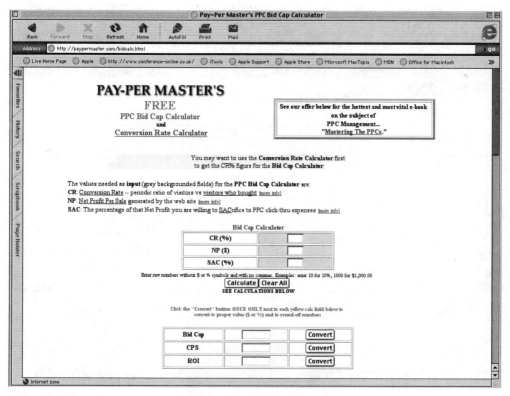

Figure 7.46 *http://paypermaster.com/bidcalc.html (reproduced with permission)*

Link and support software

Hyperseek

Hyperseek (Figure 7.47) is a piece of software that allows you to build Yahoo-like directories. You do this by developing your own hierarchy of categories, and within this you can then add links to other websites, articles, and links to industry news, and feature context-sensitive advertising. Hyperseek has built-in revenue generators throughout the program, allowing you to generate revenue for your directory. This is a useful application, and is worth looking into if you want to build your own web directory.

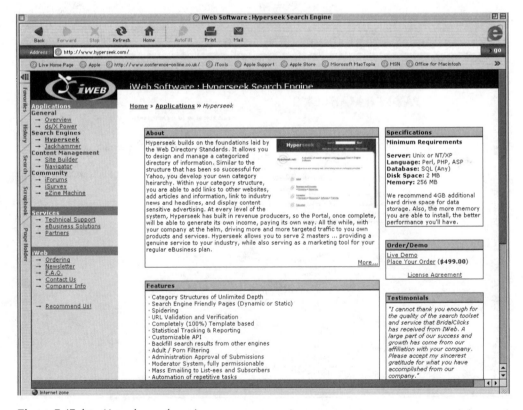

Figure 7.47 *http://www.hyperseek.com/*

Links

Links (Figure 7.48) is a package that has been modelled on Yahoo, and is a directory management tool. The package features fast searches for the end user, a comprehensive database management and repair function, a complete customization feature for your site (which can also be built using templates for the novice webmaster), and other useful features such as a 'what's cool' page. Again, this software is worth checking out if you want to build your own database of sites.

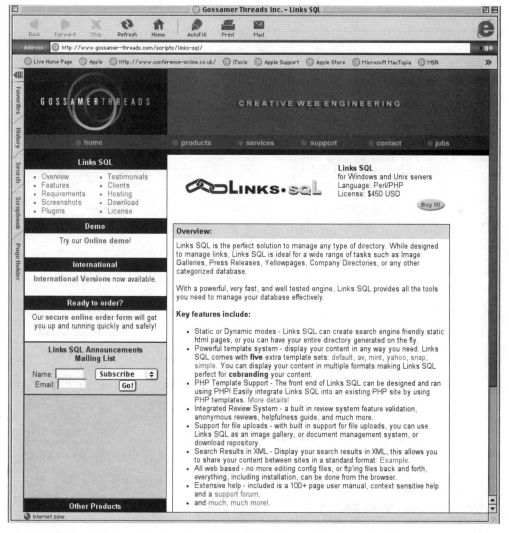

Figure 7.48 *http://www.gossamer-threads.com/scripts/links/ (reproduced with permission)*

Bookmark Us! Script

This JavaScript applet (Figure 7.49) lets Internet Explorer users bookmark your site by clicking on a link. Internet Explorer users click one text link to add your site to their 'Favorites' quickly and easily. Don't let your visitors lose you because they forget to bookmark your site – Netscape users are told the browser command to use for bookmarking. Here is the script, which can be cut and pasted from the above site:

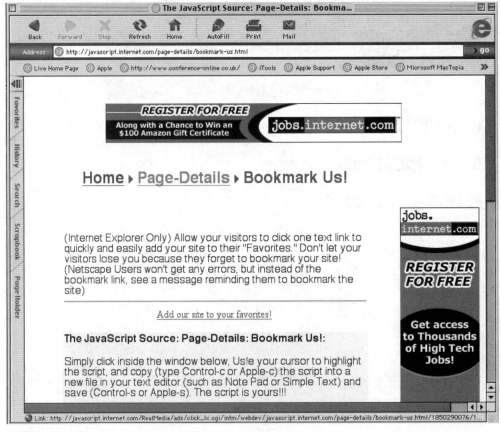

Figure 7.49 *http://javascript.internet.com/page-details/bookmark-us.html*

```
<!- ONE STEP TO INSTALL BOOKMARK US: Copy the coding into the BODY of your
    HTML document ->
<!- STEP ONE: Paste this code into the BODY of your HTML document ->
<SCRIPT LANGUAGE="JavaScript">
<!- This script and many more are available free online at ->
<!- The JavaScript Source!! http://javascript.internet.com ->
<!—Begin

if ((navigator.appName == "Microsoft Internet Explorer") &&
    (parseInt(navigator.appVersion) >= 4)) {

var url="http://www.javascriptsource.com";
var title="The JavaScript Source";
document.write('<A HREF="javascript:window.ext');
document.write('ernal.AddFavorite(url,title);" ');
document.write('onMouseOver=" window.status=');
document.write("'Add our site to your favorites!'; return true ");
document.write('"onMouseOut=" window.status=');
document.write("' '; return true ");
document.write('">Add our site to your favorites!</a>');


}


else

        {
        var msg = "Don't forget to bookmark us!";
        if(navigator.appName == "Netscape") msg += " (CTRL-D)";
        document.write(msg);
        }
        // End ->

</script>
<p><center>
<font face="arial, helvetica" size="-2">Free JavaScripts provided<br>
by <a href="http://javascriptsource.com">The JavaScript
    Source</a></font>

</center><p>
<!- Script Size: 0.91 KB ->
```

See what people are searching for

- AltaVista Real Searches, at http://www.altavista.com/sites/search/real_searches
- Ask Jeeves Peek Through The Keyhole, at http://www.askjeeves.com/docs/peek/
- Espotting Keyword Generator, at http://www.espotting.com/advertisers/register01.asp
- Galaxy StarGazer, at http://www.galaxy.com/info/voyeur.html
- Google Zeitgeist, at http://www.google.com/press/zeitgeist.html
- Kanoodle Search Spy, at http://www.kanoodle.com/spy/
- MetaCrawler MetaSpy, at http://www.metaspy.com/
- Wordtracker, at http://www.wordtracker.com/
- Yahoo Buzz Index, at http://buzz.yahoo.com/

Company: Europe Online SA

(URL: www.europeonline.com)

Business objectives

- To create a European consumer focus site, designed to give regional news and national news in local language for each European country, and Europe-wide news in English
- To identify which content to invest in and which areas of the site represent the best advertising opportunities
- To improve the effectiveness of online promotions and sponsorships.

The challenge

Europe Online was a large organization that had editors in all the countries throughout Europe. It needed a high profile and high levels of traffic to create an advertising business and a subscription business. In 1995 the dominating search engine worldwide was AltaVista, but in certain regions of Europe AltaVista was not localized (local language sites) and local search sites were directories that had a larger presence. So how was a search strategy to be implemented in a cost-effective manner?

The solution

A two-part strategy was implemented for both link popularity and page architecture. We wanted people to find Europe Online as part of a natural search for content – so if users were searching for sport they would find the sport landing pages and an option to view those pages in any of the European languages. In effect, each section page became a home page for the international pages. In this instance the focus on page architecture was all important, and the consistency of the title tag with the headlines and the META tags was an essential part of increasing the hit area for the home pages. We suddenly had fourteen country sites, each having twelve mini-sites covering everything from local theatre to education.

Link popularity was also an important feature, and the focus of this was on a local level so that every supplier, client and support site linked to the local content. Regional advertising was purchased, as well as for road shows and exhibitions. The site was Netscape 'site of the day' for nearly two weeks (in the days when Netscape had 85 per cent of the Internet market). Within twelve months it was impossible to do a search for any news, sport or lifestyle article without getting Europe Online within the top ten ranking.

Company: Disney

(URL: All European websites, including www.disney.co.uk)

Business objectives

- To ensure an informative and user-friendly website that promoted all business activities, from theme parks to movies
- To create advertising, promotions, and sponsorship opportunities.

The challenge

The Disney brand covers all aspects of the entertainment industry. What was important here was to create landing pages from things as diverse as new film releases through to retail sites for merchandise, and at the same time to support video, DVD, interactive games and the theme parks. This was a consumer service without loyalty to any of the service providers, but it was totally committed to go.com before it became a family portal.

The solution

A link strategy was implemented that linked all the publications in print, film and interactive media. In effect, the result was that each country had its many (up to twenty) sites linked up with the international sites into one big 'walled garden' that was both safe and secure for the users (mostly children or adults looking up the theme parks). Within a year we had nearly 5000 links to the site, but not a single link out of the main site.

The combination of quality and well-engineered content made the Disney sites very high-ranking in the directories, and later in the search engines. The focus was very much on building links and on paid directories, with the assumption that if these worked well then the crawlers would soon automatically rank the site.

Disney had a strong tool to promote the site, which was television. Television was the biggest driver of traffic. This also included referrals from search engines from individual searches for character names like 'Snow White'. Within a year the site moved from 5 million page impressions a month to 13 million.

Company: Grayling Group

(URL: www.graylinggroup.com)

Business objectives

- To increase the number of visitors and improve audience retention through enhanced web design and content offerings
- To become a central directory for Grayling PR activity across Europe
- To appear in the top ten of searches across Europe for PR.

The challenge

In 1998 this was a new site that was to become central to all the European PR companies within the Grayling Group. The challenge was to use web crawlers and free subscriptions as the main indexing tool. In addition we had to start a search engine strategy for the UK, but implement country-specific strategies as and when each country produced their own pages.

The solution

A strategy was implemented that turned each country page into a landing page for search engines. This meant that each set of META tags was almost unique in that they were in the local language. At that time AltaVista and Google were almost head-to-head in the popularity stakes across Europe, so we did a paid listing through Google and heavily promoted the site on AltaVista on both paid and free listings. It was more complicated to implement a successful link strategy than had been anticipated. The main drivers of traffic to the site were the crawler search engines. A strategy for promoting content through landing pages was later successful in increasing traffic. We believe that, for the type of directory site it was, it had reached its natural traffic size. The paid listing on Yahoo meant that pan-European status was achieved in a very short period of time. The growth of the Yahoo directory across Europe meant that we were able to localize all the content.

Company: Solaglas San Gobain UK

(URL: www.Solaglas.co.uk)

Business objectives

- To drive business traffic made up primarily of architects, specifiers and contractors to the definitive glass site for the construction industry
- To make every product (of 250) a landing page for search engines
- To make links from and to all the professional bodies in the construction industry.

The challenge

Solaglas needed to promote their service called GlassFacts to the industry. It was a free service that helped professionals from that industry to identify glass products. A lot of these products existed on other sites in both the UK and all over Europe, so the traffic had to be driven to the UK for the UK audience. Specifiers also needed to download specifications to put into their proposals in either pdf or word format. Therefore, the site had to be found by different means across a wide product range that was initially in database format.

The solution

The solution implemented involved publishing all the content in a flat HTML format. In 1999, no real solution existed to help the crawlers index dynamic data. We created a mini-site around each product range that was fully searchable from the non-product version of the site. This meant that the number of possible landing places was huge, but with careful wording and good architecture users would be filtered down to a few highly ranked pages. The initial task undertaken was both to set a strategy in place and then to implement it. The second part of the strategy was to set up a system to measure the success of the strategy. The links part of the strategy was more straightforward, as all suppliers and clients were happy to link to the site. Within six months the objectives had been achieved in what was at the time a fledgling industry on the Internet.

Company: DIA

(URL: www.dia.co.uk)

Business objectives
- To obtain new business for the company's print, packaging design and interactive work
- To appeal to the small professional design market.

The challenge

DIA was a multidisciplinary company whose website acted as an online portfolio for their print, packaging design and interactive work.

A search for design agencies on the Web will produce a long list of companies, from small two- or three-man operations through to big multinational companies. The main objective, therefore, was to differentiate the site from the other agencies on the Web, and to get it listed highly on specific keyword searches. The site also needed to be optimized so it could be found easily by the more niche design industry, through association websites and directories.

The solution

By 2000, when this job was commissioned, Google was becoming the dominant search engine on the Web. The main aim of the campaign was to be listed highly, so we focused on paid inclusion across the major engines. Alongside this we invested in pay-per-click listings on the top services, including GoTo (now Overture); this ensured high listings on the pay-per-click engines and their affiliates for specific keyword searches. In addition to this, the DIA site was registered on all related association websites to increase the amount of industry traffic coming into the site. Building link popularity was a very important factor, and we contacted all suppliers and related sites to build reciprocal links. Individual landing pages were also created around the various design topics covered by the site to reinforce the site's appeal and increase its visibility to design students and the industry as a whole. A year later, DIA was bought by Havas.

Company: EMB
(URL: www.emb.co.uk)

Business objectives
- To develop an international presence for EMB, an actuarial consultancy that specializes in general insurance consulting
- To promote the company's five software packages through the website
- To drive and increase the quality of traffic to the EMB site for both the software and the consultancy sides of the business.

The challenge
Traditionally, the general insurance area on the Web only serves the purpose of highlighting the location of consultancies – acting like a kind of directory. EMB wanted to be the number one ranking consultancy in the UK, which would be reinforced by a content-rich site. EMB is one of the top actuarial consultancies in the UK for general insurance, and this was to be reflected on the Web. EMB also wanted a top keyword ranking for their five software packages.

The solution
First of all, the EMB site was optimized for keyword relevance and density on each page. Relevant META and keyword tags were implemented site-wide, and the site was then submitted to the main search engines by paid inclusion to ensure a quick listing. To ensure that the software was easy to find and ranked well, landing pages were developed for each individual package. These were then submitted to the main search engines, which had the effect of driving more relevant traffic to the site. To optimise the site further, cross-links were set up with major industry bodies and other relevant websites; this ensured that the site consistently ranked highly, and also created new sources of quality traffic. The EMB site now ranks highly for actuarial keyword searches, and the software section of the site has had a large increase in relevant traffic.

Company: Voltimum

(URL: www.voltimum.com)

Business objectives

- To develop an international presence for the Voltimum website
- To drive relevant traffic to Voltimum's country-specific sites.

The challenge

Voltimum is an electrical industry portal for all professionals who work in the electrical installation industry. It was set up to assist with the day-to-day working life of electrical industry professionals, and to support their existing trading relationships. Voltimum.com is the hub of six country-specific sites, each of which launched on different dates and had different levels of SEO; this meant that the situation arose where a French electrician could search for Voltimum and be pointed towards the Germany-specific site. The challenge was to harmonize the country-specific sites and make sure that the traffic being returned to each site was relevant. Each site also ran off the back of a database, so this presented the problem of getting around the fact that the pages were dynamically generated.

The solution

First, country-specific landing points were created. Mini-sites were created for each country; these were optimized to be fully searchable and linked into each main country site. These were then submitted to the major search engines and directories, and each country's site was submitted to relevant country-specific search engines. This had the effect of returning much more country-specific traffic to each site. A link popularity campaign was also initiated, and manufacturers (whose products were featured in the product catalogue section of the site), industry associations and other relevant sites, such as the trade press, were approached to link into the Voltimum sites. The result of this strategy was that each country's site received considerably more relevant traffic, and the Voltimum brand's visibility on all the major search engines increased significantly.

Appendix A

eStrategy presentation

eStrategy

for

Search Optimization

Sprite Interactive Ltd

Presented by: Alex Michael and Ben Salter

Search engines explained

- Search engines are used by 80 per cent of web surfers as their first point of reference to locate a website

- Most users get to see only 5 per cent of all websites searched for on the Internet

- Web directories like Yahoo only have 30 per cent of the Web on their systems

What are SEO and SEP?

- Search engine optimization is the science of search positioning on the Internet

- Search engine positioning and analysis is the process of search optimization

Search engines *vs* directories

- Search engines create listings by using robots or web crawlers

- Directories create listings from registration to directory-based websites

- Hybrid search engines utilize both robots and editors to create listings

The three-part plan

1 Subscription to commercial registrations

2 Page architecture and content structure

3 Links popularity

Links popularity

- Popularity drives the web crawlers to your site

- Improves listings in search engines and directories, and is ultimately the biggest source of traffic to your site

Three parts to a search engine

1 Spider/crawler/robot – traverses the Web regularly by following links

2 Index – spidered pages are stored in the index, with UTRL for fast retrieval

3 Engine software – program organizes and sifts through millions of records to find pages and ranks them in order of relevance

Differences between search engines

- Search engines use their own algorithms to rank sites

- Search engines have different partners

- Some use fee-based submissions and some have free submissions

The importance of META tags

- Not all search engines use META tags, but most will use them in combination with page content

- The two key tags are the Keyword and Description tags

- Each page should have its own tailored landing pages

Multiple landing pages

- The site should be split into clear content areas

- Each area should have its own META data

- Submit each page from each section individually

- Use articles and features as mini-sites

Research terms

- Find all keyword combinations for your product range

- Compile a database of terms that people search for and the traffic each search engine brings you for that term

Pay-per-click engines

- Register to the top three pay-per-click services

- Measure the value of keywords against costs and conversions

- Work to clear budgets against goals

Keyword strategy

- Search engine optimization is the science of search positioning on the Internet

- Search engine positioning and analysis is the process of search optimization

Position of keyword

- Strategic keywords appear in crucial locations on the page

- The HTML page title must be relevant

- The content page title must be clear

- The first few paragraphs should include keywords

Relevance of content

- Search engines do not read graphics, so use alt tags for pictures

- Make all text visible

- Check out similar industry sites

- Make sure content matches keywords

Search engine stumbling blocks

- Make sure you have text or HTML links

- Create a site map with links to all content

- Avoid all frames

- Create static pages if all your content is database driven

- Avoid symbols in URLs

Maintain your listing

- Resubmit on a regular basis

- See what sites are appearing with your keywords

- Make sure your site is correctly categorized

- Resubmit after every major change

Performance reports

- Run reports at least monthly to identify trends

- You must include analysis reports, terms reports, verification and submission reports

- You must have ranking reports and keyword reports weekly

Site stats

- Know which search engines are referring to your site

- Study traffic factors that affect landing pages

- Find click-throughs from the landing pages

- Measure popular links to your site

Revamping strategy

- Update or redesign the content on your site

- Re-think your page titles

- Purchase multiple domains

- Create gateway pages

- Re-work your META tags

Search engine planning cycle

- Create

- Optimize

- Submit:
  Paid indexing
  Paid listings
  Paid keywords

- Analysis

Other traffic drivers

- Site reviews

- Sponsorship

- Association links

- Affiliate programs

- Banners and strategic placement

Appendix B
Overture and Espotting style guidelines

Espotting style guide

General tone and style

All submissions should be written in the third person, in an impartial manner. British spelling should always be followed. All site descriptions should be in full sentences, and not presented as a list of keywords. Espotting promotes this method of writing listings so that they do not appear to be just a list of advertisements.

For example:

> Sprite Interactive is a new media consultancy, specializing in web to print solutions.

You should avoid jargon and technical words and phrases, and stick to simple, plain English. As you have a restricted word count, make sure that every word is necessary.

Abbreviation

You should avoid abbreviations. Shorthand will also be rejected; avoid expressions such as 'e.g.' and 'etc.'. If you are referring to a company, than you should state the legal status of the company without any punctuation (for example, Co, Ltd, Plc).

Affiliates

Advertisers listing an affiliate site must have this clearly marked in their title and descriptions (for example, 'Official Amazon affiliate').

Apostrophes and quotation marks

Use double quotation marks for quoting speech and single quotation marks for words not intended to be stated in their literal sense. Make sure you use plural and possessive punctuation correctly (for example, CD's should actually be CDs).

Capitalization

All titles and descriptions should be in lower case, apart from brands/company names, days of the week, names, months, place names, geological periods, works, professions (in titles) and nationalities. You should not write words in all upper case, unless this is part of a brand name. Follow standard conventions for place names, titles and professions.

Dates, times, weights, measures and currencies

Decades should be written without the century, with an apostrophe before the decade to state that the century has been removed (for example, write '80s rather than 80s). You should express dates as numbers (for example, 1 April not 1st April). When stating time use the conventional clock in am and pm, with no spaces (for example, 10.30am). Units of measure should be abbreviated (for example, m, km, g), and actual measures should be written as a figure immediately followed by the unit (for example, 10km). When referring to prices and currencies write the unit as a symbol (£, $) and the amount as a number, using commas to mark thousands. You can write all figures as digits if there is not enough space, but Espotting states that numbers from one to ten should be written in full if there is space.

Foreign words/companies

Foreign words should appear in italics.

Online terminology

'Online' and 'website' are both single words. The Internet and the Web are only capitalized when used as nouns; they lose their capitalization as adjectives (for example, Sprite Interactive is an internet company). The term 'email' should be presented as one word and not hyphenated; 'e-commerce' should be hyphenated.

Spacing and general punctuation

Sentences should be single-spaced. There should not be spaces before colons, commas or slashes. You can use ampersands (&), and dashes should be separated by spaces. Espotting does not encourage the use of exclamation marks unless they are part of a company's brand. All composite adjectives before the noun (used attributively) should be hyphenated (for example, 'London-based web company'). All companies or organizations should be treated as singular.

Superlatives

Please note that superlatives and assertions such as 'The UK's leading. . .' or 'The UK's no.1 shop for. . .' are not deemed in harmony with our house style and are therefore no longer acceptable. To retain the reporting tone of our listings the editorial team will remove such phrasing. 'One of the UK's leading stores for. . .', however, is acceptable.

Overture style guidelines

Capitalization

Overture states that your company name should appear in the same way that it does on your website, and words in all upper case are not permitted unless they are trademarked or copy written in this style.

Punctuation

Apostrophes

You should ensure that you use plural and possessive punctuation correctly (for example, CD's should actually be CDs). When referring to a decade, do not use an apostrophe before the numeral or before the 's' (for example, write 1950s rather than 1950's).

Commas

A comma should not follow the second-to-last item in a list unless it is needed for clarity.

Dashes

Place one space before and after a single dash; double dashes are not permitted.

Ellipses

Ellipses must use exactly three dots in a row with no spaces before, between or after (for example, 'look out. . .there's more to come').

Exclamation points and question marks

Exclamation points are only acceptable if they are part of the proper name of a company or title, and should not be used simply for emphasis. If you are using a question mark you should only use one, and not multiple instances.

Quotation marks

Quotations should only be used for titles (for example, for books or albums).

Slashes

Only use slashes for fractions, dates, common combinations (writer/editor, DVD/VCR), and to indicate alternatives (inside/outside).

Symbols

Do not use the symbols '&' or '$' in place of the words 'and' or 'money'. Do not use symbols excessively (for example, '$$$', '++great deal++').

Appendix C

Site link campaign management charts

These can be downloaded from the Sprite Interactive website at http://www.sprite.net/
linkcharts

Site link chart

Name of site to link from	Nature of site	Email address of webmaster

Link request chart

Name of site	Name and email of webmaster	Home page URL	URL of page to link from	PageRank score	Date of initial link request

Link management chart

Name of site	Name and email of webmaster	Date link activated	Date link verified

Appendix D

These tables can be used to administer your search engine optimization campaign. You can download these from the Sprite Interactive website to print out, at http://www.sprite.net/ seoadmin

Keywords and META tags management table

Page: Date:
Page title:
Possible keywords:
Keywords META tag:
Descriptor META tag:

Search engine submission management table

Name of search engine:

Page submitted	Date of submission	Date of verification

Directories submission management table

Name of directory:

Page submitted	Category location	Date of submission	Date of verification

Pay-per-click engine management table

Name of pay-per-click engine:

Web page submitted	Keywords targeted	Bid amount	Rank position on engine	Date submitted

Appendix E
Search engine listings

There are a number of industry- and country-specific search engines on the Web that can be a great place to get your website listed. The engines and directories listed in this appendix are genuine and are well worth being listed in, as they receive a lot of related traffic. We have not listed any Free-For-All links sites, also known as link farms; you can read more about these in Chapter 5. It is worth professionally submitting your site to these engines, as industry-related or regional sites can provide a good new source of traffic to your website.

The first listing is of the major web search engines that return web-wide results. The second listing is of business-related directories – so, for example, if your website is food-based, it would be worth your while submitting to the Food Contact site, FoodBot.com, the Gourmet Association, the PastryWiz Food Search and The Webtender Index. All these sites will direct relevant traffic to your site. Finally, we have listed a number of sites that are specific to regions or countries; these return results specific to these areas and are widely used by residents of each particular country or region. They are worth submitting your site to as they return regional-specific traffic, which many of the other sites do not.

Search engines

Alexa
AllTheWeb/Lycos
Claymont
Entireweb.com
EZSearches
Google/AOL/ Netscape/iWon
HotBot
Inter-Change
LookSeek.com
MSN

NationalDirectory
NetSearch
REX
Searchalot
Search It
SurfGopher
TrueSearch.com
Voila!
WalHello
What-U-Seek

Business-related directories

Agriculture
AgFind.com
Agric. Search Site
Agriscape
AgriSurf

Arts/design/fashion
1stArtDepot.com
Art Guide
ArtQuarry
aRT wEB Community
Fashion Navigator
Retif's Art Index
WW Arts Resources

Automated general directories
InfoSpace
Jayde Online Directory
MallPark
Nerd World Media
On A Mission
Scrub The Web
SearchEngineProject.com
ZenSearch

Automotive
Cardealerships.com
Motor Vehicle Dealers Network
Red-Line

Award/review sites
Adze Cosmic Site of the Nite
Cool Site of the Nite
Windows Magazine HotSpot Page

Community/family
Berit's Best
Federal Web Locator

FeMiNa
Munisource
PeachPod
Via Family
Yahooligans!
Yourfamily.com

Computers/Internet
Afterpage
Cool Tool of the Day
Guide to Computer Vendors
WSearch

Construction
AecWW
Building Online
BuildNET
TradesMaster

Employment/education
CollegeNET
Education World
Studyabroad.com

Finance/accounting
AAAWorld Banks
Invest-o-rama
MoneySearch
Mortgage Mag
Stocks.com
StreetEYE
Zagury Financial Directory

Food/beverage
FoodBot.com
Food Contact
Gourmet Association
PastryWiz Food Search
The Webtender Index

General

Acclaim Search
AtoZ.Com
CoolPick.com
Funsites.com
HotRate.com
IQSeek
LinkMaster
TheEverywherePages
The Rail

General business

AllBizOpps.com
BizWiz!
QuikPages
Where2Go

Malls/marketplaces

Buyers Index
CyberXpress Mall
ePublicEye.com
i-Stores Shopping Guide
Market Suite
Planet Shopping
ShopInternet
Shoplocally.com
The WebWatchdog
World Market Mall

Manufacturing/industrial

CircuitOnline
ElectricNet
Int'l Leather Ind. Dir.
Manufacturers Information Net
Techspex
Thomas Regional
Thomas Register of Amer. Mfr's.

Music/entertainment

ClubsIndex.com
Hollywood Access Directory

MusicScene
MusicSearch
MusicTracer
Ragtime Music Links
The Local Music Directory

Personal only

Internet Address Finder
Mail.at
The Student Homepage Directory
Who Where?
World Wide Profile Registry

Publishing/media

BRS Radio Directory
DIY Search
Radiodirectory
The Dealmakers

Real estate

IRED
Reals.com
VirtualHomeSite
VivaSearch.com
WebEstate

Regional

Fireball.de

Religion/spirituality

ActiveSS
All Things Spiritual
Christian Resource Index
Churches dot Net
CrossSearch
Goshen
Hareshima
Messianic Friends Network

Our Church.Com
Sadhu!
Self Improvement Online
Spiritual Search

Science/medicine
Drug InfoNet
HealthAtoZ
HealthCare Marketplace
Health On Net Foundation
InfoMedical
Med Help
The Exploratorium's Ten Cool Sites

Small business
AllSmallBiz.com
JackStreet
SmallBusiness.com

Specialty business
A Jewelry Mall
CustomMade.com
Executive Suite Network
FindLaw
Gardenseek.com
Insur. Adjusters Resource Cntr.
LogisticsWorld
Progressive Grocer

The Aviation Directory
The Transportation Pg.

Sporting/outdoors
GolfSearch
LargemouthBass.Com
Outdoor Resources Online
PlacesToGolf.com
Search Sport
Ski-Central
SPORTQuest
The UK Football Pages Directory
WeightsNet

Travel/leisure
Accommodation Search Engine
AnteUp Gambling Links
CoinLink
Collectiques
Contestworld
Fish Link Central
Gambling.com
HotelsTravel.com
I-Net Travel Exchange
North America Resort Locator
PetStation
RailServe
The Woodworking Catalog
Travel Accommodation Directory
Travelmag Webwide

Country-/regional-specific search engines

Africa
Egypt Classifieds
Egyptian InfoCenter
M-Web
S.A. Directory
WoYaa!

Asia
Asia Directory
Asia Guide
AsianNet
Myanmar FFA
WhatSite.com

Australia/New Zealand
About Australia
Alta Vista Australia
Australian Web Directory
Cowley Australia
Cowley's Internet for Australian Farmers
Excite Australia
HitWise
NZ Explorer
OzGuide
The Australian Web Directory
Yahoo! Australia & NZ

Austria
AustroNaut

Belgium
Web Watch Belgium

Canada
Alcanseek
AltaVista Canada
Big Skeeters
Buy Canuck
Canada Business Directory
Canadianeh.com
Canadian Women's Business Network
Canuck Site of the Day
Everything Alberta
Excite Canada
InfoSpace Canada
O.S.A.I.C.
SaskSearch
Search BC
Sympatico-Lycos
Torinfo.com
Visca Online
Yahoo! Canada

Europe
EuroSeek
EUSearch4You.com

Vinkel.nu
Yelloweb Europe

France
Ecila
Excite – France
Lycos France
NetScan
Nomade
Voila France!
Yahoo! France

Germany
Aladin
Crawler.de
Excite Deutschland
FIREBALL
Infoseek DE
Kolibri
Lycos DE
Spider.de
Yahoo! Deutschland

Greece
Atlas – The Greek Index
Hellas On Business
Webindex Greece

Iceland
Iceland on the Web

India
123India.com
Indian Index
Jadoo
NewIndia

Ireland
Infosite Ireland
SearchIreland.com

Italy
Arianna
Il Ragno Italiano
Italian Business
Lycos Italy
Multisoft
Yahoo! Italia

Japan
NTT Directory

Korea
KINFO
Oomph!

Latin America
Auyantepui
Honduras Interactive Travel and Commerce
Latin World

Malta
Malta Network Resources

Manual search engines
Altavista (all languages)
Open Directory

Middle East
ArabSites.com
MEdirectory.com

MidWest USA
AllDetroit.com
Great Lakes Commerce Network
Ohio.com
SearchNWI.com

SoDa PoP
Virtual Michigan
VirtualOhio.com

NorthEast USA
Boston-Online.com
Cnynet.com
Connecticut Business Links
CT-Info.com
Delaware.com
FindMaine.com
GreaterPittsburgh.com
IndexVermont.com
Info Grove
NJave.com
Pennsylvania Visitors Network
SearchNH

Pakistan
Pakistan Web Directory
PakPowerPage.com

Portugal
Gertrudes

South Africa
Max

SouthEast USA
D.C. Registry
FloridaNetlink.com
FloridaSmart.com
Greater Hampton Roads
Orbit
TampaBayWired.com
West Virginia Online

SouthWest USA

4 OK Links
Cactus Corner
New Mexico Net
New Mexico Web Guide
NMGrande.com
Search Texas

Spain

Ozu

Sweden

Lycos Sweden
Punkt.se
SUNET's WWW Catalog

Switzerland

Swiss Search

UK

@UK
BritIndex

Excite UK
Infoseek United Kingdom
I-Stores.co.uk
Lycos UK
Mugomilk UK
NetLondon
SearchUK
ShopGuide
UKMax
Yahoo! UK & Ireland

West USA

@LA
Alaska Internet Directory
California Mall
List Vegas!
Montana Native
MontanaNative.com
Oregon Business Directory
OregonPages
Pathfinder
Planet Hawaii

Appendix F

Glossary of terms

404: The server will generate a 404 error when a visitor attempts to view a page that is unavailable.

Ad inventory: The number of page views a site has available for advertising.

Adult words: Words that are censored by search engines. Adult words are called STOP WORDS by the search engines because the indexer stops when it finds one.

Affiliate: Someone who sets up a business that is in between the original manufacturer and the end customer.

Algorithm: The way a search engine decides where a site is ranked for a particular search. Each search engine uses a different set of algorithms; factors such as a site's title, body copy, META tags and link popularity are all important.

Altavista: One of the most popular search engines, found at www.altavista.com.

ALT tag: An HTML tag that allows a browser to display text instead of a graphic. As spiders cannot read graphics, ALT tags should be used to give the spider something to read.

Apache web server: Web server software.

Ask Jeeves: A search engine that accepts queries phrased as questions, found at www.askjeeves.com.

ASP: Active Server Pages – a scripting language that provides dynamic content for database-driven websites.

B2B: Business to business. Products and services for other businesses.

B2C: Business to consumer. Products and services for the general public.

BBS: Bulletin Board System – an online text exchange.

Boolean search: The search operators AND, OR, and/or NOT, that can be used to refine a search.

Bridge page: Another name for a doorway page.

CGI: Common Gateway Interface. CGI programs are used to generate web page content dynamically.

CGI-BIN: A directory on a web server that contains CGI files. These directories usually have much tighter access privileges than normal files.

Click-through: This is what happens when a user selects a link on a web page. The click is the noise of the mouse being pressed, and the 'through' is the act of passing from one page to another. Many advertising systems are based on the number of click-throughs a banner ad has.

Client: A browser is a client, and a web server is a server. The client computer gets information from the server computer.

Cloaking: A way of hiding code or content from a user or search engine spider. There are three types of cloaking: IP based, user-agent based, and a combination of the two.

Clustering: The process that some search engines use to cluster pages from the same website in groups in order to keep any one site from dominating the top results with more than one listing.

Counter: A counter counts hits on a website and reports the results back to the webmaster.

CPC: Cost Per Click. Search engines such as Overture.com charge sites for the number of users sent to them, depending on how many times the sites listing is clicked on.

Crawler: Also known as *robots* or *spiders*, these are the tools that search engines send out to find websites, record them, and index them within their databases. They also follow links between websites, which is why it's good to have a high 'link popularity'. Different crawlers crawl in different ways, depending on the engines they have come from.

Cross linking: Linking to content from within the same site.

Dead link: An HTML link that does not point anywhere, as the destination page does not exist. Dead links used to be a serious problem on search engines, but spiders can now check to see whether a link is dead.

Deep linking: Linking to content buried deep within a website – more than a couple of directories into the hierarchy of a site.

Directory: A web search tool compiled manually by human editors. Websites are submitted with a title and description, and are then assessed by an editor and listed under one or more subject categories if accepted. Good examples of directories are Yahoo and the Open Directory Project. Users can browse through the directory of websites, which is organized in a hierarchical manner.

Domain: Domain is a generic term to describe a level of domain. Domain names can play an important part in determining a site's rankings on the search engines. There are top level domains (such as .com, .net, or .co.uk), and then there are midlevel domains such as Ford (ford.com, ford.net or ford.org).

Domain name registration: The act of registering a domain name with an approved registrar.

Doorway domain: A domain designed to redirect traffic to another page that is located on a different domain.

Doorway page: A page designed as an entrance to a website, which is located on a different page. Many doorway pages are specifically created to rank high on a search engines. Also known as a bridge page.

Downloading: The process of retrieving information.

Dynamic content: A page that is generated just as the user views it. The content delivered to the user is often updated on-the-fly, out of a database of content.

Entry page: A specific entry page to a website, which may take the form of a single page with a logo and 'click here' to enter.

Error log file: Web servers run separate logs that show website errors, which can then be viewed at a later date.

Excite: One of the original major search engines, found at www.excite.com.

FFA: Free-For-All sites are often included within the lists used by some companies or software, offering submission of your website to 'thousands of sites'. Submissions to FFA sites will usually result in your website only being listed for a short time, and in return your email address will receive hundreds of 'junk' marketing emails, many of which will require a manual opt-out. FFAs are not worth using.

Frames: This is the HTML technique that creates a static area on a web page, usually containing navigation buttons and a title bar. Frames can cause problems for search engine optimization, as they restrict the ability of some crawlers to index the site.

Gateway domain names: A domain name the purpose of which is to direct traffic to a main site.

Gateway pages: These pages are also known as *bridge pages* or *doorway pages*, and are submitted to search engines separately from the main site. They are used for a variety of reasons, such as to emphasize particular keywords or phrases or to target the optimization requirements of a specific search engine. They can also be used as a way to submit a site that has database-driven pages or that uses Flash. They can be viewed as being spam if used incorrectly, so should be prepared carefully.

Google: Now the most widely used search engine on the web, found at www.google.com.

Heading tag: An HTML tag of six sizes. It is possible that search engines rank a keyword higher if it appears in a larger heading.

Hidden text/tiny text: Placing coloured characters on the same-coloured background causes them to be hidden. This technique was popular for a while to increase keyword coverage on a site, but has been identified now and is viewed as spam.

Hit: A request for a file on a web server. If someone visits your page, it is a 'hit' on that page.

HotBot: Another popular and powerful search engine, located at www.hotbot.com.

HTML: HyperText Markup Language – the programming language of tag commands used in web pages, which web browsers read in order to present pages to a web user.

HTML link: A hyperlink within a web page.

HTTP: HyperText Transfer Protocol – the standard system to transfer data between a web server and a web browser.

Image map: A system of associating parts of an image with hyperlinks. Pictures can be split into specific areas that then link to different pages on a site.

Inbound link: Links pointing to a website. When a user arrives at a website from another site, that link is called an inbound link.

Indexer: The part of a search engine that is responsible for processing pages that a spider has visited. It will store any pages in the searchable database.

Infoseek: An older but still popular search engine, found at www.infoseek.com and now owned by Disney and the Go.com group.

Inktomi: A search engine database of sites that just services other search engines, providing search results. Inktomi provides more searches per search engine than any other site on the Internet, and can be found at www.inktomi.com.

Invisible web: The group of dynamic or large database sites and online documents that search engines will not index.

IP address: Whenever you connect to the Internet, you are giving a unique four-number Internet Protocol address (IP address). If your IP address stays the same from connection to connection you have a static IP address. If it changes each time you connect, you have a dynamic IP address. IP addresses let search engines know where you are coming from; they can then deliver customized content depending on your location (Yahoo does this).

IP delivery: The process of delivering customized content based upon the user's IP address.

ISP: Internet Service Provider – the name designed by a Madison Avenue advertising and marketing firm for Internet point-of-access sellers.

Java: A computer language designed to be delivered from websites to a user's browser. Small programs written in Javascript can be run from within the browser window.

Javascript: A language embedded within HTML that is executed after a page of HTML has been transferred to a user's browser, and adds extra functionality to a web page.

Keyword: A singular word or phrase that is typed into a search engine. Mainly refers to popular words that relate to any one website.

Keyword density: A percentage measure of how many times a keyword is repeated within the text of a page – for example, if a page contains 100 words and 10 of those words are 'house', then 'house' is said to have a 10 per cent keyword density.

Linkage: A count of the number of links pointing (inbound links) at a website. Many search engines, most notably Google, now count linkage in their algorithms.

Link farm: Otherwise known as free-for-all links. These are places that allow anyone to add a link.

Link popularity: The term used to describe the number of hypertext links coming into a website from other websites. Building link popularity is a great way to get a higher listing on many search engines. Google is the most high profile engine to place a large emphasis on link popularity.

Logger: A program that logs web page views.

LookSmart: One of the largest directories on the Internet, found at www.looksmart.com.

Lycos: A large search engine, found at www.lycos.com.

Metasearch: A process of searching several databases simultaneously and combining the results.

Metasearch engine: A type of search tool that conducts a search across a number of search engines and directories in one go; it does not hold its own index.

META tag: Author-generated HTML commands that are placed in the head section of an HTML document. The META keywords and META description can affect a site's listing on most major search engines. The Robots META tag is used to control certain aspect of how a search engine indexes the page, and can stop a spider from indexing certain parts of it.

Mirror site: A duplicate copy of a website at a different address, which allows websites to spread their resources. Search engines view the multiple duplicate pages of mirror sites as spamming.

Misspellings: The technique of making a spelling mistake in META keywords or META tags to catch search engine users who also misspell words when searching.

Multiple keyword tags: Using two or three keyword META tags to increase the relevancy of a page. This technique is considered spam by most search engines, and should be avoided.

Obfuscation: The act of misrepresenting META tags or content. The user is presented with a page that looks normal, but it is not the page submitted to search engines.

Open Directory Project: The Open Directory Project (ODP) is a site directory run by volunteer editors, and found at www.dmoz.org.

Optimization: Creating a page that is specifically intended to rank well at search engines. Basics optimization includes keywords and a description paragraph, no frames, and making sure that keywords are repeated across the page (e.g. in alt tags).

Opt-in: A program that gives the user the choice of whether to participate.

Opt-out: Any program or process that requires a user to take action to stop being included in some action – e.g. opt-out email lists.

Outbound link: A link that points away from your website.

Overture: A search engine that sells keywords via auctions, found at www.overture.com.

Page view: The number of times a page is viewed.

Perl: One of the main CGI programming languages, which has an easy-to-use syntax built from several common languages.

Pigeon ranking: Web searching in clusters – the name comes from the way pigeons scavenge for food. Google uses this technique to index sites.

Pop-up: An ad that opens in a new browser window.

Portal: A once popular term to refer to a site that is an entry point to other sites on the Internet. Portals are also known as online communities, and usually offer a range of services. Yahoo could be described as a portal.

Positioning: The position of the site's entry in the results list returned by a search engine query.

PPC: Pay Per Click. A pay-per-click search engine charges websites on a per-click basis. Charges operate on an auction-style basis.

Proximity search: Defines how close words are together in any search query result.

Query: The act of typing search terms or keywords into a search engine in order to get a result. A single search of the search engine's database is called a query.

Ranking: In the context of search engines, it is the position of a site's entry in a search engine results screen.

Reciprocal link: When two websites swap links so they point at each other.

Referrer: The address of the web page from which a user came to another site. Referrer strings can report where a visitor to your site has come from, and record what a user has typed into a search engine to get your site.

Refresh tag: The META refresh tag reloads a page at a set time.

Registration: The act of submitting a website to a directory for inclusion (such as registering with Yahoo).

Relevancy: The accuracy of results that a search engine returns.

Results page: A page at a search engine that displays the results of a search. This is the page that appears after the user has typed a search query into the engine. The order the results are presented in is called the rankings.

Robot: In the context of search engines, robots are the programs that go out onto the Web and follow links to record web pages, which are then stored in the search engine's database. A spider is a type of robot.

robots.txt: A file in the root directory of a website that is used to control which pages spiders can access. When a spider or robot connects to a website, it checks for the presence of a robot.txt.

ROI: Return On Investment. In relation to search engine advertising, this refers to the amount of return in relation to the amount of money invested in a particular campaign. This can be hard to measure in relation to search engine optimization.

Search engine: A web-based search tool that visits websites and records and indexes them to its database. It then uses this database to provide results based on user queries. Examples of search engines are Google and AltaVista.

Search engine marketing: SEM is the term used to describe the process of making a website visible on search engines and directories so that it will attract more visitors. There are a number of different techniques, including site optimization, submission to directories and search engines, and the use of pay-per-click services.

Search engine optimization: SEO is the term used to describe the preparation of a website in order to improve its chances of being ranked highly in search engine listings.

Search terms: The words that are typed into a search engine search box. Also called search words, keywords, and queries

SEO: Search engine optimization, the act of preparing a website for search engine submission.

Server: A computer that is designed to provide information for clients' computers. Servers store documents, which are then supplied to the client computer.

Spamdexing: The submission of pages that have been modified in an unethical way to rank highly. Techniques include submitting hundreds of different pages designed to rank high, or small invisible text to increase the keyword count of a page.

Spamming: See spamdexing. A broad term mainly used to describe unsolicited junk email.

Spider: The main program used by search engines to retrieve web pages to include in their database (see Robot).

Spidering: The process of a spider downloading a web page. Most modern spiders download pages and store them raw in a database. Different search engines use different custom spiders.

Static IP address: An IP address that remains the same each time a person logs on to the Internet.

Stop words: A stop word is a word that causes an indexer to stop indexing in the current procedure and do something else – most commonly when an indexer encounters an Adult word.

Submission: The act of submitting a web page to a search engine, or a website to a directory.

Submission service: A service that will automatically submit your page or website to many search engines at once. These were once popular, but many search engines now ban these types of services. One that is still widely used is Submit It, part of Microsoft's bCentral suite.

Theme engine: A theme engine is a search engine that indexes entire sites as one giant page. Theme engines then use only the most relevant keywords found to determine your site's theme. By determining a theme, search engines hope to return more accurate results.

Title: The part of an HTML page that is displayed on a browser title line. The text of a title is important, as it is the text displayed on the search results page as the link to that page.

Traffic: The number of visitors a website receives.

Unique user: A single individual website visitor. Unique users are important, as these give an indication of success of a website. If you have a high unique user count but a low hit count this means people are not staying on your site; the opposite would mean less people are visiting your site, but they are staying on it longer and looking at more pages.

Upload: The process of retrieving information from any computer is called downloading. When one computer sends information to another, it is called uploading.

URL: Universal Resource Locator. URLs form the basis of how we find websites; your URL is basically a web address, and by typing it into a web browser you will be taken to that page.

URL submission: The process of submitting a web page to search engines.

Yahoo: One of the oldest site directories on the Internet, found at www.yahoo.com.

Index

Yahoo, xii, 12, 39, 41–53, 56, 65, 102, 105, 134,
190, 233
directory, 44–5
Dynamic Submission, 2000, 145
and Espotting, 78
free submission, 91
and Google, 42, 44, 50, 51, 52, 133
how searches work, 43
listing, 48–52
location of link partners, 100, 106
origin, 4

and Overture, 49, 75
preparing your website for submission, 45
special tactics to get listed, 52–3
submission methods, 46–8
submitting your website, 45–6
Yahoo Express submission program, 46, 47
Yahoo Buzz Index, 186
Yang, Jerry, 41, 42

Zeal, 60, 62–3, 65, 103, 104, 106

Marketing titles from Butterworth-Heinemann

Student list

Creating Powerful Brands (second edition), Leslie de Chernatony and Malcolm McDonald

Customer Relationship Management, Simon Knox, Stan Maklan, Adrian Payne, Joe Peppard and Lynette Ryals

Direct Marketing in Practice, Brian Thomas and Matthew Housden

eMarketing eXcellence, PR Smith and Dave Chaffey

Essential Law for Marketers, Ardi Kolah

Fashion Marketing, Margaret Bruce and Tony Hines

Innovation in Marketing, Peter Doyle and Susan Bridgewater

Internal Marketing, Pervaiz Ahmed and Mohammed Rafiq

International Marketing (third edition), Stanley J. Paliwoda and Michael J. Thomas

Integrated Marketing Communications, Tony Yeshin

Key Customers, Malcolm McDonald, Beth Rogers and Diana Woodburn

Marketing Briefs, Sally Dibb and Lyndon Simkin

Marketing in Travel and Tourism (third edition), Victor T. C. Middleton with Jackie R. Clarke

Marketing Plans (fifth edition), Malcolm McDonald

Marketing: the One Semester Introduction, Geoff Lancaster and Paul Reynolds

Market-Led Strategic Change (third edition), Nigel F. Piercy

Relationship Marketing for Competitive Advantage, Adrian Payne, Martin Christopher, Moira Clark and Helen Peck

The Fundamentals and Practice of Marketing (fourth edition), John Wilmshurst and Adrian Mackay

The New Marketing, Malcolm McDonald and Hugh Wilson

Relationship Marketing: Strategy & Implementation, Helen Peck, Adrian Payne, Martin Christopher and Moira Clark

Strategic Marketing Management (second edition), Richard M. S. Wilson and Colin Gilligan

Strategic Marketing: Planning and Control (second edition), Graeme Drummond and John Ensor

Successful Marketing Communications, Cathy Ace

Tales from the Market Place, Nigel F. Piercy

The CIM Handbook of Export Marketing, Chris Noonan

The Fundamentals of Advertising (second edition), John Wilmshurst and Adrian Mackay

The Marketing Book (fifth edition), Michael J. Baker (ed.)

Total Relationship Marketing (second edition), Evert Gummesson

Professional list

AdValue, Leslie Butterfield (ed.)

Brand New Justice: the upside of global branding, Simon Anholt

Cause Related Marketing, Sue Adkins

Creating Value, Shiv S. Mathur and Alfred Kenyon

Customer Relationship Management, Simon Knox, Stan Maklan, Adrian Payne, Joe Peppard and Lynette Ryals

Cybermarketing (second edition), Pauline Bickerton and Matthew Bickerton

Cyberstrategy, Pauline Bickerton, Matthew Bickerton and Kate Simpson-Holley

Direct Marketing in Practice, Brian Thomas and Matthew Housden

e-Business, J. A. Matthewson

Effective Promotional Practice for eBusiness, Cathy Ace
Essential Law for Marketers, Ardi Kolah
Excellence in Advertising (second edition), Leslie Butterfield (ed.)
Fashion Marketing, Margaret Bruce and Tony Hines
Financial Services and the Multimedia Revolution, Paul Lucas, Rachel Kinniburgh and Donna Terp
From Brand Vision to Brand Evaluation, Leslie de Chernatony
Go-to-Market Strategy, Lawrence Friedman
Internal Marketing, Pervaiz Ahmed and Mohammed Rafiq
Marketing Made Simple, Geoff Lancaster and Paul Reynolds
Marketing Professional Services, Michael Roe
Marketing Strategy (second edition), Paul Fifield
Market-Led Strategic Change (third edition), Nigel F. Piercy
Relationship Marketing (second edition), Martin Christopher, Adrian Payne and David Ballantyne
The New Marketing, Malcolm McDonald and Hugh Wilson
The Channel Advantage, Lawrence Friedman and Tim Furey
The CIM Handbook of Export Marketing, Chris Noonan
The Committed Enterprise, Hugh Davidson
The Fundamentals of Corporate Communications, Richard Dolphin
The Marketing Plan in Colour, Malcolm McDonald and Peter Morris
Total Email Marketing, Dave Chaffey

Forthcoming

Creating Powerful Brands (third edition), Leslie de Chernatony and Malcolm McDonald
Creative Arts Marketing (second edition), Liz Hill, Terry O'Sullivan and Catherine O'Sullivan
Customer Relationship Management, Francis Buttle
Hospitality Marketing, David Bowie and Francis Buttle
International Retail Marketing, Margaret Bruce and Christopher Moore
Marketing Finance, Keith Ward
Marketing Graffiti, Mike Saren
Marketing Logistics (second edition), Martin Christopher and Helen Peck
Marketing Research for Managers (third edition), Sunny Crouch and Matthew Housden
Market Segmentation, Malcolm McDonald and Ian Dunbar
Marketing Strategy (third edition), Paul Fifield
Political Marketing, Phil Harris and Dominic Wring
Principles of Retailing, John Fernie, Suzanne Fernie and Christopher Moore
Public Relations: contemporary issues and techniques, Paul Baines, John Egan and Frank Jefkins
Retail Strategy, Christine Cuthbertson et al.
Strategic Marketing Planning, Colin Gilligan and Richard M. S. Wilson

For more information on all these titles, as well as the ability to buy online, please visit
www.bh.com/marketing